Withdrawn

D0123023

MAYDAY

MAYDAY

The Decline of American Naval Supremacy

SETH CROPSEY

OVERLOOK DUCKWORTH
NEW YORK • LONDON

This edition first published in hardcover in the United States and the United Kingdom in 2013 by Overlook Duckworth, Peter Mayer Publishers, Inc.

NEW YORK
141 Wooster Street
New York, NY 10012
www.overlookpress.com
For bulk and special sales, please contact sales@overlookny.com,
or write us at the above address

LONDON
30 Calvin Street
London E1 6NW
info@duckworth-publishers.co.uk
www.ducknet.co.uk

The illustrations appearing on pages 40, 71, 85, and 101 were provided by the Library of Congress. The photos appear on pages 91, 103, 115, 215, 238, and 242 were provided by the U.S. Navy. The map appearing on page 143 was adapted from a report by the Heritage Foundation. The map appearing on page 163 was adapted from a report by the Council on Foreign Relations. All others are in the public domain.

Cataloging-in-Publication Data is available from the Library of Congress

Book design and typeformatting by Bernard Schleifer
Manufactured in the United States of America
ISBN US: 978-1-59020-789-5
ISBN UK: 978-0-7156-4581-9

Dedicated to the memory of my parents,
Lilian and Joseph Cropsey

Contents

MAYDAY

POSITION OF U.S. NAVY FLEETS

2ND FLEET
North Atlantic
HQ: Norfolk, VA

3RD FLEET
East Pacific
HQ: San Diego, CA

4TH FLEET
South Atlantic
HQ: Mayport, FL

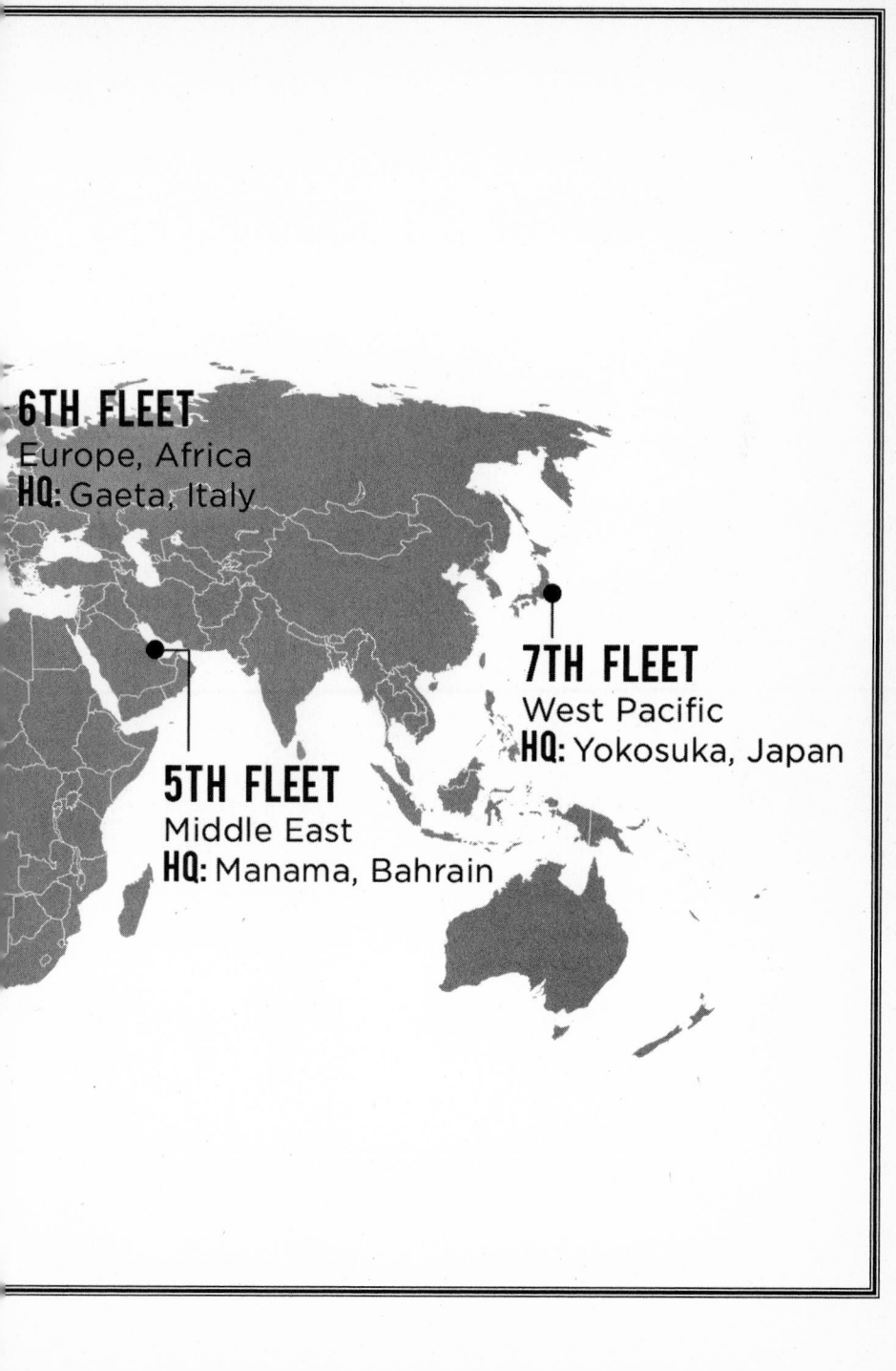

6TH FLEET
Europe, Africa
HQ: Gaeta, Italy

7TH FLEET
West Pacific
HQ: Yokosuka, Japan

5TH FLEET
Middle East
HQ: Manama, Bahrain

1

American Seapower in Distress

MERICAN SEAPOWER TODAY is heading for shoal waters. With 286 or so ships, the navy is less than half the size of the force that existed at the end of the Reagan administration and about the same size as America's fleet at the midpoint of the twentieth century's second decade. The U.S. Navy is stretched paper thin between operations in Afghanistan and the Persian Gulf, plus maintaining a presence in the western Pacific where impressive Chinese military modernization and assertiveness in the South China Sea, a bubbling regional naval arms competition, and the likelihood of additional North Korean mischief point toward trouble ahead. Neither the Middle East nor the western Pacific is likely soon to become less important for the United States. To paraphrase what is often ascribed to Trotsky, "The United States may no longer be interested in the Middle East, but the Middle East is decidedly interested in the United States." Nevertheless, the U.S. Sixth Fleet is no longer a power in the Mediterranean. Besides the U.S. combatants that are temporarily assigned to the Sixth Fleet as they steam between Gibraltar and the northern end of the Suez Canal, the U.S. Mediterranean Fleet is more or less a flagship based in a harbor up the road from Naples. When American citizens had to be evacuated from Libya in February 2011, the United States rented a Greek ferry. If the departure of Americans from Libya had been contested, the United States might have found itself in a difficult situation with diplomatic hostages, one that looked unpleasantly similar to the crisis of 1979 when Iranian students and militants held fifty-two American citizens hostage at the U.S. embassy in Tehran for almost fifteen months. Other states in the region had already noted the U.S. Sixth Fleet's virtual departure. In the same week that the absence of U.S. naval combatants required a Greek ferry to extract potential American hostages, Iran and Syria signed an agreement for the former to build a naval base at the Syrian port of Latakia on the Mediterranean. This will help Iran, its terrorist proxies Hezbollah and Hamas, and Syria—if the Assad regime survives—in making Lebanon a nation-size safe house for terror and allow the easy import of more and larger weapons for use against Israel and commercial shipping that operates in the eastern Mediterranean. Nature is said to abhor vacuums. So does power. It swiftly fills voids when they are of strategic value.

Nothing seems able to stanch the fleet's contraction to date or halt a similar future ebb. The responsibility for this unfolding strategic miscalculation is nearly evenly divided between the leadership of both political parties and can be apportioned equally between the executive branch and most of the legislative branch's concentration on such other issues as the wars in Iraq and Afghanistan and the increasingly dismal state of the nation's finances. Efforts to check the ascending spiral of ship costs have not succeeded. Measured in constant (2009) dollars, the average cost of a combat ship has increased from $1.2 billion during the 1980s to the $2.1 billion per ship that Congress appropriated in 2010—with predictable results in the number of ships purchased. During the 1980s the navy bought 17.2 vessels annually. The 2011 shipbuilding plan calls for 9.2 ships to be constructed and 276 ships in all for the thirty-year period ending in 2040. The navy's 2012 plan would have purchased 270 ships in the thirty-year period that ends in 2041. The 2013 plan drops the thirty-year plan for new ship construction to 268 ships. Achieving even this may turn out to be more difficult than anyone had anticipated, and growing the total fleet to the size naval leadership says is necessary will be even more elusive. The nonpartisan Congressional Budget Office states that at the rate the navy plans to retire ships, the thirty-year plans for fiscal years 2011, 2012, and 2013 were each "insufficient" to meet the navy's gradually declining goals for the size of the fleet.[1] This is hardly a surprise. The Department of Defense announced in the first month of 2011 a $78 billion budget cut over the succeeding five years. Nearing the end of his tenure as secretary of defense, Robert Gates said in mid-2011, "All told, over the past two years, more than 30 programs were cancelled, capped, or ended that, if pursued to completion, would have cost more than $300 billion."[2] By the fall of 2011 President Obama substantially increased this figure. He proposed, and succeeded in securing, bipartisan support in Congress to cut $489 billion from the U.S. defense budget over the next ten years—although as Secretary of Defense Gates prepared to leave office in the late spring of 2011, he warned publicly against "hollowing out" the current U.S. military.[3] The Obama proposal will cut $48.9 billion per year until 2023, a little more than three times the $15.6 billion per year that Secretary Gates had initially proposed for a five-year period. If monies are sequestered as a result of a congressional super-committee's failure to agree on deficit reductions in the late fall of 2011, an additional $500 billion will be subtracted in defense spending over the next decade. These cuts cannot be achieved by consolidating bases, reorganizing departments, or looking in the usual places for fat to trim. They will require cuts in forces. *Before* these proposed reductions, the navy had decided that even if the investments it makes in new ship construction—$10.8 billion for fiscal year 2013—were to remain steady into the future, the size of the fleet would continue its decline. For most of the past ten years the navy has said that 313 ships are needed to perform the missions it has been assigned. The Congressional Budget Office's senior analyst for naval forces and weapons told Congress in January 2010 that the 2011 draft proposal would reduce the size of the fleet to 237 ships at the end of the thirty-year period—2040—for which the navy traditionally plans.[4] A worse way to decide the size and shape of a military force is hard to imagine. The end should determine the means, not the other way around. A prudent architect designs a building to remain standing under foreseeable pressure. Where cost—not structural integrity—determines construction, buildings are at greater risk of falling down, and as news reports occasionally show, some do. Defense needs should be established by measuring the threat, deciding an acceptable level of risk, conceiving a strategy that addresses both threat and risk, and then building forces that the strategy requires. Good strategy succeeds in the case of a navy when it complements and makes possible the execution of a coherent national security strategy. This determines what tasks combat ships are intended to achieve and dictates what kinds and numbers of vessels are built—from capital ships to those that support them and perform related supporting tasks. Whether this orderly process is ignored because of a failure to adapt to political or technological changes, or the subordination of strategy to domestic political requirements, the result is ultimately and inevitably the same: the inability to defend a nation's interests.

This inability snowballs gradually but recovery is much slower. Mothballing ships is accomplished with the stroke of a pen. Building new vessels—after as little as a decade at the current pace, technological advance shows the folly of the original decision—means catching up technologically in design and then the lengthy process of building, testing, and evaluating replacement vessels. No state that has allowed its seapower to decline has succeeded at recovering it. Another seldom-noticed consequence of gradually disappearing seapower is the contraction of the industrial base that builds ships, naval aircraft, missiles, and weapons, and on which the nation's ability to defend its seaborne commerce and project global power depends. This is already happening. In the summer of 2010 Northrop Grumman, one of the United States' largest defense contractors, said that it would close its Avondale, Louisiana, shipyard and planned to sell off two other shipyards, Ingalls in Mississippi and Newport News in Virginia. This follows years of consolidation of ship-building capacity and the closing or reduction in size of yard after yard. The results are fewer ships to build, decreasing profit, and, most important, a disappearing force of skilled workers who know how to build modern naval combatants. So, not only are combat vessels lacking when needed, but the ability to make them has also vanished.

The obvious result of a shrinking fleet is either reducing the scope of American seapower or increasing the workload of the sailors who make it possible—or both. This would be ill-timed and dangerous. China has transformed its navy from the small and insignificant coastal force that Mao knew into a technologi-cally impressive blue-water fleet supported by cyber warfare, satellites, capable surface combatants, ground-based aircraft, and submarines—both nuclear and conventionally powered. Aircraft carriers are being built and China put its first aircraft carrier, *Liaoning*, into service in late September 2012. Aircraft carriers signal intent to project power beyond the range of land-based aircraft. Moreover, China has publicly stated its intent to deny access to large portions of the western Pacific to the U.S. fleet and is readying the world's only antiship ballistic missile, one whose high speed and range would threaten large-deck U.S. air-craft carriers and large-deck amphibious ships that have approached the Asian mainland closely enough to protect our allies in the region. China is not the only problem. The prospect of nuclear proliferation, the need to defend the United States and its allies against missile-borne weapons of mass destruction, the political and security threats that accompany failed states, the likelihood that the uprisings in the Arab world that began in 2011 may not yield positive outcomes, terrorism, piracy, youth bulges, and heightened competition for raw materials and food—to name a few—all point toward an increasingly chaotic and unstable international political climate.

The imposing Chinese carrier, the Liaoning, *was put into service in September 2012.*

In this unsavory stew preponderant seapower remains key to protecting freedom of transit for America's burgeoning international trade and commerce, while also deterring conflict, assuring allies, preserving alliances, responding to crises, and, if necessary, defeating an enemy. These desiderata serve not only American interests. They also protect an international system that favors security, stability, and prosperity, and in the end nourishes realistic hope for a more democratic world. For most of history the world's oceans had been lawless. Piracy, human trafficking, state-sponsored commerce raiding, and plundering descents from the sea on land targets were normal. The rise of the Royal Navy as a transoceanic force and the subsequent transfer of power to the U.S. Navy changed this. Beginning with their intercession, the international slave trade was largely ended. The right of free passage on the high seas was enforced, as were the dividing lines that separate sovereign from international waters. Piracy, while not eliminated, was reduced. International commerce flourished and grew as it never had. The Royal and U.S. navies reflected the self-governing values of the nations in whose service they sailed. At its apogee much of the Royal Navy protected England's ability to communicate with the empire. The United States used its naval forces to communicate with and defend its allies, to prevent regional crises from expanding, to deter war, and, as in World War II, to defeat aggression. Powerful regional naval forces existed in antiquity. The confluence of increased wealth required to build and maintain great fleets, together with the self-governing polities that emerged with the European political Enlightenment, demonstrated that, unlike ground or air forces, transoceanic seapower is at least as useful in preserving peace and shaping its future as it is in defeating an enemy. The loss of such abilities would reduce the United States to a second-rate power. It would smooth the path to naval supremacy for states that cherish neither self-governance nor the rule of law that are at the heart of the international order that a strong U.S. Navy protects.

America has enough experience to know better. Post–Civil War exhaustion in the form of congressional indifference and skimpy budgets lasted three and a half decades after the end of the Lincoln administration. Other nations—like England, Germany, and even Japan—modernized their fleets as U.S. seapower lost the technological edge and manufacturing skills it had honed in the Civil War. President Grant's navy secretary mended old ships and tried to preserve the fleet with caulking and patches, which is ultimately more costly than keeping abreast of technology, since sooner or later the expense of modernization must be added to the price of repairing an aging fleet. But it didn't matter. The United States faced neither a naval peer competitor in the second half of the nineteenth century nor the prospect of a serious one. With the War of 1812's disputes behind us—and with the exception of the Civil War—the United States turned its energies to developing infrastructure and expanding international trade in large measure protected by England's dominant seapower.

The English navy's global reach coincided with and permitted England's acquisition of an empire whose legacy to its former colonies is freer, more democratic, functional, and prosperous than that of the states that were once colonies of other European powers. India, for example, the world's largest democracy, is more stable and has greater prospects for wealth than those of its Central Asian neighbors to the north that were folded into the Russian Empire. Singapore, also colonized by Great Britain, is a model of security and prosperity compared to the nearby Philippines, which were part of the Spanish dominion. Kenya's prospects for stability and rising standards of living remain more promising than French-colonized Algeria. Spanish-conquered Mexico is beset with violence, poverty, and chronic widespread corruption. The contrast to the United States and Canada could not be greater. Without the Royal Navy's ocean-spanning fleet and its ability to protect and transport, the sun would surely have set upon the British Empire far sooner than it did. Instead, command of the seas safeguarded the empire, discouraged potential opponents, encouraged some—like Kaiser Wilhelm—to divert valuable national resources toward building a fleet of dubious strategic value, and, in a time when large armies could not be easily moved about on land, spared England the expense of large land forces. The Royal Navy performed other important global services. Its blockade of French ports and destruction of the combined French-Spanish fleet kept Napoleon from subjugating all of Europe. Its pursuit of slave ships that began two years after the Battle of Trafalgar effectively ended the world's slave trade. A little more than a century later the Royal Navy's overtopping power virtually confined the German fleet to its continental ports during World War I, dashing once again the hopes of a continental hegemon.

The Royal Navy's comparative power waned at the end of the nineteenth century as mature rail systems chipped away at continental states' dependence on the oceans. At the same time other navies—like those of the United States and Japan—rose. In Europe, the military utility of large continental railway systems was compounded by unwieldy, countervailing alliance structures and conscription. Forced to find ways to save on defense, Great Britain settled on alliances, modestly increased her land forces, and looked to Japan to relieve the cost of maintaining security in the West Pacific and to the United States for similar purposes in the western Atlantic. The United States turned out to be a good bet. Sometime between the beginning of the twentieth century and the invasion of Poland, superior global naval power passed from Britain to the United States as imperceptibly as a submarine gliding silently below a great ocean liner's keel.

No one noticed. Franklin Roosevelt held a famously dim view of the British Empire. But Churchill's idea, as expressed in *A History of the English-Speaking Peoples*, of two peoples bound together by language, political culture, liberty, law, habits of self-reliance, and the confident belief in self-determination proved a more accurate insight into what the Anglo-American relationship did for the world. The United States turned out to hold the same broad international objectives of free markets and untroubled access to the world's oceans, political liberty, rule of law, sovereignty, nonintervention, and international order for which Britain at its best had stood. American foreign policy after World War II reflected these large goals and American seapower responded accordingly.

When Stalin demanded a measure of control over the Dardanelles after the war and Turkish ambassador Mehmet Münir Ertegün died of natural causes in Washington, DC, Truman returned his body to Istanbul in the largest class of surface ship of the U.S. fleet, the battleship U.S.S. *Missouri*. This act of respect successfully demonstrated American support for Turkish sovereignty. It was transmitted in the form of deliberately impressive naval power. There are shops in Istanbul today named "Missouri."[5] The Soviets failed to equal their predecessor regime's influence in Asia Minor. Turkey joined NATO before Eisenhower was elected to the White House.

Seapower played a major supporting role in the Korean War. The navy and Marine Corps' surprise landing at the heavily defended port of Inchon opened the way to drive North Korean forces from Seoul, which remained contested territory for much of the conflict. The conclusion of major combat in the Korean War of the early 1950s preserved the independence of South Korea and with it a beachhead of freedom in East Asia.

The applications of seapower since the burden of demonstrating it around the globe shifted to the United States from Britain are numerous. Several examples follow in succeeding chapters. The constant that links the uses of American seapower to one another as well as to the Royal Navy that preceded it is the pursuit of a stable, secure and—in the United States' case—increasingly democratic global order. What varies is the enlarging use of seapower as technology, missions, politics, and threats have changed since the end of World War II.

Those changes are interesting, but they are not the subject here. Far more important is a basic grasp of how U.S. seapower shapes the world today and what would be the consequences of its reduction or absence.

Transoceanic Force

The U.S. fleet today numbers 286 ships. They sail in all the world's oceans on the surface and below it. Their planes patrol above both land and water. Off the coast of Southwest Asia U.S. carriers launch strikes that support the war against the Taliban in Afghanistan. Navy commandos (SEALs) stalk the dusty paths of valleys and mountains in the provinces beyond Kabul, provide intelligence, kill terrorist chieftains, and fight on the ground. Naval forces performed similar missions during and after the most heated combat in Iraq. Farther to the south and west American seapower patrols the Persian Gulf, protecting this most strategic of international arteries and assuring the safety of its narrow approaches at the Strait of Hormuz. Over a thousand miles southwest—and beyond—other navy ships protect international shipping off the Somali coast, where pirates threaten commerce, much of it bound to or from the Suez Canal through the Bab el Mandeb Strait at the southern narrows of the Red Sea. Farther south, down the east coast of Africa around the Cape of Good Hope and up the west coast, is more peaceful duty: building working relationships with coastal states' navies—which helps them prevent human trafficking and smuggling; inoculating animals against diseases that endanger humans; and delivering food and medicine to refugees, as one of the navy's high-speed vessels did in Cameroon in February 2011.[6] If American seapower could no longer assure safe passage through the international waters of the Middle East's strategic choke points, those who depend on the region's natural resources must expect either wild fluctuations in the cost and supply of oil or the imposition of a very different international order that would determine rules for commercial shipping—or both. The same consequences would flow from the United States' inability to lead an international naval coalition against piracy. The contagion would raise costs as shippers sought other—longer—routes, and the disease would spread as would-be pirates in other strategic choke points around the world quickly saw the benefits of piracy. The seas would revert to chaos, with catastrophic effects on American commerce.

The Mediterranean Reverts to Form

The yet unknown results of the Arab Spring aside, the central Mediterranean is calmer now than during the Balkan ethnic-cleansing conflicts of the mid- and late 1990s. But the eastern reaches of that often troubled sea are becoming more treacherous. If the Egyptian uprising of early 2011 had descended into widespread violence, the navy amphibious ships U.S.S. *Kearsarge* and U.S.S. *Ponce*, with large marine forces, would have evacuated the thousands of American citizens who live and work in Egypt. Divining the effects in the region of the political tremors that cast down the Tunisian, Egyptian, and Libyan rulers in 2011 is difficult. But if force is required—as it often has since the United States became a great power—to rescue Americans, assist allies, assure the safety of commercial or military shipping, or calm an explosion in the making, U.S. naval forces will repeat the role they have been playing in the Mediterranean since Thomas Jefferson decided that he'd had enough of the Barbary pirates. Middle Eastern volatility—in the shape of Iranian rockets that could someday carry nuclear weapons that threaten Europe—will also demand American naval presence in the Mediterranean. The United States has promised that naval vessels capable of destroying ballistic missiles in flight will prowl the eastern Mediterranean. This is instead of the original plan of stationing similar defenses on land in Poland and the Czech Republic to protect Europe from the threat of Iranian missiles. Unabated gradual defense cuts delay the time when the United States will struggle or fail to meet this commitment. Radical cuts all but assure a broken promise. In either case, Europe and America's defense against Iranian-launched ballistic missiles would suffer grievously while Iran's ability to conduct terror globally would grow exponentially, protected by the potential threat of nuclear weapons.

Mediterranean of the Americas

As Europe and Africa are separated by an inland sea, a large body of water with a far more open passage to the Atlantic divides the northern and southern halves of the Western Hemisphere. U.S. seapower in the form of both naval and Coast Guard ships search the Gulf of Mexico, Caribbean, and eastern Pacific for drug runners, many of whom come from or pass through Columbia with their illicit and often deadly cargo. Illegal drugs that enter the United States divert money from the economy, encourage corruption among law-enforcement authorities, generate crime from the source of the origin to their end use in the United States, increase addiction along with the cost of its treatment, and are a bountiful source of revenue for foreign criminal groups that conduct the trade. According to U.S. government officials, the money from this illicit harvest is now becoming a source of revenue for criminal groups that may sympathize with al-Qaeda.[7] U.S. military commanders familiar with the region are more blunt. They see an increasing presence in the region of Islamic extremists with illegal drugs to sell and a nurturing of ties between jihadists and the often less ideological but equally profit-minded drug cartels of Latin and Central America. The seas are an important means of moving illegal drugs north. Retreating U.S. seapower offers a carte blanche invitation for an abundant and deadly increase of imported illegal drugs. These would add to the already large economic, social, and criminal consequences of drug use in the United States

Each year, the U.S. Navy sails, exercises, and meets together with the naval forces of South and Central American states. The navies that participate—and almost all do—practice a range of skills that cement military partnerships, encourage greater diplomatic cooperation, and improve the hemisphere's ability to defend its coastal approaches. Instead of the antagonistic relations that small states often have with large powerful ones, the U.S. Navy allows South American states to benefit from superior American seapower, which helps unify the entire hemisphere in a shared taste for flourishing commerce and expanding liberty.

The U.S. Navy is also an abiding source of humanitarian assistance and disaster relief. When a large tropical storm struck Guatemala in the spring of 2010, a navy frigate, U.S.S. *Underwood*, was ordered away from its antidrug patrols and dispatched to deliver several tons of food to the victims. A detachment of navy SEALs was also ordered to pitch in with the relief effort.

The best-known recent example of such assistance was in Haiti. The United States sent an aircraft carrier, three large amphibious ships, and elements of two Marine Expeditionary Units, as well as the hospital ship U.S.N.S. *Comfort*[8] as part of the relief effort following the earthquake that killed an estimated 230,000 Haitians in January 2010. No other naval force in the world can provide such relief so quickly or in such abundance. American seapower earns goodwill. The loss of this goodwill as a result of increasingly limited American seapower cannot be compensated for by diplomatic nicety or the capability of other American military services. The navy's loss would be the nation's loss.

Keeping the Pacific Pacific

The span of more than six thousand miles from San Diego to Shanghai is, as the name of the ocean that separates the two cities suggests, peaceful. But nearing the Asian continent and reaching beneath it into the Indian Ocean, the strategic map starts to pitch. There are China's dependence on the sea to supply essential raw materials, evidence of the Chinese state's growing prosperity and expanding navy, territorial disputes with neighbors over islands and seabed mining, unremitting tensions on the Korean Peninsula, and India's rising wealth and strategic position astride the ocean that bears its name. The history of enmity among many of the region's states blurs in antiquity and parallels their growth as great civilizations.

Because of ancient discord sewn among huge populations, accumulating wealth, ambition to match, and strategic location, there is no other portion of the globe that is of more immediate or greater importance to U.S. foreign policy or security. In no other part of the world is so large a U.S. naval presence based. The Seventh Fleet, the largest of the United States' six numbered fleets, consists of over seventy ships, two hundred to three hundred aircraft, and forty thousand sailors and marines. They are not idle.

When North Korea bombarded the South Korean island of Yeon-pyeong, killing four in November 2010, the aircraft carrier U.S.S. *George Washington* sallied from the U.S. Seventh Fleet's home-port at Yokosuka, Japan, along with its escorts to the Yellow Sea, there to conduct exercises with the South Korean navy. The nearby presence of easily moved and highly potent naval forces helps prevent recurring violence in and around the Korean Penin-sula from turning into major incidents that, unleashed, could eas-ily lead to war. American seapower's shrinkage or departure would nudge events in this direction.

This was not the first occasion that a U.S. naval force smoothed the western Pacific's unsettled waters. In 1996 Presi-dent Clinton sent two carriers, U.S.S. *Nimitz* and U.S.S. *Inde-pendence*, to the waters off Taiwan after China tested missiles in the vicinity of an island off the northern end of Taiwan. These proofs of U.S. resolution in the face of armed intimidation are the firm and high contours of American seapower in the region. At a lower but also effective level is the series of exercises that the U.S. Navy holds regularly with friendly navies in East and Southeast Asia. For example, as part of a regularly scheduled exercise—Keen Sword—with Japan's Self-Defense Force, which offered up scores of ships and hundreds of aircraft, the U.S. Navy also sent a large detachment of ships and aircraft to operate together off Japan's south coast, not far from the Korean Peninsula during the 2010 crisis. Sixty warships sailing safely and effectively together is not like playing pickup ball at the park. Ships and aircraft from different countries must coordinate their standard procedures for keeping apart safely, communicate, respond to emergencies including simulated attack, exchange vital tactical information, and turn plans for such necessities as command and control into working practice.

In the western Pacific, sharpening these skills is quotidian business. During 2010 ships and aircraft of the Seventh Fleet also exercised with many of the nations on or near China's periphery: Bangladesh, Brunei, Cambodia, Malaysia, the Philippines, Singapore, and Thailand. In the same year the Seventh Fleet dispatched a mine warfare detachment, which shared its expertise and technical skills with naval forces from most of the previously mentioned states along with India and Indonesia. The entire region, which lives under the threat of growing Chinese ambitions, is increasingly versed in practiced and coordinated naval operations as a result of American seapower. Such exercises help create unity of action and its necessary complement, political unity in the face of potential threats. Removing or shrinking these effective bonds helps tip the scale of power in Asia toward Chinese hegemony.

A regular part of the western Pacific Fleet's responsibilities, as with other forward deployed naval forces, is humanitarian assistance. The hospital ship U.S.N.S. *Mercy*, a converted oil supertanker, provided medical and veterinary services in Cambodia, Indonesia, Timor-Leste, and Vietnam in 2010. U.S. Navy ships brought similar services to Palau and Papua, New Guinea. Again, the availability of these services earns the United States respect and influence while the withering of this support diminishes our stature, commerce, and influence in the region.

The Global Theater

Other seapower tasks overlap regional needs. To keep track of potentially hostile shipping, terrorist or criminal plans, dangers to coastal regions, and infrastructure, naval vessels routinely collect intelligence as they go about their regular duties. In the movie version of the Tom Clancy thriller *The Sum of All Fears*, a nuclear device that is later detonated arrives in Baltimore aboard a freighter. Terrorists would use such weapons if they could get their hands on them. In 2009, the last year for which accurate records were maintained, more than 154 million cargo containers passed through the world's ten largest ports[9] that specialize in moving these twenty-foot-long metal containers. Hence, naval intelligence has good reason to watch international shipping carefully. If money is unavailable to build or operate the ships and aircraft that are part of the network of watchers, the risks that made Tom Clancy's book a bestseller will rise dramatically.

Other seagoing duties also transcend the regional political circumstances that determine the fleets' work. Foremost among them is nuclear deterrence. Submarines are the least detectable and most survivable part of the three-part force that could respond with similar or greater power if the United States or its allies are the objects of a nuclear attack—the other two elements are intercontinental missiles and long-range bombers. The navy has fourteen submarines whose lengthy unseen patrols remain critical in the eyes of defense planners against such a strike. The question of whether so large a ballistic-missile submarine fleet whose size was dictated by the Cold War doctrine of mutual assured destruction (MAD) offers better protection against nuclear weapons in the hands of terrorists or in case of another state's accidental launch than a strong defense against ballistic missiles remains open. But until the Cold War doctrine is rethought or replaced, massive retaliation remains, for better or worse, a keystone of U.S. defense against nuclear attack. A lack of funds that keeps the United States from building the needed replacement for the nation's aging ballistic-missile force and simultaneously skimps on seaborne ballistic-missile defenses will increase the risks to the United States and its allies of existing and proliferating nuclear weapons as it self-pierces the shield that protects us if such weapons are actually fired in anger. Land-based rockets and long-range aircraft might still deter an attack, but they are much easier to target than submarines. The United States would have taken a large and important step down from its once-dominant position as the world's great power and increased the risks to the nation and its allies of nuclear attack.

The supporting beams that subtend the totality of navy and marine forces on duty around the world are nearly as invisible to the public as the undulating terrain of the sea's bottom. These supports include maintenance and repair facilities, ammunition dumps, a logistical chain unparalleled in human history, research facilities, testing ranges, education and training programs, recruiters, and doctors as well as one ship and its complement being readied to take the place of a similar class of a ship at sea once the latter's deployment ends and the crew returns home.

In short, U.S. seapower is a globe-encircling moat defensive to the American house. It shelters the pathways to and from the nation on which commerce depends and alliances rely. In peace its appearance and implicit power keep allies from the pull of other powers—like China—that may seek regional hegemony. The partnerships it constructs add to the safety of the world's oceans and the stability of important states that abut them. American seaborne civic, humanitarian, and disaster assistance are not merely good deeds, but materially support stability and security against criminal and terrorist subversion. America's protection of untrammeled transit through the world's trade routes directly benefits all who use them and indirectly and quietly supports the international order at which American foreign policy has aimed for a century. As has been shown time and again since the end of World War II, the mere appearance of massive seaborne power discourages aggression and encourages diplomacy rather than force to resolve crises. Indeed, seapower encourages peaceful resolution of disputes and crises, since without it U.S. diplomacy has little or no leverage from afar.

When necessary—as it was to stop a brutal Serbian's ethnic cleansing or Saddam Hussein's invasion of a neighboring state—American seapower in the form of air and missile strikes, amphibious feints, and Special Operations Forces have helped enforce accepted norms of international behavior. This, too, advances the United States' interest in an orderly international system that respects rule of law, sovereignty, and the security and stability on which the progress of democratic institutions rests. Seapower, defense planners hope, deters war by the threat of fearsome retaliation and the assurance of its mobile defense against hostile missiles that could carry nuclear weapons. In war itself American seaborne force including amphibious power supports ground troops by diversion, direct strikes against key infrastructure, the preservation of safe passage into enemy territory, and the ability to destroy enemy fleets and sink the commerce that sustains a hostile power.

A World Without Dominant American Seapower?

However, the straits that American seapower finds itself in today, along with the part it continues to play in defending the nation and its international prestige, have been virtually erased from public understanding in part because benefits long enjoyed are often taken for granted. Just as important, the nation's land engagements going back nearly a generation—in Panama in 1989, in the First Gulf War the following year, in the Balkans during the mid-1990s, and then again in the current conflicts in Afghanistan and Iraq—all have been chiefly ground actions. Seapower played a major supporting role in these actions but one that the essentially land character of the conflict eclipsed. The tedious job of protecting against the threat of a seaborne terrorist attack remains equally obscure to the general public.

But if dominant U.S. seapower were to vanish, substantially diminish, or find a significant challenge from a competitor that seeks to achieve peer status as a naval power, the consequences would be profound and impossible to ignore. The real possibility of the continued decline of our own maritime position, combined with the growth of China's ability to project naval power in its own spacious backyard as well as beyond, demands considering such a reversal that today seems so unthinkable.

First, unlike what the British encountered as their relative naval power diminished and the United States stepped into the breach, there is no other state that both shares our political values and possesses the maritime power to assume the United States' current responsibilities. Japan fields one of the world's largest navies. Although anxiety over the future of U.S. presence in the region and sharpening tensions with China over possession of the South China Sea's disputed Senkaku Islands have increased domestic political pressure to rethink its interpretation, the Japanese constitution's Article 9 effectively keeps the nation from using force as a means of policy. India has no such compunction, but while its navy is a growing regional force it could not today substitute for the global presence of the United States. It possesses a single aircraft carrier. So does France, whose fleet is less than one-fourth the size of the United States' fleet. Russia still operates some large naval combatants including submarines, but just a handful, and a large infusion of new ships does not seem likely. China is a naval power on the rise. Its flotillas call on a growing list of foreign ports as it acquires more access to bases in a widening geographic arc. An effective coalition of these fleets is as politically unimaginable as it is tactically unmanageable. If the United States were to vacate or substantially abbreviate its global maritime duties, a power vacuum would be the certain outcome. Power vacuums are unlike physical ones. Instead of inhibiting the growth of organisms, as a physical vacuum does, power vacuums positively encourage the nourishment of a host of toxic elements: piracy, for example. The United States today provides the strong glue that binds together Combined Task Force 150 and its antipiracy mission off the Horn of Africa including the specially designed ship from which whatever senior naval officer, U.S. or foreign, commands operations. Other nations don't possess the combination of intelligence, command and control vessels, and logistics to stand in for the United States if we reduce our role in providing maritime security at this vital oceanic choke point. The end of antipiracy patrols and enforcement in the Gulf of Aden would encourage piracy in other critical choke points around the world, for example, the Strait of Malacca through which many oil tankers transit on their voyages between Asia and the Middle East. The immediate effect on the global economy would be as shattering as the longer-term negative effects on the region—and the world—if the United States allows this pillar of support for freedom of transit through international waters to fall.

The same issues must arise about the partnerships that the United States builds with other coastal states the world over. What effect would the dissolution of this broadening network have—on U.S. relations in Africa, Southeast Asia, and the southern half of this hemisphere? Who would replace our presence, and to what end? What other state would supply the United States with intelligence about suspicious vessels whose cargoes could allow one rogue nuclear state—or terrorist group—to aid another in turning itself into a similar threat? What nation would dispatch combatants to keep a crisis from becoming a war? And in which crises would another nation with such capability choose to intervene—and with what result for U.S. diplomacy, international influence, and security?

Most important, the same question applies to keeping a crisis from erupting in the first place: American seapower remains visible around the globe today in the form of port visits. The U.S. flag whips at the stern of surface combatants entering and departing harbors from Busan in South Korea, Umm Qasr in Iraq, Bata in Equatorial Guinea, and Cartagena in Colombia. Their presence in the region is a flashing beacon of the United States' ability to support friends and produce daunting combat power, as well as a reminder of American political values, in particular the interests advanced by U.S. seapower of stability and security as represented by the assurance of peaceful transit through international waters. What effect would a radical decrease or elimination of these standard visits produce around the world?

If the U.S. ballistic-missile-carrying fleet were to be diminished or eliminated, would our threat to retaliate under attack remain as believable as it currently is? And if not, what would the opening of a credibility gap in our retaliatory ability mean for U.S. and allied security? Having fewer U.S. cruisers and destroyers equipped with radar and missiles that can shoot down ballistic missiles raises similar questions. If their ability to protect is limited or removed, what will be the likely effect on friends and allies within range of, for example, North Korea and Iran as these states continue their development of longer-range missiles and weapons of mass destruction? The answer is simple. If a shrinking U.S. fleet is unable to protect Asian allies and friends such as Japan, South Korea, the Philippines, Singapore, Vietnam, and Indonesia, their historical enmity militates against forming their own naval coalition. Temporizing with China is the more reasonable course. Resisting until diplomatic and military intimidation left them with no choice but to capitulate invites only humiliation and the worst terms once an accommodation is reached. Such an accommodation would force remaining influence in the Pacific back to Hawaii, chill expanding American commerce in Asia, and end East Asia's prospects for increasing democratization. Wide-ranging seapower is not so much an instrument of force—although that it is—as a condition of stable commerce, effective diplomacy, and regional influence.

But seapower not only allows force to be projected. It is also the least expensive and most efficient route for delivering war matériel to friends and allies in a serious crisis or war. Oceans separate America from its major allies and alliances, the Pacific from the United States' Asian allies, and the Atlantic from most of the NATO states. Knowledge of this fact helps restrain enemies from precipitous action. In terms of force, America is by far the senior partner in each case. The United States' anticipated ability to supply allies in the event of a war depends on commanding the seas—or at least that portion over which a supply convoy is passing. A loss of this command due to the absence of either auxiliary vessels or combatants to protect them concludes the United States' ability to convey vital military logistics to our major allies. And in that loss is the end of alliance no less than the inability to provide actual combat support.

War itself seems the least likely danger, at least today. But it is foolish to think about naval forces—which take years to design, build, and test before they can be deployed—without considering what the world may look like two or three decades hence. The biggest and most likely single challenge at sea comes from China so long as it continues its current path toward building naval forces that can deny the United States access to the western Pacific. The likelihood that China could prevail in a naval conflict with the United States would displace power relationships in Asia. China's defeat of the United States in any naval engagement would establish an unchallenged hegemony in Asia and shatter America's trading relationships in the region. It would confirm the end of the United States' existence as the world's great power and would draw a dark curtain over the hope for an international system that, in serving America's interest in democratic international norms, advances most of the world's.

In fact, the same unwelcome consequence is limned in the answers to most of the questions that are raised above. A severe curtailment of intelligence collection aimed at potentially dangerous international shipping as a result of diminished U.S. naval patrols or the yielding of the oceans to the predations of would-be nuclear proliferators, armed thugs, and the illicit activity of drug runners and human traffickers would be a large step backward to medieval times when even great powers countenanced pillaging on the high seas. The difference today is there's a lot more to steal. A world in which expensive cargoes could be plucked from the ocean's major choke points would start to look like Edward Gibbon's description of the Roman Empire's failing effort to safeguard even nearby provinces that "were constantly exposed to the invasion and passage of the barbarians."[10] The international norms that U.S. seapower has encouraged do not aim, as did the Roman imperium, at conquest for the sake of the state's enrichment. But the stable world that both Rome and the United States sought for different reasons is equally susceptible to corrosion that begins in small bites and ends with an insatiable appetite for civilization itself.

The complete or near elimination of American seapower as

a stabilizing presence to keep crises from erupting or to smother them when they do would recapitulate the substitution of barbarian for Roman order in the West as it signaled the terminal decay of America's position as a great power.

Global Fleet, Discreet Use, and American Power

Comparisons of U.S. seapower to a global police force are absurd. The police must respond to all reported serious crimes. The United States doesn't. When large numbers of Vietnamese from the South took to the sea to escape Hanoi's reeducation camps and extreme mistreatment in the late 1970s, pirates set upon them with a ferocity that equaled if not surpassed the conditions from which they had fled. Ships at sea often responded to the boat people's distress, but the United States—which could have used decoys to lure and sink pirate vessels or attack the pirates as they emerged from their lairs—ignored the issue. The United States said it was displeased when Russia invaded Georgia in the summer of 2008 but turned its attention elsewhere. American ships could have entered the Black Sea and moderated Russian behavior either by threat, military resupply of Georgian units, or more forceful means. When Mu'ammar Gadhafi turned on his own people in February 2010, the United States issued expressions of displeasure and then deployed limited naval power. The admonitions did not protect Libyans from their government. The United States used minimal force. Its actions resembled more a solitary constable sent to investigate a possible crime than a large-scale police response to an episode of mass murder.

But when, in 1986, the same Colonel Gadhafi claimed sovereignty over the large bight in Libya's Mediterranean coastline known as the Gulf of Sidra, U.S. seapower challenged the assertion. President Reagan ordered naval vessels into the international water of the Gulf of Sidra. They successfully engaged units of the Libyan military and the principle of free navigation through international waters was forcibly upheld. Naval and amphibious power was also prominent in destroying Iraqi military infrastructure and pinning down Iraqi forces during Operation Desert Storm, the 1991 attack that forced Iraq to withdraw from Kuwait, which it had seized by force in August 1990. Applying seapower to the land helped support a basic tenet of U.S. foreign policy, the proscription against using force to invade and capture another state. Sometimes the simple appearance of impressive seapower has produced the same desirable result. Large U.S. naval and amphibious forces—as well as British carriers—were sent to supplement the U.S. Sixth Fleet in 1970 when Syrian forces invaded Jordan and the possibility of a wider war loomed. The arrival of U.S. and British naval and amphibious forces was enough to keep the crisis from worsening. By threat or actual use of combat force, seapower has been a fulcrum of American influence since World War II. Its virtual disappearance would either encourage another power or powers to assume a similar role for their own purposes or else result in an increasingly violent world.

For the United States as it was for Great Britain, Spain, Venice, the Netherlands, and Athens, the loss of superior seapower would crumble a lengthy stretch of the foundation that supports America's claim to great power status. The United States might still retain a high standard of living. It might lead other states in ratios of per capita GDP. Its military could still be ranked among the world's largest and technologically most proficient. And its universities might still be those to which students from around the world flock. But as with the other states throughout history that have descended the same path, the United States would by degrees lose its ability to protect itself at a distance, look on helplessly as control evaporated over the lines of communication on which its economy in large measure depends, surrender the ability to influence events within the reach that its strategy encompassed, see its overseas allies scramble for stronger partners, and stand by as its international prestige and global influence shriveled.

In his famous 1630 sermon—written and perhaps delivered to colonists aboard their ship, *Arabella*—John Winthrop envisioned a "city on a hill" as a way to "avoid the shipwreck" of communal dissension that would incur the unfavorable judgment of his own generation as well as those to follow. Neither the exemplary polity that Winthrop envisioned nor any other can survive by virtue alone. And Winthrop knew it. He closes his sermon with Moses's final admonition to Israel to "choose life."[11] Choices are needed in the world of the spirit no less than in the related world of hard knocks. The choices that the American people and their elected leaders have taken since the United States' founding showed their twin understanding that political liberty must continually be defended and that the peculiar geography of the United States is best advanced by keeping threats from reaching America's borders. The ideas and practices that inform American seapower today are strikingly similar to those that were present at the creation of the American polity. Nowhere are those ideas more deeply understood or better expressed than in the writings of naval thinker Alfred Thayer Mahan (born September 27, 1840; died December 1, 1914).

2

Alfred Thayer Mahan: Seapower as an Instrument of Democratic Expansion

BESIDES THE INDUSTRIAL REVOLUTION and a significant interval of peace among the great powers, the nineteenth century was characterized by intellectual efforts to understand the governing principles of very large phenomena. Hegel tried to explain history. Marx wanted to account for what he believed were the determined movements of economics, politics, and society. At the beginning of the twentieth century Einstein related gravity to space and time in trying to understand the universe itself.

Similar efforts at comprehensive understanding were applied to human conflict. The German military thinker Carl von Clausewitz and the French nobleman general Antoine-Henri Jomini tried to codify the principles of war. An American naval officer, Alfred Thayer Mahan, applied the same attempt to understanding the unchanging characteristics of naval warfare.

Today, outside of a small circle of naval officers—including Chinese officers who admire his idea that under the right circumstances seapower is the key to national greatness—Alfred Thayer Mahan is largely forgotten. Yet at the turn of the century Mahan's thought, coupled with Theodore Roosevelt's energy and

Admiral Alfred Thayer Mahan

influence, built and launched America's first global navy. This moment marked the beginning of the United States' status as a great seapower and mapped the strategic path that U.S. commerce pursues to this day. Mahan's famous work, *The Influence of Sea Power upon History 1660–1783*, examines the central importance of naval power to democratic prosperity and commercial empire.

Yet Mahan has fallen out of favor today among those who study foreign affairs. Some contemporary international relations theorists examine social norms of the day to explain relations among states. Others hold that the legal coordination of mutual self-interest between competing states establishes a certain kind of international order. Such abstract theories focus almost exclusively on economic relations between states.

Still other international relations theorists look to Immanuel Kant's hope for perpetual peace in politics. Democratic peace theories occupy the thoughts and efforts of academics around the world. The main tenet of democratic peace theory argues that, in politics, lasting peace exists only between democracies. As evidence, proponents often claim that democracies never go to war against each other. The University of Chicago's Charles Lipson, for instance, contends that democracies honor contracts and rely more firmly on legal agreements than authoritarian states. Both of these peculiarly democratic virtues, he argues, support a long-term credibility and diminish the insecurity and uncertainty that often drives states to war.[1] However, such theories avoid the disproportion in size and power of the American democracy compared to its trade allies. They also overlook the influence of military—and especially naval—power's protection of the political conditions that we today see as the normal state of things, commerce's free access to the world's oceans. The question of how this stable international environment developed out of the piracy and plunder that once made oceangoing commerce risky business is asked no more than what facilitated the development of friendly democracies. Current international relations theories often exclude the military's—and especially the navy's—influence on commerce and trade.

Over 90 percent of the world's trade is conducted by water. The world's waterways are and will remain the most efficient means for transporting goods. However, the decades of stability on the high seas since the end of World War II have encouraged us to take for granted that the oceans are safe for navigation. American seapower created this freedom. Should a competitor state arise to challenge America's influence on the oceans, the world's waterways are not likely to remain as friendly to liberal commerce as they have been since 1945. The consequences to America's economy would be significant.

Naval power exists and operates, as Mahan wrote, "more silent than the clash of arms," yet as influential as it is quiet.[2] If

Mahan's history had continued beyond the Treaty of Paris in 1783, he might have illustrated his explanation of naval power's silent influence by pointing to England's success following the Battle of Trafalgar in 1805: England used the constant presence of its menacing naval squadrons to bottle up the French and their continental allies in ports from the Low Countries to Toulon. There was little noise, but much influence.

The result of ignoring the influence that seapower wields over commerce and national security exposes it to negligence and inattention each time the nation feels domestic financial pressures. One reason is because it is difficult to quantify seapower's strategic gains. Seapower lies beyond the horizon of economic forecast models. Seapower is not a variable in an economic equation but instead creates the conditions for establishing stable commercial relations on the world's waterways. If one of the most important results of naval power is difficult to quantify, what are the likely consequences for American commercial and national security once the memory of danger to trade by sea recedes and disappears?

Mahan viewed seapower as the protector of *democratic* freedom because he understood that Americans have a talent for creating wealth. Seapower is needed to increase that wealth by overseas trade. Mahan saw—as did Alexander Hamilton—that expanding wealth would move the international system toward a commercial competition that was more productive than military contests, as well as one in which the United States was likely to hold the upper hand. An additional benefit of successful commercial competition is being able to afford the most advanced military equipment. Thus for Mahan, commerce not only offers democracies a special economic advantage but national security as well. More than assuring the continuation of liberal commerce on the seas and securing freedom from domination by other states, seapower wins the greatest power: commercial supremacy.

Peace and War

Mahan argues that a thriving commercial shipping industry naturally produces a healthy navy, not a force that exists by whim of a monarch or the command of an autocratic regime—like that of Kaiser Wilhelm's or the Soviet navy. Mahan almost always sees the power of commerce as an aspect of national strength, inseparable from effective seapower. Mahan articulates a widely overlooked part of our military strategy: seapower's significance during *times of peace*, or what today is called force projection.

A peacetime superpower like the United States can send powerful mobile force to any place in the world's oceans or on their coasts at any time—and keep it there indefinitely. Seapower is the most cost-effective and efficient means of indirectly diverting the efforts of other states. Its mobile power can persuade competitors to develop commercially and militarily in accordance with our strategic interests. Attempting the same goal with ground forces is neither practicable nor desirable. More than any other military instrument, seapower can serve as a *preventative* force, one that if maintained vigorously reassures friends of support, reminds allies of American commitment, and can prevent states without navies from developing them. It can accomplish these objectives from a great distance. During the Punic Wars, Rome's absolute control of the Mediterranean Sea, Mahan argues, convinced Hannibal to abandon naval development and compelled him to march across the Alps—a diversion that drained his expenses and manpower.[3]

Mahan writes that naval strategy during peace is guided primarily by three principles: a great seafaring commercial state must (a) build and sustain a large merchant fleet; (b) prevent potential competitors from constructing their own merchant fleet; and (c) determine if its interest is best served by encouraging a competitor or potential competitor to build a fleet of questionable strategic value.

Mahan argues that the first error commercial states make is outsourcing their shipping to other states. Mahan's judgment on this as it applies to the United States must for now weigh in the balance. The outsourcing of shipping was the silent though immediate cause of the decline of the Spanish navy in the seventeenth century. Although thousands of Spaniards left Spain to colonize the New World, their labor yielded relatively little merchandise to send home. The absence of goods to ship home and an underdeveloped manufacturing industry in their colonies ensured the decay of Spain's shipping fleet. This in turn magnified the decay of her naval fleet. An underdeveloped merchant fleet compelled the Spanish to rely on Dutch shipping, and the Dutch, ironically, gained significantly from Spain's colonial exploits. In the end, Spain's fictitious wealth was squandered on shipping costs, instead of being spent more wisely on manufactures and trade, or simply lost to piracy and bad weather.[4]

Thus, the second error great commercial states make is allowing competitors to develop their own merchant shipping to support their foreign trade. Mahan argues that commercial powers can dissuade competitors from developing their own shipping industry by undercutting shipping costs directly or by restricting competitors' access to raw materials or technology in constructing a robust commercial fleet. This policy was never attempted by the United States toward China, which now owns several of the largest shipping companies in the world. The question of such a policy's merits is one that history will have to answer. The U.S. bet on China during Washington's struggle with Moscow, and those who placed this bet—Henry Kissinger foremost among them—have not reconsidered whether, by seeking to offset one danger, they helped to create another.

Mahan contends that it may even be a good idea for a state to encourage its competitor to build a blue-water navy independently of a commercial fleet. Such a navy will likely have the appearance of strength but will be short-lived and financially disastrous. Germany, for example, invested huge sums in large, powerful surface ships in both world wars and in the end had little to show for it. The ambition to build a global navy can harm a rival by compelling it to devote large resources to naval power, and all the more so if the rival simultaneously seeks to dominate on land and at sea. Mahan argues that "the strength of [Holland] was early exhausted by the necessity of keeping up a large army and carrying on expensive wars on the sea to preserve her independence; while the policy of France was constantly diverted, sometimes wisely and sometimes most foolishly, from the sea to projects of continental extension. These military efforts expended wealth: whereas a wise and consistent use of her geographical position would have added to it.[5]

The more subtle strategy, the one best undertaken in peace, is to secure and hold territories useful for commerce or territorial management, or as preparation for the possibility of determined commercial competition or armed conflict itself. As a theorist Mahan would have nodded approvingly of China's efforts to develop the naval facilities and supporting bases in the Indo-Pacific region called the "string of pearls." He observes that "in peace [naval strategy] . . . may gain its most decisive victories by occupying in a country, either by purchase or treaty, excellent positions which would perhaps hardly be got by war.[6] The United States, for example, maintained a naval base at Subic Bay in the Philippines for over ninety years following the Spanish-American War of 1898. Times of peace are devoted to quietly securing strategically valuable territories with an eye toward the possibility of war—ends best pursued in the form of humanitarian aid, disaster relief, and commercial or shared security interests. Peace for Mahan is a breather, a time when architects of foreign policy look to the direct and indirect effects of far-flung seapower in a future when gun ports are once again opened.

Thus, without spending enormous sums of money on stationing garrisons abroad or maintaining military bases, and without facing the logistical, monetary, and public relations difficulties of establishing what amounts to military colonies, the navy becomes an armed chess set whose global maneuverability equals its adaptability to use force, threaten to do so merely by appearing, or assist states in need. This flexibility allows a state that possesses dominant seapower to influence, either directly or indirectly, other states, as the United States has done from the Barbary Wars to today when—as noted above—combat vessels have been dispatched to reassure South Korean and Taiwanese friends who face threats from neighbors. Moreover, restricting or limiting a strategic rival's access to global waters also indirectly controls their military development by forcing a competitor to choose between developing on the sea or on land. The example of contemporary Russia is a good one. Even at current oil and natural gas prices, Russia cannot yet afford a competitive blue-water fleet—they have even turned to selling off old Soviet equipment while keeping active their naval industrial base to produce submarines and destroyers for sale abroad. The lack of global naval power pressures Russia to maintain its continental forces. As a result, the monopoly of Central Asia's energy dominates Russia's strategic concerns as it cannot afford to challenge U.S. control of the seas.

A powerful navy with a global reach can persuade a strategic competitor to rely on trade with its neighboring states or at least restrict a competitor's trade abroad by controlling its access of the sea. If used wisely, seapower can—from a great distance—prevent the rise of a competing power. While limiting himself to strategy exclusively, Mahan supplies a powerful example of indirect influence: "At the present day, looking only at the geographical position of Italy, and not at the other conditions affecting her seapower, it would seem that with her extensive sea-coast and good ports she is very well placed for exerting a decisive influence on the trade route to the Levant and by the isthmus to Suez. This is true in a degree, and would be much more so did Italy now hold all the islands naturally Italian; but with Malta in the hands of England, and Corsica in those of France, the advantages of her geographical position are largely neutralized."[7]

Though ultimately competing against each other, France and England together silently neutralized the potential naval threat of Italy. In taking away Italy's freedom of movement around its shores, France and England curtailed Italy's economic development before it could begin. Strategic projection of force at a distance shapes a competitor's behavior without war. If friends and potential enemies in the region believe that the United States cannot or will not maintain its naval presence in the western Pacific, six thousand to seven thousand miles from California, alliances will shift, instability will follow, and the likelihood of Chinese hegemony in Asia—which accomplishes the same objectives as war without conflict—greatly increases. Maritime strategy has the power to reverse the benefits of geography in the service of strategic interests.

Conversely, a failure to project force at a distance also has consequences. The evisceration of China's navy that followed the end of the third Ming emperor's reign began a long descent into national weakness, which eventually led to China's colonization by European powers in the nineteenth century.

Beneath Economics—the Conflict Between Comfort and Efficiency, and Scarcity

Liberal commerce orders relations between states through the principle of interest. But Mahan questions whether *international* commerce is possible without the support of global seapower. He asks whether in the absence of such power only variations of disorder, war, and piracy persist on the seas. For Mahan, combat seapower—whether or not exercised by democratic states—is the force that first establishes the grounds for trade on the sea and safeguards its continuation.

Mahan opens the argument of his most famous work with a philosophical observation that explains the necessity of force: scarcity. He starts his narration of seventeenth-century European history by explaining the motives of states: "to secure to one's own people a disproportionate share of benefits, every effort was made to exclude others, either by peaceful legislative methods of monopoly or prohibitory regulations, or, when these failed, by direct violence."[8] Nations not only have endless appetites, but these appetites inevitably conflict with the interests of other states. Mahan reasons that nations both desire to and must seek gain. By implication he contends that there is no permanent status quo. From this assumption comes the primary question: *How do nations seek wealth?*[9]

The acquisition of wealth is not limited by commercial markets but by geography as well. The possession of geographic choke points and clear passages affects the commercial interests of nations. Geographic limits such as vulnerability to invasion or inaccessibility to the sea affect both prosperity and security. To protect themselves, states must take and hold strategic positions, usually at the expense of others.[10] The English-Dutch force that captured Gibraltar in the War of the Spanish Succession gave the Royal Navy not only a logistical perch for projecting power into the Mediterranean but a choke hold over entrance to the inland sea that by treaty is to remain under British sovereignty forever. The British use Gibraltar today as a logistics base. It served the same purpose during the 1982 Falklands War. If the Mediterranean becomes a flash point of international tension, for example, as a result of the possible radicalization of a large part of the Middle East following the Arab Spring of 2011, a destabilizing Islamist takeover of Turkey, the need to protect Israel against growing Islamist militancy, and Europe against Iranian missiles, England's possession of this key choke point will again demonstrate its usefulness.

If Mahan is right that scarcity is the overarching *economic* determinant of states' behavior, and if modern democracies are constituted to pursue comfort and well-being, competition is an unalterable fact of international life that always ends disproportionately. The same truth applies to nondemocratic states: their rulers may seek to enrich the state's coffers by selling mineral wealth, practicing mercantilist economic policy, seeking monopolies, or some combination of each of these. But the visible hand of scarcity touches all: competition always yields winners and losers.

If states relate to one another through either alliance or competition, as Mahan believes they do, successful commercial states follow one of three tracks: they either seek to (a) turn other states into allies by guiding them toward democratic laws through commercial pressure or military influence, as the United States did in Japan and Korea; (b) control the world's waterways for the purpose of "managing" trade; or (c) send out colonies.

Mahan cites history to provide three examples of states that pursue militarism either for imperial conquest or for commerce: Spain, France, and England. All three represented forms of commercial expansion that depended on seapower. The Spanish had the advantage of arriving in the New World before the rest of Europe. Mahan sees in the Spanish character great national spirit, boldness, an enterprising nature, and enthusiasm, which contributed to their quick accumulation of wealth. However, their "fierce avarice" for gold and silver prevented the development of new fields of industry and private enterprise: Spanish interest in bullion was not matched by a talent for trade and manufacturing.[11]

The French, on the other hand, lacked boldness, particularly in their financial investments, which, Mahan observes, reflected the private and restricted character of their ambition. Moreover, those who were motivated to acquire enough wealth to gain a title of nobility promptly left the world of commerce altogether. This deprived the commercial class of its best exemplars and practitioners. Vanity, Mahan argues, was the French motive for acquiring wealth.

The British and the Dutch, on the other hand, "sought riches not by the sword but by labor"—a path that required the longest and most farsighted kind of industrial organization and investment.[12] The British and Dutch looked at the world in terms of production and extracting from the earth raw goods for production. They developed lands both agriculturally and through manufacturing, which multiplied the commerce between colony and mother country. But most important, both peoples were free and did not need the heavy hand of a mother state to guide their industriousness.

Manufacturing and Service Economies

If, as Mahan argues, the United States mirrors England more than seventeenth-century Spain or France, a new problem exists, one that Mahan did not foresee. Manufacturing economies, as Mahan argues, rely on naval power to protect commerce. However, service economies—such as the United States has in important measure become—*appear* to rely less and less on seapower as the need to protect the ocean-borne import and export of raw materials and finished goods decreases. But service economies in fact depend even more on seapower because of the absence of a shipping fleet.

Commercial ships can disappear from waters they once dominated without ruining the combat fleets built to protect them. The U.S. example proves this. A large merchant fleet hasn't existed in the United States since the Civil War. But even for a nation that is replacing manufacturing with a service economy and has rented foreign hulls to carry its own goods—as the United States has—the ability to control strategic choke points, along with such other advantages as projecting power and command of the seas, remains critical to the order on which freedom of navigation depends. The sea routes to whose safety such states have become accustomed risk the imposition of new forms of rule based on new interests and different ideas of international order. When the Royal Navy abandoned its forward presence in the western Pacific to Japan in 1904, a new and destructive order established itself there. This order led soon to Japanese aggression in Asia and eventually to war with the United States.

This helps explain the popularity Mahan has enjoyed in China.[13] Their rapidly enlarging merchant fleet and developing manufacturing economy are linked to a rising naval fleet. Mahan would have seen this at once. If at the same time the U.S. combat fleet's prospects for long-term health dim, international conflicts— which harm trade—will not subside; they will increase. And the strategic fall from grace worsens. Without dominant seapower, what are the choices? Land intervention—the costliest and most politically unpopular option—or impotence. The United States loses strategically as well as commercially. The replacement of English with American naval power meant little to the international order since England and the United States shared similar views of international order. The replacement of America's dominant position as a global seapower by another state's, for example, China's, would have much more serious consequences. China has an idea of national sovereignty that encompasses international waters: we see the same waters as essential to untrammeled navigation. Preserving command of the seas supports the competitive advantage that the United States hopes to maintain. It allows communication with the alliances that we hope to keep if we do not voluntarily disarm. And it gives the United States broad strategic options. If the debt crisis the United States must address is resolved at the expense of commanding the seas, the cure to our financial woes will prove a Pyrrhic victory.

Equality, Wealth, and Democracy

In both peace and war, the goal of maritime strategy is the increase in the strength of a country, and "its study has an interest and value for all citizens of a free country."[14]

Unlike Spanish avarice or French vanity as the motive for commerce, the democratic disposition toward commerce encourages efficiency. Commerce is a means toward gain for the purpose of well-being, comfort, and security. In democracies, the cheapest means win the day, and rationally developed commerce will always prove least expensive.

But equality itself fosters social conditions that favor liberal commerce. Characteristic of democratic societies, "wealth, as a source of civic distinction, carried with it also power in the state; and with power there went social position and consideration."[15] Moreover, "in a representative government the power of wealth could be neither put down nor overshadowed. It was patent to the eyes of all, it was honored by all; and in England, as well as Holland, the occupations which were the source of wealth shared in the honor given to wealth itself."[16] Egalitarian states honor wealth as a mark of social distinctions that are otherwise lacking, unlike aristocracies, where titles are granted. Egalitarian states also look favorably on trade because wealth is among the few available means to political power in democracies.

Alexis de Tocqueville observed nearly one hundred years before Mahan that "almost all the tastes and habits that are born of equality naturally lead men toward commerce and industry," which he sees as distinct from agriculture.[17] The middle class desires to better one's lot and to apply rational principles to satisfy this desire; the private, apolitical character of the middle class leads citizens to pursue the most direct ways to attain wealth, which are always commerce and industry.[18] Tocqueville also rightly saw that in America "the greatest industrial enterprises are executed without difficulty, because the population as a whole is involved in industry and because the poorest as well as the most opulent citizens willingly unite their efforts in this.[19] However, Tocqueville warns that because all Americans are "occupied with industry at the same time . . . they are subject to very unexpected and very formidable industrial crises" together, and all at once.[20] As an effect of social equality, all Americans are, in Tocqueville's view, economic beings dependent on the state of the economy as a whole. Their efforts together must ensure the means to safeguard commerce, or they must all equally suffer the losses.

But with democracies, as with individuals, virtues often come with darker sides. The pursuit of efficiency can blur the long-term vision of democracies. Observing the democratic character of his people, the Dutch statesman Johan de Witt writes: "Never in time of peace and from fear of a rupture will [the Dutch] take resolutions strong enough to lead them to pecuniary sacrifices beforehand. The character of the Dutch[21] is such that, unless danger stares them in the face, they are indisposed to lay out money for their own defense. I have to do with a people who, liberal to profusion where they ought to economize, are often sparing to avarice where they ought to spend."[22]

Aristocracies, Mahan argues, do not suffer from similar problems. He saw the English landed classes' political power as a highly effective bulwark of support for maintaining superior and effective seapower.[23] The wealthy aristocracy feels financial burdens less and, "not being commercial, the sources of its own wealth are not so immediately endangered, and it does not share that political timidity which characterizes those whose property is exposed and business threatened—the proverbial timidity of capital."[24]

Ensuring and protecting the preparedness of the industrial base, knowing what parts of society to call upon for sea service if crises arise, and knowing citizens' aversion to military spending are all dilemmas that Mahan advises democratic statesmen to understand.[25] "It behooves countries whose genius is essentially not military, whose people, like all free people, object to paying for large military establishments, to see to it that they are at least strong enough to gain the time necessary to turn the spirit and capacity of their subjects into the new activities which war calls for."[26]

The world's waterways are of themselves neutral and without a preference for the state that governs them. Different states bring their own order of governing the seas. The United States brings with it liberal economics. It is difficult to imagine serious discussions of international maritime law or treaties that establish a law of the seas had the Soviet Union emerged victorious in the Cold War. The fragility of commerce—for instance, the control over such strategic territories and regions as Taiwan, the South China Sea, and the Philippines—can disrupt the smooth trade we have with Asia.

Commerce between states—especially between states that engage in both strategic and economic competition—does not exist within a predictable and rational system, but depends on strategic planning, economic competition, and chance. The Chinese, for instance, are deeply conscious of their trade advantage over the U.S. and EU high currency valuation. China's insistence in undervaluing the yuan maintains a competitive advantage over its large trading partners. That is, such principles as allowing currencies to find their own value in relation to other currencies play a role in commercial relations and commerce does not simply tend toward a common good arising from self-interested liberal economics. Such orders are not only initially established but later maintained and safeguarded by naval presence.

America's allies in the Pacific are currently being pressed more immediately than we are. Their predicament demonstrates the importance of American seapower as an assurance of agreements and good relations with our Pacific allies. The U.S. Navy's 2007 maritime strategy focused on humanitarian assistance and disaster relief. The word "China" did not appear in the entire published strategy. This plus recent administrations' reluctance publicly to discuss or act in response to China's growing naval power suggest that American leaders neither look at strategic competition with China in the long term nor recognize the Chinese desire slowly to push U.S. seapower out of the international waters in their proximity.

Mahan offers the intellectual arguments to understand what the United States stands to lose economically and militarily—and all that China will gain if there is a profound shift of power in the western Pacific. Commerce, he believes, plays to the natural advantage of an enterprising people who are largely free to act upon their judgment. But commercial advantage relies equally on the ability to keep open the oceanic arteries through which decisively superior commerce must be able to flow. This equation is set on its head when prosperity becomes an important instrument to justify rule—as in China. There, freedoms of commerce are restricted by the state's pressing requirement, for example, to employ millions; by an understanding of commercial freedom that is wholly separate from political freedom or consideration of a larger international order; and by a parallel view of seapower that sees the interruption of commerce no less as a national economic challenge than as a threat to those who rule the state. This idea of order is inconsistent with free commerce, which Mahan understood serves the objective of democratic expansion and rests on dominant seapower as its means. Or, if Mahan had been more inclined toward Euclidean formulae, he might have put it this way: democracy is to commerce what commerce is to seapower. To the degree that the spread of democracy depends on the wealth gained in commercial mastery, the same success in commerce depends on seapower. But Mahan was not exclusively a theorist. His practical ideas about command of the sea, defense at a distance, and the importance of choke points and bases had precedents in America's use of seapower, geography, and the quality of naval leadership. Mahan, in sum, believed that Americans' talent for business directed them toward substantial participation in international commerce and that naval force was needed to protect this commerce along with the sea-lanes over which it flows. He argued that the international order that follows in the wake of a modern liberal democracy's seapower contributes mightily to such a democracy's strategic defense and status as a preeminent power. Mahan's insights remain especially applicable over one hundred years later as a potential competitor, China, sees in his idea of the link between commercial activity, large fleets, and increasing international influence a means of extending their power, which is not rooted in the same values of free markets, free access to open seas, and political liberty that have generally characterized the use of American power and the conduct of American foreign policy. The next chapter traces the rise of American seapower and its general conformity to Mahan's major ideas on democracy, commerce, geography, naval force, and international influence.

3

The Roots of
American Seapower

ECAUSE THE UNITED STATES DEVELOPED from a small to a great power so quickly—in only a little more than a century—the rise of American seapower is similarly compressed. One of its persistent characteristics is tactical and operational flexibility. Other unchanging elements include technological innovation and the clear, if not always articulated, objective of projecting power internationally for the purpose of preventing conflict from reaching our shores. Beneath this sturdy superstructure and coeval with its emergence appeared the frame of intellectual justification of Mahan. Mahan helped transform seapower into a focused instrument. His ideas about command of the seas became popular around the time that American leaders started thinking—as Woodrow Wilson did—that relief from catastrophic global confrontation might be sought in adherence to universal principles. Wilson's League of Nations was a conspicuous failure. But whether by osmosis or happenstance, the idea of international order took real shape as growing American seapower encompassed the globe and gradually, although not deliberately, assumed responsibility for preserving a form of international order.

But the story begins with simple self-defense. By the end of the American Revolution, British forces had captured most of the

Continental navy that Congress authorized, and the better part of what remained was burned or scuttled to keep ships out of enemy hands. Yet less than four decades later American frigates were engaging and defeating Royal Navy combatants on the high seas. American maritime strategy evolved parallel to the nation's growth and national crises. But it was constructed from the beginning on the same thoughtfulness and perception that characterized the founders' political judgments. John Adams and other founders looked to their own times for the European Enlightenment's ideas about natural right. Locke and Hobbes sought to establish fundamental political principles—such as the universal desire to preserve life, enjoy liberty, and prosper—by examining human nature as recorded by ancient historians and characterized by later political philosophers. The American founders embraced European Enlightenment political theory and focused on the practical benefits and weaknesses of ancient democracies and republics, including how they defended themselves. This made sense. There was no other recorded experience of the workings and details of popular government practiced on a grand scale. John Adams, the chief proponent of a strong navy for the new American republic, wrote about Athens, other Greek city-states including Corinth and Sparta, and, of course, Rome. But he describes Carthage first.

The ruins of Roman baths look northeast to the spreading arms of the Gulf of Tunis. Framed by these widely separated promontories is the swelling Mediterranean, where the arms join at the base stood Carthage. Americans' understanding of seapower sprang as much from John Adams's seagoing New England background as his thoughts on Carthage, whose government he claimed "resembles those of the States of America, more than any other of the ancient republics, perhaps more than the modern."[1] Adams wrote admiringly of the Carthaginians' enterprising habits, military prowess, and balance of political powers. He was also keenly aware of the link between the ancient African city's spirit, its geography, its commerce, and its reliance on controlling the seas. "Their commerce and riches," Adams wrote, "their empire of the sea, and extensive dominion of two thousand miles on the sea coast, their obstinate military contests with Rome . . . prove both that their population and power were very great, and their constitution good . . ."[2]

Adams was a student of the Roman historians Polybius and Livy, the principal ancient sources of our knowledge about the wars between Rome and Carthage. He understood the strategic advantage to Carthage of its combat fleet. He realized, as did the Allied and Axis high command two millennia later, the truth in Polybius's comment that the Romans could "not abandon Messana [today's Messina] and thus allow the Carthaginians to secure a bridgehead for the invasion of Italy."[3] He saw how Carthage's navy countered Roman victories in contested Sicily with raids against Italy itself. He could not have overlooked Rome's eventual success in denying Carthage access to central Mediterranean bases, including Sicily, thus forcing Hannibal's circuitous invasion of Rome through Spain and over the Alps. Nor could he have failed to see how naval power allowed Rome both to resupply its ground forces in Spain and to choke Carthage's Spanish supply center—New Carthage—the present-day Cartagena, a frequent port of call for U.S. Navy ships that visit the Mediterranean today.

Big Coast, Little Navy

Adams's published work indicates that he took from Polybius and Livy an advanced grasp of the benefits that controlling the seas offer where ambition, commerce, and defense strategy coincide with a state's geographic proximity to the sea. His policy and public statements show that he applied these lessons to his presidency.

The treaty that Supreme Court Chief Justice John Jay negotiated with England in November 1794 put to rest issues that remained from the Revolutionary War. The treaty was finalized seven months after George Washington signed the legislation that directed the construction or purchase of six powerful—for their size—and swift frigates. Jay's Treaty also followed Washington's announcement of neutrality in the war between England and France by a year. This irritated France's revolutionary rulers, who were already angry that the United States had declined to repay monies borrowed during the Revolution, arguing that war debt was owed to the French crown and not the First Republic. France began issuing writs to privateers to prey on American shipping bound for British and British colonial ports and declined to accept the new American ambassador, Charles Cotesworth Pinckney, when he arrived in Paris at the end of 1796 to present his credentials.

Tensions continued to rise as France set aside the alliance of the American Revolution and threatened American neutrality and trade with England. At the time the American navy consisted chiefly of one out of six of the frigates authorized by Congress, the recently launched *United States*, and she was not yet ready to sail, much less to fight. Even if it had been sea-ready, *United States* could not have protected the coastal areas from southern New England to the Middle Atlantic states, where French privateers waited to descend on American merchant shipping. In June 1797 Secretary of State Timothy Pickering told Congress that French privateers had seized over three hundred American merchant ships in the preceding year. When Congress vacated existing treaties with France in the summer of 1798 and authorized attack on French ships, the Quasi-War smoldered into existence, characterized by single-ship engagements often in the West Indies and the protection and recapture of American merchant vessels.

The United States' dearth of West Indies bases pulled American combatants back to U.S. homeports for repairs and supplies, leaving commerce in peril, but still naval presence proved effective. The seizure of American merchant ships fell dramatically in 1799 and Congress reported that U.S. naval force had prevented

$9 million in merchant losses on the high seas. Late in the same year, Napoleon took power and saw monarchic England as a greater strategic threat than the American republic. He swiftly ended the Quasi-War in 1800.

But the ideas that sprang from this almost-war were far more important than its strategic results. Adams's message to the special session of Congress in May 1797 was the intellectual keel on which American seapower would be built. He argued that a coastline of two thousand miles—precisely the same length he calculated Carthage's to be—guaranteed that Americans will apply their energy to the seas in commerce, fishing, and navigation. He warned that serious or permanent damage to this commerce would be crippling and insisted that it must be protected. The United States depended on commerce. Commerce was borne by the sea. Adams completed the syllogism: "A naval power, next to the militia, is the natural defense of the United States."[4]

Adams did not overlook the parallel military point. America's interest in defending seaborne trade was as great as the nation's strategic ability to deny the seas to a potential enemy. England's control of the coastal seas during much of the Revolutionary War "baffled many formidable transportations of troops from one state to another . . ."[5]

Reminding Congress that toothless neutrality in the dispute between France and England had been useless in protecting against the French and that apparent defenselessness had encouraged French privateers, Adams concluded that "the establishment of a permanent system of naval defense appears to be requisite."[6] He asked Congress to ensure that the frigates under construction were properly supplied, and he encouraged the construction of smaller naval vessels to "convoy" unarmed merchant ships.

Nor did Adams's strategic conception stop here. He argued that a seafaring nation must also protect the ports through which trade as well as naval logistics flow. "The distance of the United States from Europe and the well-known promptitude, ardor, and courage of the people in defense of their country happily diminish the probability of invasion. Nevertheless, to guard against sudden and predatory incursions the situation of some of our principal sea ports demands your consideration."[7]

The articulation of naval theories was still more than a century in the future, but here Adams had laid down four of the most fundamental ideas: (a) the importance of geography to seapower; (b) the inflexible requirement of defending seagoing trade for a commercial state with large exposure to the seas; (c) the strategic imperative of being able to transport troops and military equipment by sea; and (d) the pivotal role of ports or, more broadly understood, bases, in maintaining seapower. Although unformulated as general propositions, plentiful strategic justification for Adams's arguments existed.

The naval portion of the mid-eighteenth-century War of the Austrian Succession, for example, was a good recent example that supported John Adams's concern about defending merchant shipping. The war was a struggle for dominant power on the European continent in which the maritime states of England and Holland took Austria's side against Prussia and France, which objected to the succession of a woman—Maria Theresa of Austria—to the Habsburg throne as a convenient excuse for a war to bolster their strategic position to the east and south. Because of the geographic spread of the contestants' colonial possessions and alliances on both sides, the conflict came as close to a world war as would be seen until the twentieth century.

Although the fighting took place primarily on the Continent, naval exchanges occurred around the European littoral including the Mediterranean. They reached into the Caribbean and extended to both sides of the Pacific and the Indian Ocean. Decisive results did not characterize the conflict's end. Maria Theresa kept her throne and Silesia, part of today's Poland, changed hands from Austrian to Prussian control. At sea, however, as Alfred Thayer Mahan observed, the commercial trade of England, France, and Holland was decimated. France and Spain lost more than thirty-four hundred merchant ships while England lost some thirty-two hundred, an apparent equality that is belied, Mahan argued, by England's far larger shipping industry. Moreover, in the commerce raiding war, England came out £2 million ahead of her French and Spanish rivals. Mahan quoted the French count Lapeyrouse Bonfils's 1845 *Histoire de Marine Française*: "The French flag did not appear at sea. Twenty-two ships-of-the-line composed the navy of France, which sixty years before had one hundred and twenty. Privateers made few prizes; followed everywhere, unprotected, they almost always fell a prey to the English. The British naval forces, without any rivals, passed unmolested over the seas. In one year they are said to have taken from French commerce £7,000,000 sterling."[8]

Lacking the means to protect one's commerce is expensive and strategically crippling. England was better equipped to bear losses because its seaborne commerce greatly exceeded that of her enemies. France proved vulnerable to severe merchant shipping losses in its home waters because it lacked the naval strength that Adams told Congress was needed to protect American commerce from French privateers in 1797.

Jefferson and the Pirates: Principles vs. Facts

Jefferson's presidency expanded Adams' principles although, as was often the case with Jefferson, his conclusions looked inconsistent with his stated theories. In 1806 as the dispute between France and England sharpened, both states attempted to restrict each other's trade. The sanctions they declared hurt neutral shippers who tried to do business on both sides of the English Channel, including American merchantmen who traded with England or sailed among the French ports looking for business in the carrying trade or selling goods. In his 1807 message to Congress, Jefferson explicitly rejected "protecting our commerce on the open seas even on our coast." He hoped for European hostilities to end but proposed building a large fleet of small gunboats armed with a single bow gun and constructed to operate in shallow waters. These, he proposed, would be distributed for "defensive operation" "among the ports and harbors of the United States."[9]

Jefferson recoiled at the idea of paying for a navy to compete with the great European powers. Notwithstanding the host of ships that England and France deployed across the Atlantic during the Revolutionary War, Jefferson argued against a naval force that could challenge the great European powers. Distance from American shores and the uncertainties of traversing it, he thought, guaranteed that "a small part only of their naval force will ever be risqued [sic] across the Atlantic."[10] Nevertheless, he was adamant about the Barbary pirates.

England protected its American colonies' trade against Mediterranean pirates until the War of Independence. The 1778 alliance between the United States and France that Adams and Franklin negotiated shifted responsibility for protecting U.S. Mediterranean trade to French hands. After the war ended officially in 1783, the United States became responsible for protecting itself. American merchant ships' trade in agricultural products, including lumber, as well as salted cod in exchange for Mediterranean olive oil, citrus crops, and wine, was measured in the tens of thousands of tons. Pirates operating out of the Barbary States of Algiers, Morocco, Tripoli, and Tunis took more than note. They started seizing American ships, cargoes, and crews. Jefferson and Adams, who were both serving as diplomats in the mid-1780s, disagreed over meeting the ransom demands of pirates who had captured two American ships. Adams agreed with the prevailing international approach: paying tribute was cheaper than equipping a naval force to put the pirates out of business.

Jefferson demurred. Echoing the ideas and rhetoric that he had marshaled so elegantly in the Declaration of Independence, he argued that honor, justice, and the respect of other states required the United States to use force against the pirates. He proposed an international coalition to conduct operations against

the pirates "beginning with the Algerines" with the object of compelling "the piratical states to perpetual peace without price."[11]
Jefferson recommended "constant cruises on their coast" composed of "half a dozen frigates, with as many Tenders or Xebecs
[small, highly maneuverable two or three-masted lateen-rigged
and oared coastal vessels used by the pirates]."[12]

For Jefferson, the honor and respect risked by submitting to
the pirates' blackmail in the Mediterranean surpassed the losses
that U.S. merchant shippers suffered in the form of collateral damage inflicted by the northern European powers' mutual pummeling.
Defending against the former was also much less expensive than
building a navy to prevent the latter. Jefferson enlarged Adams's
idea of defending shipping in coastal waters by applying the same
notion in a very limited form to protect American shipping at the
other side of the Atlantic into the central Mediterranean. Limited
defense of sea lines of communication would be affordable and
achievable as it served the larger purpose of warning foreign states
that the United States would not be bullied—at least up to a point.

Jefferson was as good as his word. In February 1804 Lieutenant Stephen Decatur led a detachment of U.S. Navy officers
and men who boarded and burned the captured frigate U.S.S.
Philadelphia, which was riding to anchor in the port of Tripoli.
The Tripolitans had seized and renamed her *Gift of Allah* after
the vessel grounded while on blockade duty the previous October.
The Tripolitan authorities also controlled the fate of the ship's
crew of more than three hundred men. Jefferson learned of
Philadelphia's capture and the detention of her crew before
he received news of Decatur's exploits in March. The president
immediately told Congress that the ship, "its officers and men,
had fallen into the hands of the Tripolitans."[13] He urged the
national legislature to increase spending required to prepare
additional naval forces for the conflict with the Barbary States.
Congress responded affirmatively and swiftly. Four frigates and a
supply ship were prepared for service in the Mediterranean and
set sail in late June.

Meanwhile Captain Edward Preble, commodore of the Mediterranean squadron, had become convinced that while deep-draft American frigates could perform useful blockade operations and provide cover against shore batteries, only smaller, shallow-draft vessels armed with shorter-range guns could contest the Tripolitan coastal navy and deliver effective fire into the city. He used these tactics throughout much of August, during which the larger ships whose outfitting Congress had authorized, completed their journey from the east coast of the United States. Despite setbacks and changes in command, American naval force wore down the Tripolitan leader, Yusuf Karamanli. Jefferson's resolve persisted. It supported a combination of blockades, bombardments, more frigates with long-range guns, and a U.S. Marine–led column that marched on Tripoli from the east in a combined operation with U.S. ships off the coast that captured the port city of Derna. Karamanli turned reasonable and agreed to a conclusion of hostilities that ended the practice of demanding tribute from American merchantmen, but he insisted on and received a ransom for Americans still held in his prisons.

This ended the first war with the Barbary States, but not the source of the problem. The treaties signed by the Barbary chieftains and warlords who sanctioned and profited from preying on commerce were no stronger than the North African rulers' fear of their enforcement. The War of 1812 concentrated U.S. naval effort on the Atlantic and homeland defense. Barbary attacks on American shipping in the Mediterranean increased. With the 1812 war concluded, James Madison sent a squadron of ten ships under Stephen Decatur, now a captain, back to North Africa to end attacks on American shipping permanently. A second squadron of seventeen American combatants followed Decatur by several weeks. Decatur sailed through the Strait of Gibraltar in the late spring of 1815 and captured two Algerian warships. He brought his prizes into the port of Algiers and refused to negotiate any terms except a cessation of all tribute paid for American passage through the area. The captured Algerian warships, the size of the

American naval presence, Decatur's intransigence, and the Algerian dey's likely knowledge that England had failed to defeat the United States in the recently concluded war yielded the objective Madison sought. The large U.S. naval squadron paid similar visits to Tunis and Tripoli and met with equal success. Tribute for passage of American shipping in the Mediterranean was over. The Barbary rulers understood the risk of breaking their word: the appearance of a large and powerful American naval force that could seize their naval power, raze their capitals, and shatter their rule.

Jefferson projected naval force at a large distance from the United States with the limited objective of protecting sea lines of communication. He put into practice the principle of defending seaborne commerce that Adams asserted and defended when he sent U.S. warships to safeguard American shipping in the West Indies during the Quasi-War with France. The derivative blockading and amphibious operations that helped secure Jefferson's war objectives had been tools of naval force since Agamemnon's coalition landed at Troy and sought to prevent the besieged city's reinforcement from the sea. Jefferson's use of these traditional naval instruments increased the U.S. Navy's operational experience but, more important, national leadership's flexibility and understanding of the uses of seapower to apply force and defend American interests at a great distance from home.

The War of 1812 and Its Lessons

Madison's use of naval force was constructed on Jefferson's. The objective of protecting the sea-lanes for U.S. shipping was the same for both presidents. But Madison's use of overwhelming naval force showed the Barbary rulers that the United States could top anything they could muster.

The British tried to apply this principle during the War of 1812, but the length of the American coastline frustrated them and the impossibility of patrolling all of it prevented them. For the American navy, the ability to escalate over and above an enemy's strength—or what is called "escalation dominance" today—was never an issue in the 1812 conflict, which was the next significant marker in the development of U.S. naval strategy and thought.

Still, the war marked an important advance in America's reputation as a naval power, ability to project force, and understanding of the economics of seapower. Following Admiral Nelson's crushing defeat of the French-Spanish fleet off Cape Trafalgar in 1805, Napoleon abandoned hope of an amphibious invasion of Britain. He issued the Berlin Decree the following year, which forbade French, allied, or neutral ships from trading with Britain. England answered in late 1807 with an Order in Council that prohibited French trade with Britain along with her allies and neutrals. Under these edicts America's neutrality severed it from trading with either side or their allies. George III increased tensions with the United States by ordering the Royal Navy to remove British-born seamen from serving on foreign ships. This provided the royal imprimatur for a policy of impressment that was already a decade and a half old. American merchant shipping had expanded at the same moment that war with France spurred the Royal Navy's demand for sailors. British warships looked for crews in prisons, in pubs, in the streets, and on the high seas. The unlucky victims often deserted and impressment turned out to accentuate the problem it was intended to address.

Events slowly lit the wood that English policy had desiccated. In June 1807 a Royal Navy frigate, H.M.S. *Leopard*, intercepted the American frigate U.S.S. *Chesapeake* in the waters of the Virginia Capes and then attacked her after the American commanding officer refused to muster his crew for impressment. Jefferson took small steps. He ordered Royal Navy vessels to leave American ports and asked Congress for money to build single-gun gunboats to defend home waters. H.M.S. *Leopard* was a relatively small British combatant equipped with about fifty guns, or half the number carried aboard Nelson's flagship, H.M.S. *Victory*, and other Royal Navy capital ships. Writing more than seven decades later, Theodore Roosevelt was openly contemptuous. He called "President Jefferson's ideas of having an enormous force of very worthless gun-boats—a scheme whose wisdom was about on a par with some of that statesman's political and military theories."[14] Jefferson also succeeded in shepherding through Congress an Embargo Act intended to end the export of American agricultural products and the carrying trade on which British merchants partially depended. The Embargo Act complemented an earlier congressional measure that banned import of British goods, and was as porous as the scantlings of U.S.S. *Chesapeake* after suffering several of H.M.S. *Leopard*'s broadsides.

Ridiculed, opposed, and violated in sea and lake ports throughout the nation, the Embargo Act still had a powerful effect. Exports sank like an anchor—from $108 million in 1807 to $22 million the next year.[15] The act succeeded in damaging the American economy but failed to influence British restrictions on American trade. Smuggling, nearly universal contempt for the law, loopholes, and Jefferson's eventual all-but-revocation of the Embargo Act left the newly inaugurated James Madison in March 1809 with a diplomatic and military dilemma that had changed little in two years. The British still seized American sailors on the high seas and battling the great European powers choked but by no means impoverished American traders.

Despite British and French predations on neutrals, American trade measured in tonnage exceeded its preembargo level, reaching 910,059 tons in 1809.[16] In April 1811, as the result of what was likely a case of confused communications at night, an American frigate and a smaller British corvette fired at each other briefly. The smaller vessel suffered greater losses. Congress approved the return to service of two frigates that had been mothballed, and recriminations followed on both sides. Congress acted more assertively the following April, enacting a ninety-day embargo that was commonly understood to clear American merchant shipping from British ports in advance of a formal declaration of war. Madison delivered the formal declaration to Congress on June 1 and Congress approved it less than three weeks later.

The war is the textbook example of a global navy's—Britain's in this case—difficulty in applying effective seapower against a capable, determined, and far smaller regional power. The Royal Navy fleet numbered over 600 ships, with another two hundred vessels in yards for completion or repair.[17] Two years before the war began nearly one-fourth of Britain's combat-ready fleet were wooden ships-of-the-line, many of which equaled or exceeded in displacement America's steel destroyers of World War II. Britain was a transoceanic power. Her great ships prowled the Mediterranean between the Levant and Gibraltar, blockaded French ports from the Channel to Toulon, and crossed the Atlantic to protect trade with Canada and the West Indies. The Admiralty was conducting operations against the French in the Indian Ocean half a century before the War of 1812 and had successfully contested Napoleon's navy for control of France's Indian Ocean bases in 1811. The American navy's frigates were designed to be larger, faster, and more heavily armed than their British equivalents, but only seven existed when war was declared. Between Canada and the West Indies the Royal Navy had based 135 ships. With five of England's large, multidecked combatants similar to those that had played a decisive role in the Battle of Trafalgar and another thirty-two smaller but still powerful frigates, as well as a swarm of smaller corvettes and other minor fighting ships, Britain maintained a small but robust naval force in the western Atlantic theater.

Even with reinforcements, it wasn't enough. The difficulty of blockading America's two thousand miles of coast with its growing number and size of port cities, as well as swarms of privateers and early U.S. naval victories, frustrated the Royal Navy and withheld decisive victory from its grasp. The U.S.S. *Constitution* outmaneuvered an entire squadron of British warships in July

1812 and made for Boston to replenish supplies. Anxious about a possible blockade, her commanding officer, Isaac Hull, stayed in port briefly and headed for the routes traversed by British supply ships bound for Canada's maritime provinces. In mid-August, about four hundred miles south of Newfoundland's eastern capes, the *Constitution* sighted and, in a battle that lasted thirty minutes, raked at close range with double-shotted broadsides the British frigate H.M.S. *Guerrière*. De-masted and stripped of motive power, *Guerrière* surrendered.

A print from 1813 depicting the U.S.S. Constitution *during its dramatic escape from the British Navy*

Constitution returned to Boston harbor as three of her sister ships arrived from their eastern Atlantic patrol. Again, navy leadership moved swiftly to put its frigates back to sea before a powerful British squadron could blockade Boston. U.S.S. *President* and U.S.S. *United States* departed Boston in early October. Two weeks later in the middle of the Atlantic *United States* with Stephen Decatur commanding sighted the frigate H.M.S. *Macedonian*. The two ships made for each other and went into action at nine a.m. on October 25. American fire swiftly incapacitated

Macedonian's masts, splintered the hull throughout, and killed or wounded a large part of the crew. *Macedonia* surrendered at once.

Sailing south to prey on British commercial shipping, *Constitution* left port in mid-October and encountered H.M.S. *Java* off the southeast Brazilian coast at the end of December. *Constitution* poured raking fire into the British frigate, whose officers and men tried unsuccessfully to board the American ship. Again, the Royal Navy crew saw their masts and spars shot away, leaving a blood-soaked deck, a severely damaged hull, and nearly 50 dead or mortally wounded and another 102 injured.[18] Command had passed to a lieutenant when American sniper fire grievously wounded *Java*'s commanding officer. The junior officer surrendered the ship.

Despite naval successes against French warships as the conflict with Napoleon smoldered, the most powerful seapower in the world had lost three combatants to the little American navy in just over four months. The Royal Navy high command ordered its captains to steer clear of single-ship combat with the victorious American frigates, but the damage was not only to British pride. James Madison's several messages to Congress in 1813 and 1814 resounded with praise for both the navy's and for privateers' achievements. "Our public ships of war in general, as well as the private armed vessels, have continued their activity and success against the commerce of the enemy . . ."[19] On this point the Americans and English agreed. Royal Navy Admiral John Borlase Warren, who commanded the North American Station, wrote to London in late December 1812. He asked for more ships and warned of "the Swarms of Privateers and Letters of Marque, their numbers now amounting to 600" that threatened to strangle British trade in the western Atlantic.[20] There was nothing idle about this threat. Four months after Admiral Warren sent his letter the *London Pilot* commented on British losses during the war's first seven months: "Five hundred merchantmen and three frigates!"[21] The same paper described the scope of American privateer operations: "They traverse the Atlantic; they beset the West

India Islands; they advance to the very chops of the Channel; they parade along the coasts of South America."[22]

The loss of her three frigates twisted British strategy. When Royal Navy numerical superiority was eventually brought to bear, it concentrated on the East Coast ports into which the successful American frigates had fled for safety. This allowed privateers and merchantmen to come and go elsewhere, for example, from southern and Gulf Coast ports. Still, American naval vessels escaped the blockade. U.S.S. *President* and U.S.S. *Congress* threaded a curtain of Boston fog and slid past a pair of vigilant but purblind British frigates in May 1813. Emerging, they sailed toward the Azores and separated about 750 miles east of the north coast of New Jersey. *Congress* patrolled in the southeastern Atlantic and returned to port eight months later after capturing only four merchantmen. *President* experienced as little good luck in the seas around Newfoundland as she did after navigating south to search for a Jamaican convoy. Her luck changed in British waters. *President* cruised among the Shetland and Orkney Islands, landed on the Norwegian coast to replenish her water supply, headed for Ireland, and returned to Newport, Rhode Island, with twelve prizes in late September. Even as the war was drawing to a close as the result of increased unhappiness in the English business community at mounting losses at sea, spiking maritime insurance rates, and growing political opposition to the war's cost, American naval leadership sharpened its focus on British commerce. Stephen Decatur in *President* received orders to attack British trade with India, at its source halfway around the globe. The cruise ended in failure and capture, but the orders to undertake it demonstrate American leadership's dawning strategic conception of seapower. With so small a fleet, command of the seas was out of the question, but raiding enemy commerce as a means of reducing his economy was possible. Sea lines of communication were as important to the United States as they were to Britain, and American political leadership had grasped the fact as it deepened its strategic understanding that the United States must be able to project power at a distance.

The Treaty of Ghent, signed in December 1814, negated small territorial gains the British had achieved in northern New England and the Great Lakes. It secured a return to the status quo before the war. Hostilities between England and France had ceased, and with them ended the need to recruit by impressment. American naval successes and Andrew Jackson's victory over British amphibious forces at the Battle of New Orleans also discouraged any lingering temptation to fill the Royal Navy's ranks by boarding American ships.

The War of 1812 demoralized England but far less so than it uplifted America. *Constitution*'s—*Old Ironsides'*—victories immortalized her. The other American frigates' success in defeating Royal Navy combatants punctured the supreme invincibility on which the British Admiralty had prided itself. But the single-ship victories were as strategically unimportant as was the burning of Washington's public buildings in the summer of 1814. The Royal Navy retained its huge numerical superiority, and the Executive Mansion was rebuilt by the time Madison's successor, James Monroe, took office in 1817.

The war held several important strategic lessons for American seapower. Most important was the economic damage that armed vessels on the high seas could wreak. American privateers proved very effective. Insurance rates for British shippers had far exceeded levels reached while Napoleon was setting fire to all of Europe. Businessmen from a single city, Liverpool, claimed in 1814 that American attacks had resulted in the loss or capture of 800 ships since the war began.[23] Lloyds of London recorded a loss of 108 merchant ships for the month of September in the same year.[24] Offensive naval warfare directed at an enemy's economic underpinnings could be strategically decisive.

The obverse side of this lesson came from the damage that the British blockade had inflicted on the American economy. In the year after the blockade was lifted, the capacity of ships arriving in American ports as measured in tons increased by a magnitude of more than eight.[25] During the same period American exports increased from $7 million to $53 million.[26] As an effective seagoing force could stagger an opponent's economy, a powerful and well-distributed enemy navy could deny access to the sea with equally grave consequences for the American economy. For nations that were surrounded or nearly encircled by oceans, the ability to constrict seaborne trade substantially could determine the outcome of conflict. Seapower's potential decisiveness makes it a strategic instrument.

Applying the Last War's Lessons

Most American leaders saw the importance of the navy to America's future. The same message in which Madison submitted the Treaty of Ghent to Congress contained his request that added to a ship construction measure adopted in 1812 by providing "for the gradual advancement of the naval establishment."[27] Jefferson grumbled privately that building large naval combatants was a concession to American prejudices. He argued that in the recently concluded war the navy's frigates "rendered a great moral service . . .but they have had no physical effect sensible to the enemy."[28] Admiralty Lords who had poured resources into blockading a handful of American frigates while privateers swarmed out elsewhere to prey on British commerce would have disagreed. So did Congress. A year after the Senate ratified the Treaty of Ghent, Congress voted $8 million over eight years for the construction of nine ships-of-the-line armed with at least seventy-four guns each, or half again as many guns as *Constitution* and her sister ships carried, as well as a dozen large frigates. The war had embedded in American minds the strategic notion that seapower is linked to economic survival.

The War of 1812 nourished another fundamental idea, one that Jefferson himself had planted by sending naval forces into the Mediterranean: the little American state possessed security interests thousands of miles distant. British merchant targets were scattered around the globe, from their home waters to Canada, the West Indies, the South Atlantic, the Pacific, and India—among others. American naval leadership never saw as an obstacle the distances between their homeports and the areas where enemy shipping could be interrupted and captured. American combatants were ordered to all these places. The navy might be small, but its sense of itself was as global as the enemy's, the world's most powerful naval force.

Self-conception led to action. The navy established a Pacific Squadron in 1821, almost three decades before the first U.S. state that bordered the Pacific, California, joined the Union. Five years later the navy formed and dispatched, at a distance of almost five thousand nautical miles, a South Atlantic Squadron to protect American shipping as Brazil and Argentina fought over what is today the general area of Uruguay. The Pacific Squadron had to sail an additional nine thousand nautical miles to protect growing U.S. shipping along the west coast of North and South America as well as the sea-lanes to Hawaii. Provisioned by local purchases and supply vessels, the Pacific Squadron combined with the East India Squadron in 1835. The joining of forces expanded the navy's operating area into the western Pacific. Showing the flag, paying port visits, and transporting diplomats became standard missions. The idea of seapower as a critical instrument was embedding itself in the strategic conception of America's political leadership.

American presidents also used force to defend American commerce at sea. When Sumatran pirates attacked and killed a few crew members of an American merchantman who were trying to buy pepper in 1831, Andrew Jackson sent a U.S. warship. U.S.S. *Potomac* arrived a year after the original provocation, fired on local fortresses, and sent ashore lightly armed small boats that sank three of the pirates' vessels. Despite the American naval officer's warning, another similar attack on American shipping in the same place occurred six years later. A second punitive naval expedition sailed halfway around the world to defend

American commerce. Neither the immensity of distance nor the relative infrequency and small size of the aggressor prevented what was for those times a swift and forceful response. Commerce was as ingrained in the activities of the young republic's citizenry as it was central to the Declaration of Independence's assertion that the pursuit of "happiness"—Jefferson's higher-minded restatement of John Locke's original term, "possessions"[29]—is a fundamental human right. Seapower served the nation's evolving strategic interest in trade and demanded the ability to project effective naval force around the world.

From Blockaded to Blockader

Territorial greed, manifest destiny, and the expansion of slavery animated political debate during the 1846 to 1848 Mexican-American War. The consequences for U.S. seapower matched in scope the lands ceded by Mexico to the United States in the Treaty of Guadalupe Hidalgo that ended the war. This area amounted to roughly the southwestern quarter of the continental United States. The missions of the American navy in the Gulf of Mexico reversed the experience of the War of 1812. Instead of trying to break through a naval blockade, U.S. combatants were responsible for establishing one. Protecting American commerce in the Gulf region from Mexican privateers and gunboats was also part of the navy's responsibilities. At the same time an American squadron sailed along the Pacific coast of the continent, capturing the small and largely undefended towns of San Francisco, Monterey, Los Angeles, and San Diego. Mexican-led forces occasionally resisted, but the virtual seizure of California stuck. More important strategically, the U.S. Navy now found itself operating in two theaters separated by nearly fourteen thousand miles. With great difficulty, America grappled with the problems of keeping its ships supplied while fighting on one hostile and another largely uninhabited coast.

A small coastal navy may triumph on the strength of good leadership, imaginative tactics, and superior seamanship. These are necessary but not sufficient for a global naval power, which must supply itself through bases or an efficient procession of logistics that produce the needed supplies at the right moment— or some combination of the two means of supply. The Mexican-American War provided the seeds of experience from which American seapower's ability to sustain itself around the world grew. The American navy also conducted a successful major amphibious landing, and its first, at Vera Cruz that put ashore marines whose hymn's first line, "From the Halls of Montezuma," is a reminder of their role in the six-month campaign that ended with the fall of Mexico City in September 1847.

The Mexican-American War stretched the American navy into a stronger and more flexible instrument than the one that emerged at the end of the previous war. Where it had depended on privateers to assist in preying on British shipping and its own combatants to break the Royal Navy blockade in 1812, now the navy protected American shipping against possible enemy privateers and established blockades to help cripple the enemy. Wherein the previous war the United States had been the subject of enemy amphibious attack, now the American navy was conducting amphibious operations itself and on a much bigger and more strategically important scale than the British expedition that burned Washington in August 1814. The single or paired ship operations that characterized the American navy's offense in the war against England were replaced by larger numbers of deployed ships, twin theaters of operation separated by vast distance, and challenging logistics problems.

Although the Polk administration's support for the navy during the war was scant, events bypassed the domestic political debate over naval expansion. Although it would not find as eloquent an advocate as Alfred Thayer Mahan for another half century, the extent and breadth of naval operations in the Mexican-American War planted the idea of command of the seas as essential to future

American seapower. Command of the seas was indispensable to establish and maintain a blockade, stage and then conduct amphibious landings, descend upon California's towns, protect the seaward flanks of moving army columns, and supply and replace the ships that performed these missions. War with Mexico elevated the navy's strategic focus while the war's outcome deepened the nation's dependence on naval force to protect its commerce.

The scope of the Mexican-American War tracked alongside the enlargement of the United States into a growing commercial power whose rail system would link the Atlantic and Pacific Oceans within two decades. In the approximate decade between the Mexican-American War and the Civil War, the total tonnage of American foreign trade that passed through U.S. ports grew by 123 percent.[30] Statistics over a broader span of time tell the same story of an enterprising nation's need for good order at sea to guarantee its uninterrupted and astonishing commercial success. Measured in constant (1996) dollars, the value of combined imports and exports borne to and from American shores largely by sea in 1830, the first full year of Andrew Jackson's first administration, amounted to $2.3 billion. In the year Abraham Lincoln was elected president for the first time, 1860, this figure had more than quadrupled.[31] The Civil War began with Southern batteries' bombardment of a Federal fortification that sat amid the seaborne approaches to the port of Charleston, South Carolina. The watery location turned out to be ironically appropriate. It underscored what would be proved in the conflict that followed: America's encirclement by the seas and the riverine highways through which the nation's trade coursed were strategic keys to the country's existence.

In the Civil War the Union navy recapitulated the role reversal that separated the conduct of the Mexican-American War from the War of 1812. Instead of being blockaded, the Union naval command moved quickly to capture bases along the Southern coast as the logistical anchors for a blockade that isolated the

South, staggered its economy, and restricted its access to war matériel. The Union naval assault on the South Carolina haven of Port Royal in November 1861 provided a deepwater base for the South Atlantic Blockading Squadron midway between Charleston, South Carolina, and Savannah, Georgia, two of the Confederacy's major East Coast harbors. Later naval captures of New Orleans in 1862 and Mobile two years later aimed successfully at controlling key ports themselves rather than apprehending those who tried to run the blockade at sea. The economic effects reduced King Cotton to a minor knighthood. In real terms, the price of a bale of Southern cotton in Liverpool more than tripled from the beginning of the war to 1864.[32] Estimates of the South's loss of revenue from cotton as a result of the naval blockade range from one-third to two-thirds of prewar levels, a substantial hemorrhage in revenue and a waste of labor.

Union naval strategists did not need to be reminded of the comment attributed to Napoleon that "an army fights on its stomach." As the naval blockade choked exports, it also interrupted the South's internal supply lines. Confederate armies massed and consumed available livestock, but Federal forces extended their reach into the border states that had been principal suppliers of meat. Meanwhile the navy closed its grip on the Mississippi River, across which Texas cattle might have been sent eastward, and Gulf ports, including Galveston, from which beef could have been shipped to feed Confederate armies in the field. When Southern purchasing agents offered economic incentives for Texas livestock in the form of Confederate currency, Union quartermasters countered by offering to pay in gold. Gold against virtually worthless Confederate paper was no match. Texas cattle would not grace the Confederate armies' cooking fires for most of the war.

The Union blockade also helped create shortages of imported weapons, which were at a premium in the Confederate states because of the South's insignificant ability to manufacture small arms. Well-heeled Federal purchasers arrived in Europe and drove up the price of rifles. This multiplied costs for Confederate financial resources already strained by blockade-induced revenue losses. To the higher prices forced on Southern arms purchasers were added substantial transatlantic shipping costs that included losses sustained attempting to run the blockade. General Winfield Scott had originally proposed a naval blockade that encircled the South from its East Coast ports through the Gulf and up the Mississippi River. The coils of Scott's so-called Anaconda Plan grew more muscular and tightened as Union shipyards' output increased, the blockade solidified, key Southern ports fell, and Confederate riverine highways were blocked by naval or combined assault.

The Union blockade remains a subject of debate over the extent of its permeability and economic influence. Those who dispute its effectiveness note the success of blockade-runners. Those who disagree list the substantial economic dislocations the South experienced as a result of blockade-imposed shortages and observe that the loss to Confederate states in revenue from cotton equaled or exceeded the $567 million spent on the entire navy throughout the war.[33] However, there can be little dispute that the South was increasingly an international outcast as European states recognized the blockade to avoid the risk of armed conflict with the Union and its enlarging capacity to wage war on a numerically and technologically unprecedented scale.

The naval blockade and the military power it represented played a strategic role in isolating the South and hastening the war's end. Riverine vessels were critical in transporting and defending Union troops as Federal forces succeeded in controlling the lower Mississippi River. Ironclad combatants, mines, submarines equipped with compressed air, the replacement of steam-driven side-wheelers with screw-propelled warships, and rotating turrets first appeared or were more fully developed in the Civil War. They demonstrated American inventiveness in further applying to naval warfare the talent for innovation that began in the Revolutionary War, continues today, and represents the

Founders'—especially Alexander Hamilton's—success in constructing a commercial republic based on entrepreneurial skill and free enterprise. The Union's naval experience in the Civil War again proved that seapower was a powerful economic and diplomatic instrument that could—and did—make a decisive contribution in suppressing the rebellion and accomplishing the moral purpose to which Lincoln turned the conflict, ending slavery.

The nation's trading commerce, which had suffered during the Civil War, revived vigorously in the postwar years. Unvexed by conflict and unfettered by regulation, enterprise burgeoned. Between the end of the Civil War and the beginning of the Spanish-American War, the annual value of exports and imports multiplied by a factor of more than eight. The navy that had been enlarged by the addition of riverine craft and ships intended for broad blockade duties as well as a few for commerce raiding during the Civil War shriveled. It returned to its antebellum role as global protector of transoceanic routes for American shipping, and concentrated on internecine bureaucratic disputes over such issues as the future applications of steam propulsion. During the same period, reorganization of the naval staff, officer professionalization, and, most important, the development of strategic thought about the use of seapower showed a slow but undiminished national interest in expanding maritime power.

The idea of seapower up until the end of the nineteenth century had been anchored in protecting American commerce. The exercise of seapower fluctuated according to circumstances, from defending the safety of transit between American ports in the Revolutionary War to transoceanic voyages to protect merchants in the Mediterranean during the Barbary Wars to defending national honor in the War of 1812 to power projection in the conflict with Mexico. Commerce raiding afar and blockade duty along the American coast during the Civil War brought the navy back to its prior strategic foundation as an instrument of national power rooted in protecting economic interest. Events and ideas at the end of the nineteenth century transformed ideas about how best to defend global economic interests, and the transformation expanded Americans' understanding of seapower as an instrument to help achieve the increasing role that the nation saw for itself internationally.

Alfred Thayer Mahan and the Emergence of America as a Global Seapower

The Spanish-American War roughly coincided with the wide circulation and acceptance of navy captain Alfred Thayer Mahan's ideas and the presidency of Theodore Roosevelt. The fundamental Mahanian argument we've already explored—which he based on his reading of European navies from 1660 to 1783—is that defending a maritime state by placing armed vessels along its coast, commerce raiding, and punitive attacks on a seaborne enemy matter far less than the larger category that subsumes them all: control of the seas including choke points, defensible bases, and such critical passages as major canals. Sea control might be achieved by strangling an enemy's productive capacity and thus its ability to put naval and merchant ships to sea. But Mahan argued that the direct route to command of the seas was a powerful navy capable of defending the United States at transoceanic distances from its borders by sweeping the seas of a competitor and protecting the commerce on which national power including seapower depend.

Evidence to support Mahan's idea predates the era that he examined. Two centuries prior, the contrast between the Venetian and Ottoman use of seapower offered watertight proof that sea control is the strategic keystone of maritime power. As the Ottomans ascended, they used newly built fleets as a seagoing mirror image of their Ghazi warrior style of raiding. For example, they descended on and drove the Venetians from their western Aegean strategic base at Negroponte (modern-day Boeotia) in 1470 and then withdrew. Ten years later the Ottomans successfully attacked Otranto at the heel of Italy's boot—the strategically placed western approach to the Adriatic—only to withdraw shortly afterward. They could pluck the fruit, but they would not seize the tree. The Venetians, however, had long understood that a series of Aegean bases that allowed their naval and merchant vessels to control the vital sea lines of communication that linked them to Byzantine and Black Sea markets was essential to their preeminence as both a naval and a commercial power.

The 1898 Spanish-American War's outcome helped nurture this idea of seapower. Decisive naval actions were fought in Cuba and, on the other side of the world, in Manila Bay. They resulted in the collapse of the global colonial empire that Spain had built over the preceding five centuries and in U.S. territorial acquisition of Guam, the Philippines, and Puerto Rico. This hardly constituted an empire, but the United States now held important responsibility for territory at the western extremes of the Pacific Ocean. The Spanish-American War's extension of the transoceanic distance at which lasting American interests were engaged complemented Theodore Roosevelt's expansive idea of naval power, which in turn paralleled if not preceded Mahan's thought that command of the seas is the heart of seapower.

Driven by French and German blockades of Venezuela for nonpayment of debt, Roosevelt as president added a corollary to the Monroe Doctrine that claimed a U.S. obligation to intervene to prevent economic collapse in Central American and Caribbean states. His advocacy in favor of war against Spain following the U.S.S. *Maine*'s destruction in Havana harbor in 1898 also vigorously supported the Monroe Doctrine whose successful application in the Spanish-American War drove the last great European power out of the Western Hemisphere. It took no great leaps of logic for Roosevelt to grasp that the final departure of European power from the Western Hemisphere established the foundation of U.S. hemispheric superiority as it formally separated European threats to American security by the Atlantic Ocean. The retreat of European power from the Western Hemisphere and return to

*The wreckage of the U.S.S. Maine, adorned with a memorial flag
in 1902 by order of President Tomas Palma of Cuba*

the continent of its origin joined Mahan and Roosevelt's idea of
defending U.S. security at a distance by controlling the seas. The
1899 annexation of Hawaii along with effective possession of
American Samoa and Wake Island confirmed the navy's global
reach as it supported the idea and fact of a wide-ranging seagoing
perimeter defense for the United States. Roosevelt built a large,
powerful, and demonstrably transoceanic fleet along with the
canal through which it could be shifted between the world's great
oceans.

America's outward-looking foreign policy, like Rome's, was
rooted in geography, political constitution, and national character. But with both states, the expression of a broad and powerful
interest in external affairs produced little of significance until
security in the immediate neighborhood had been assured. In

each case, command of the seas was indispensable to the shift outward. America's war with Spain ignited in the Caribbean, the southern end of the Mariana archipelago, and the eastern boundary of the South China Sea; similarly, Rome's struggle with Carthage spanned the Mediterranean from its Atlantic mouth to the Hellespont. Naval superiority in the central Mediterranean was as important to Rome in preventing Carthage from conducting a frontal amphibious invasion of the Italian peninsula and eventually choking off Hannibal's logistic support as it was to U.S. naval victories at Manila Bay and Santiago in Cuba. Both Rome and the United States emerged with larger, more robust naval forces and more activist external policies that, while they differed profoundly in objectives, shared a sophisticated understanding of the strategic rationale for using maritime power to achieve foreign policy goals by control of the seas.

Japan's 1905 naval victory over a Russian fleet divided between the Pacific and Baltic reinforced Mahan and Roosevelt's strongly held opinion in favor of concentrating—as opposed to dividing—naval force. The victory left Japan as the dominant naval force in the western Pacific. U.S. naval planners fretted over this, constructed logistics vessels to compensate for the Pacific's long distances, and sought to beef up the Pacific Fleet with less success under William Howard Taft than during the administration of his predecessor, Roosevelt. But as European fleets increased in size and firepower during the first decade and a half of the twentieth century and the continent's great powers circled, the U.S. Atlantic Fleet mattered most.

Woodrow Wilson's order to U.S. military officers to avoid public statements about the unfolding war in Europe underscored American neutrality at the beginning of World War I. American policy looked to a postwar world through a lens ground by Alfred Thayer Mahan. The ability of a large, powerful, concentrated fleet to sweep the seas of potential enemies would assure command of the seas, supply the force to defeat whoever emerged victorious from the European war, and guarantee safe passage on the high seas. Irritated by disagreement with Britain over questions of neutrality, President Wilson told a close confidant: "Let us build a bigger Navy than hers and do what we please."[34] The Naval Act of 1916 aimed at doing just that. It ordered the construction of ten battleships, six battle cruisers, fifty destroyers, dozens of submarines, and a host of other supporting combatants.

The act had the good fortune to be debated by Congress a few weeks after the Battle of Jutland, which, measured in tonnage and firepower, ranks as the largest naval engagement in history. It proved to be the last major contest between great battleships but became the subject of such intensive scrutiny at the Naval War College in Newport, Rhode Island, that a waggish naval officer termed Jutland "a major defeat of the United States Navy."[35] The same engagement helped persuade Congress that doing "what we please" demanded a big, heavily armed fleet that could meet and defeat other similarly armed naval forces. But diplomacy ultimately echoed the indecisiveness of the battle itself, resulting in the United States' postwar offer to limit naval armament if other powers followed suit in the construction and tonnage of capital ships.

American action in World War I had needed no such vessels. U.S. objectives included turning back Germany's declaration of unrestricted submarine warfare in the Atlantic. This required supporting the Allied powers by conveying American troops and war matériel safely across the ocean. Command of the seas would not be won in the strict Mahanian sense by offensive action against the enemy fleet, which had retreated to German ports after the carnage at Jutland. Sea control became the defense of surface vessels against submarines. As it would a quarter century later in World War II, holding the upper hand in the Atlantic and its confined approaches to Britain meant using defended convoys to keep German submarines at bay and occasionally destroying them. Command of the seas in World War I turned out to look like a successful version of today's discredited counterinsurgency tactic of clearing a village of the enemy and then moving on. But what counted at sea was the stretch of ocean over which large numbers of men, equipment, and supplies sailed in convoy at a given moment, not the ability to secure large swaths of the surface by sinking enemy combatants that might endanger it. Protecting a convoy against U-boats was a job for light and maneuverable destroyers and escorts, not the great steel-walled oceangoing fortresses with wide turning radii and fourteen-inch guns that could throw a fifteen-hundred-pound shell twenty-one miles. The cobra watches for the mongoose, not the elephant.

The U.S. Navy built elephants in the interwar years. Battleships proved useful in bombarding the enemy during amphibious landings in the Pacific, and rarely—as at Guadalcanal in 1942—in providing decisive gunfire against an enemy fleet. But although command of the seas would indeed be a pivotal tool of national power, World War II did not support Mahan's idea that massive long-range fire would secure such command.

A Field Marshal Looks at Seapower

For U.S. seapower, the interwar years, however ill-funded, were a period of innovation and useful thought transformed into effective action. Technology, tactical imagination, and a strategic grasp of how war would be fought against Japan turned naval aviation and amphibious warfare into potent tools that were central to victory in the Pacific—as was the submarine's ability to cripple the enemy's merchant fleet. Unlike the previous world war, the second one was fought on two oceans. In the Atlantic, U.S. seapower performed missions similar to those that had been learned in World War I. The successful convoying of American equipment across the Atlantic helped sustain Soviet opposition to the Nazis until enough men and matériel could be amassed in Britain to open a second front against Hitler. As they did in 1917 and 1918, escorted convoys proved their worth in countering German submarines. So did the expertise that the U.S. Marine Corps had developed for use in the Pacific as it was applied to the beaches of Normandy.

World War II's Allied leaders would have agreed heartily with Adams, Jefferson, and Madison in their understanding that seapower is critical to American grand strategy. Field Marshal Bernard Montgomery told an audience nearly a decade and a half after the end of World War II that "the Second World War was fundamentally a struggle for the control of the major oceans and seas—the control of sea communications—and until we had won that struggle we could not proceed with our plans to win the war."[36] The Anglo-American alliance was a partnership of two states, one an island and the other surrounded on three of its five sides by the seas. Their combined coastline amounts to a distance that equals 80 percent of the earth's circumference at the equator. Without the movement of men and matériel from the United States to England and Russia, the continent could not have been invaded or the enemy diverted on his eastern flank. And while the defense of Britain including its ports was conducted by airpower, Adams's understanding of the importance of secure seaports and Jefferson and Madison's confidence that American security could be endangered by events thousands of miles from our borders was no different from Roosevelt's or Churchill's.

By every measure of maritime strength, America emerged from the Second World War as the internationally acknowledged great naval power. In tonnage, firepower, number of ships, and geographic reach, the U.S. combat fleet surpassed all others and had indeed performed as Field Marshal Montgomery later observed. The question became: What now? With the Nazis defeated and most of the rest of the world exhausted after its war efforts, what was the navy's purpose? Would long-range bombers armed with atomic weapons, which were cheaper than heavily-manned fleets, provide the most cost-effective and powerful security for the United States and its allies? And what of the

Marine Corps? Was one still needed, and if so, why? The U.S. Army air force had been separated to form its own service, the air force. The military service chiefs eyed each other suspiciously and set a watch for additional predations. Could the navy's aviation arm also be swallowed by the air force? Would the marines be folded into the army's maw? U.S. policy makers offered few clues about the nation's strategic direction and—as with China in the early twenty-first century—were reluctant to identify the Soviet Union as a possible future threat.

Drift

Through this toxic climate of interservice anxiety over mission objectives and strategic uncertainty over its future role in defending the nation, U.S. military leaders sought to chart a course for their respective branches. Clarity came slowly but not soon enough to avoid pitched turf wars whose echoes have not ceased. George Kennan's "X" article published by *Foreign Affairs* in mid-1947 helped shift U.S. policy toward containing the Soviet Union, whose ambitions in and around the Persian Gulf as well as the eastern Mediterranean were growing clearer and more ominous. The navy created a Mediterranean Fleet—the Sixth Fleet—a departure from long-standing policy of sending ships to trouble spots from home waters and calling on logistical assistance as needed in welcoming ports. Naval strategic thought shifted from a strictly Mahanian idea of sweeping the seas of enemy fleets to controlling them as part of a broader national effort to use the oceans for a variety of military purposes. In 1946 hearings Chief of Naval Operations Admiral Chester Nimitz told Congress: "Fleets do not exist only to fight other fleets and to contest with them the command of the sea. Actually, command of the sea is only the means to an end. Wars cannot be concluded by naval action alone or by air action alone. Wars are conducted and concluded by the combined action of sea, land, air, diplomatic, and economic effort. . . . Upon our seapower hinges our ability to seize, hold, and cover strategic positions, to build them into adequate bases, and to transport to them the personnel, services, equipment, food, and fuel vital to carry the war to a successful conclusion."[37]

Soviet forces occupied central Europe into Germany, were superior in number to Allied strength that remained on the continent after the Nazis were defeated, and enjoyed the flanking protection of Stalin's large submarine force. Nimitz's modified and diversified idea of sea control made strategic sense. U.S. Navy carrier-borne aviation would attack and destroy the bases from which Soviet submarines swarmed. It would strike deeper and support allied land forces by destroying airfields used to support the Atlantic-aiming advance of Soviet troops. Amphibious attacks would increase pressure along the Soviets' flanking western thrust.

Postwar disputes over strategy led to such other questions

The U.S.S. Nimitz, *named for the admiral who championed the idea of American control of the seas*

as the use and delivery of atomic weapons, which, based on the war-ending attacks on Hiroshima and Nagasaki, led to air force proponents' notion that future wars could be ended similarly. But the unanswered question of political leadership's willingness to initiate such measures muted the debate. More important, naval thinking succeeded at expanding the idea of sea control from its Mahanian roots in the destruction of an enemy's fleet to the sturdy trunk and limbs that supported the application of force from the sea to the land as a means toward the same end, that is, profoundly influencing events on land. In the event the navy also presented a convincing argument for marshaling American military force as a unitary instrument of national power and preserved its carriers and their aircraft in the melee to demonstrate value that accompanied demobilization and strategic drift in the wake of World War II. Most important, the navy showed that the mixture of developing technology—in this case carrier aviation—and imagination offered adaptable force that could flex and protect the nation by achieving large strategic results. Seapower's malleability is rooted in strategic conception but linked to technology. The core of its flexibility is tripartite: the unchanging need to protect human commerce, the immense exposure of the earth's landmasses to the ocean, and the ease and ability—which has been growing since before Darius used amphibious force to begin Persia's assault on the eastern Aegean in 490 BC—to apply decisive power to the land from the sea.

But the afterglow of victory purchased by bomber-delivered nuclear weapons in Japan did not quickly fade. Five years later the argument between the air force and navy over nuclear bombing from the air continued. The Truman administration ordered more intercontinental bombers with payloads equal to the then-heavy weight of atomic weapons, and canceled a new class of aircraft carrier that would have been large enough to launch planes with nuclear payloads. The administration also dallied with organizational changes to create a general staff in which the navy would have been outvoted by the army and air force, thus risking the military prizes for which each of the other two services hankered, the marines and naval aviation.

Of course, the argument over naval delivery of atomic weapons was never put to the proof. Senior naval officers gave conflicting testimony about broad naval strategy to Congress. Admirals were fired. But the navy kept its carriers and marines. Also retained and reinforced was the important idea that naval force could be used to advance national security as effectively to sweep the seas of enemy ships as to preserve links with allies, defend a growing network of distant bases, establish beachheads in strategic locations, and protect ground forces' flanks.

The 1948 confrontation with the Soviets over supplying Berlin concentrated attention on Europe and the Truman administration's dedication to frugality turned national security strategy into a serf of financial necessity. The navy's Pacific Fleet languished as repeated requests for aircraft carriers were denied. When the Korean People's Army crossed the 38th parallel at dawn on June 25, 1950, the U.S. Navy had a single carrier deployed in the western Pacific.

Hot War Then Cold

Still the sea services played key roles and demonstrated their ability to perform a range of vital missions. The navy cleared mines, allowing its ships to approach Korea's Wonsan harbor and get close enough to deliver effective naval gunfire in support of amphibious landings that aimed at the North Korean capital. Unimpeded control of the seas permitted free transit of North Korean waters, which would be critical later for large amphibious operations such as the surprise landing at Inchon in September 1950 and the successful evacuation of UN forces by sea from Hungnam in December of the same year. A blockade prevented seaborne resupply to North Korean ports. Hostilities ended without a peace agreement, but the peninsular position of the enemy suited the diversity and facilitated the effective use of U.S. naval/amphibious force in preventing South Korea from being overrun.

Geography and the navy's several complementary competences were equally important in the Cold War that followed. The Soviet Union was no island, but it was surrounded in part by water and to a large extent by powerful members of the democratic alliance with oceanic frontiers. History proved instructive. Closing off Britain from continental trade had been an important motive for France's invasion of Russia. Czar Alexander I's 1810 decision to sell grain to England cracked Napoleon's "continental system,"—the Emperor's ban on trading with England—both commercially and politically. The U.S. policy of containment recognized in reverse the same opportunities in Russian geography that Napoleon saw: as an England cut off from continental trade might be choked, the U.S.S.R. and its self-imposed economic infirmities—combined with an interruption in commercial intercourse with its wealthier neighbors—might also wither. The Atlantic, Pacific, and their abutting seas became the connective tissue over which naval power bound together allies in Western Europe and Asia, and the United States. Pulled by centripetal force toward the United States, this network of alliances would throw the Soviets back on their own increasingly constrained resources. The victories of seapower are often silent. Without much public notice, U.S. dominance on the seas discouraged the Soviets from a more powerful global presence and helped direct their energy on a continental alliance, NATO, that stood fast despite its shortcomings.

Changes in the technology of atomic weapons, the balance of forces, and the development of intercontinental ballistic missiles (ICBMs) complicated the military task of containing the Soviet Union. Air force proponents argued that nuclear weapons offered a low-cost option to end a war quickly. The Soviets developed atomic weapons and placed a satellite in orbit before the United States did. Critics noted that "bouncing the rubble," as Churchill described a nuclear exchange, was an unacceptable cost to pay for a dubious victory. Naval advocates pointed out the vulnerability of intercontinental bombers to enemy missiles and argued for submarine-based ICBMs as a secure deterrent against Soviet attack. Moscow continued to build submarines, including ones that could strike the United States with nuclear-tipped missiles. The Soviets also added to their conventional forces in Europe.

U.S. maritime strategy sought to address this range of multiplying threats. Attack submarines would search out and destroy enemy submarines that threatened the lines of communication between the United States and its NATO allies. Ballistic missile–carrying submarines would provide a secure and certain strategic retaliation if the United States or its allies were attacked. Carrier-borne aircraft with antisubmarine warfare capability would help maintain the sea control required to communicate with allies. Other carrier aircraft would destroy the bases from which enemy submarines emerged and on which they depended for logistics and maintenance support. As the range of carrier aircraft increased, targets whose destruction would abrade the Soviets' ability to wage conventional warfare in Europe and the Near East increased.

Throughout the 1960s the range and accuracy of submarine-launched ICBMs increased proportionally to the decrease in importance of carrier-based aircraft as a means of delivering nuclear strikes against the Soviet Union. The new division of labor made strategic sense. Unheard and unseen, submarines' threat of effective and lethal retaliation deep into the Soviet heartland would help deter catastrophic nuclear exchanges. Carriers could be redirected away from ranges at which enemy ground-based bombers might reach them and focused on skirmishes around the globe where Soviet ambitions of the mid–Cold War period ignited. Ballistic missile–carrying nuclear-powered submarines helped deter the large conflagrations. Carriers, the surface fleet, and amphibious operations helped prevent smaller fires from turning into larger ones—for example, amphibious landings in Lebanon in the final years of the Eisenhower administration, air strikes into Vietnam over the next decade and a half, the naval blockade of Cuba during the Kennedy administration, as well as a multitude of other flash points around the world.

As national defense policy recovered from Vietnam leaning more heavily on détente and reaching agreements that it was hoped might moderate the Cold War, the Soviet Union's decades-long effort to be taken seriously as a naval power bore its steel fruit. Much as China is now building a large modern naval force while today's American military is fixed on the Middle East, the U.S. defense preoccupation with Vietnam forty years ago came at the expense of its seapower. The Soviets used the decade between the mid-1960s and mid-1970s to outbuild the U.S. Navy by 121 ships.[38] Admiral of the Fleet Sergei Gorshkov sent his new squadrons to ports and patrols farther and farther from Russia's coastal waters—from the Arctic to the South Atlantic to the Indian Ocean. The question of sea control in the event of a Soviet invasion of Europe arose, along with its parallel imponderable, whether the United States could simultaneously answer another, albeit lesser, crisis elsewhere. The large naval armada that the Kremlin deployed to the eastern Mediterranean as U.S. forces gathered to support Israel in the 1973 war demonstrated how far the Soviets had progressed at sea.

The post-Vietnam years did not demonstrate the American public's appetite for footing the bill to reassert preeminent seapower. The navy shifted about with ideas for cheaper but less capable vessels to complement its carriers and large surface combatants. But could the navy execute all its missions, especially keeping communications with allies on either side of both great oceans secure, with less capable ships that might have to go in harm's way against a force that had become a real menace? And if it couldn't, what was the navy's role in defending the United States? These questions produced debate, self-doubt about such critical issues as the future of the aircraft carrier, and irresolution.

Successful Maritime Strategy

The answer proved to be a maritime strategy that supported the more assertive national defense sought by U.S. policy in the Cold War's closing years. American seapower would not be justified by pecking at Soviet provocations in the Third World intersections of free and Communist competition. Its purpose would not be merely to respond where control of the seas might be contested. Seapower would take the fight to the enemy. It would project power to the flanks of a war in Europe. It would use naval aviation to help divert a Soviet drive westward, and destroy Soviet attack submarines, thus providing security for Atlantic shipping lanes and placing at risk the Soviet strategic ballistic-missile fleet that lay in silent wait beneath the northern seas' roiling waters. This strategy was disputed, criticized, and disparaged. It proved immensely successful. It offered a coherent and sensible raison d'être that took full advantage of all the Navy Department's capabilities. The new maritime strategy undertook missions that supported the other military services and advanced the United States' interest in opposing U.S. strengths to Soviet weaknesses for the purpose of achieving strategic advantage over the Soviet Union. It was comprehensible, capable of being articulated, and inseparable from the navy's successful effort to increase the fleet from its forty-year nadir of 464 combatants to nearly six hundred ships in less than a decade.

But the question "What is the purpose of seapower?" is never answered with finality. Changes in international power relations, the location of populations centers, technology, domestic politics, the political objectives of warfare, and geography itself—as is demonstrated by the possibilities of using the heretofore frozen Arctic seas for commercial exploitation and transport—suspend the use of naval force in a permanent three-dimensional state of usually gradual animation. Yesterday's strengths are as subject to deathly fissures as the ideas that governed the application of those strengths.

When the Cold War ended, the Soviet fleet retired to its far-flung ports to rot. The possibility of nuclear bombardment receded. So did the requirement for a robust force of U.S. submarine–based ballistic missiles along with a strategy to conduct flanking operations against an invasion of Western Europe by a state that had expired.

Saddam Hussein's 1990 invasion of Kuwait and the war to oust Iraqi forces that followed in 1991 shifted American foreign policy attention to regional threats. The navy changed its emphasis from maintaining control of the seas to applying power to the shore from the sea. Missiles, aircraft, amphibious force, and gunnery remained useful instruments of national power but were directed increasingly toward land. Cruise missiles launched from the sea initiated the bombardment of Iraqi forces in Operation Desert Storm and carrier strikes, naval commandos, amphibious feints, and naval gunfire support followed. Seapower would be applied again a decade later in the invasion of Iraq and operations in Afghanistan where naval aircraft provided a large portion of aircraft strike missions.

The idea of superior force applied from the sea remains as fixed today as it was in early America. Naval forces deployed in a crisis must be able to dominate an enemy—and a crisis includes serious threats to America's commercial interests. Its clearest expression in contemporary times has been the heretofore unchallenged American advantage in fleet size, numbers of large combatants, tonnage, and firepower that can be positioned in harm's way. The United States sent four aircraft carrier battle groups and two battleships to the Persian Gulf as well as dozens of surface and amphibious ships and submarines to the Persian Gulf to help drive Iraqi forces out of Kuwait in 1991. Missiles and aircraft launched from them helped destroy Iraqi air defenses and command and control centers from as far as seven hundred miles away. This massive use of naval force—mirrored by a 2:1 superiority in coalition ground troop strength—paved the way for U.S. and allied ground forces' single-week campaign that concluded with the rout of Iraqi units that had invaded Kuwait and were fleeing north. Eight years later, when NATO used force to stop the Serbian ruler Milosevic from annihilating or displacing the Albanian majority in Kosovo, the U.S.-led coalition massed three carriers in the Adriatic, supported again by surface and amphibious ships and submarines, against a potent but numerically inferior mixture of air defenses, aircraft, and mechanized forces. The ability to dominate an enemy was decisive in both campaigns.

Control of the seas can demand traditional blue-water patrolling no less than the application of force from the sea to prevent a threat from contesting sea control—as U.S. maritime strategy during the Cold War proved. The history of American seapower, in fact, is an education in the flexibility of dominant maritime force.

What has not changed are the oceans that surround the United States and separate it from friends and enemies. Nor has the idea that Jefferson eventually and reluctantly accepted that events at transoceanic distances are critical to American security and prestige. The Constitution's drafters differed over the sources of the nation's future economic strength. But presidents' protection of American commercial shipping became a fixture of U.S. strategy. It remains so today in the expanded understanding that American interest lies in the security of global international waters and ultimately in the good order that reflects American values and that seapower helps to uphold. Jefferson and Madison's prosecution of wars against the distant Barbary States is the direct lineal ancestor of American strategy that to this day prefers meeting threats at a distance to countering them at our shores. James Monroe's doctrine against European colonization or interference in the Western Hemisphere was the diplomatic expression of the same defensive impulse. Theodore Roosevelt's expansion of the Monroe Doctrine to include U.S. intervention where economic disaster threatened Caribbean and South American states carried over the same idea into the twentieth century.

At its core, American seapower is anchored in the entrepreneurial, innovative character that the Constitution's framers saw in their fellow citizens and sought to encourage. Among hundreds of other inventions, this spirit moved in Paul Revere's protective copper sheathing of U.S.S. *Constitution*'s bottom. It blossomed in John Ericsson's original design of the turreted Union ironclad, U.S.S. *Monitor*, and it lives today in the revolutionary use of electromagnetic propulsion to replace steam catapults aboard American aircraft carriers. This enterprising democratic spirit has persevered in the American character from the beginning of the Republic. Indeed, U.S. naval superiority does not merely consist of outnumbering the enemy but of outdistancing their seagoing technology. From helping to open new commercial markets to assuring their stability by the reliable enforcement of maritime order, America's innovative spirit finds new economic outlets for innovation.

Ironically, the other changeless element of American seapower has been its ability to change. The earliest naval missions tried to break blockades. During the Mexican-American and Civil Wars the navy imposed blockades. Commerce raiding was a common mission and suited the small navy's narrow purpose of imposing a cost on the enemy and demonstrating America's ability to project power—even small amounts of it—at a distance. But commerce raiding was reconsidered when the United States' security needs and responsibilities grew.

As the nation's wealth began to rival and then exceed that of the most prosperous European states toward the end of the nineteenth century, the groundwork was prepared for a transoceanic, globe-spanning navy, a large transformation from the riverine and blockading force of the Civil War. The Panama Canal allowed U.S. fleets to move quickly between the Atlantic and Pacific. Theodore Roosevelt's interest in building the Panama Canal was born in his vision of a global navy that demanded control of strategic choke points to support its free movement. Large increases in fleet size and capability that could now be easily shifted back and forth

TERRIFIC COMBAT BETWEEN THE "MONITOR" 2 GUNS & "MERRIMAC" 10 GUNS.

The U.S.S. Monitor, *depicted here in its famous battle with the* Merrimac, *was an early example of the ironclad ships that would become the heart of the modern navy.*

between the Atlantic and Pacific helped demonstrate the canal's usefulness. The fleet's increase compensated for the wholesale naval self-disarmament that followed the Civil War. And Alfred Thayer Mahan's ideas of command of the seas fit the United States' broadening worldview and maritime capabilities.

Mahan's ideas became a source from which the navy drank selectively. Command of the seas was indispensable for keeping England alive in World War II and supplying Russia, as well as for moving the American force across the Atlantic to return to the Continent. But such command did not count as much as when the U.S. amphibious campaign clawed its way toward Japan. The important point, however, is that seapower repeatedly demonstrated the resilience and adaptability to triumph in the event.

The same qualities described postwar naval force. Amid false starts, reduced budgets, interservice quarrels, and uncertainty over how best to contain the Soviet Union, American sea-power redrew itself, adapted its equipment and ideas of warfare to the development of nuclear weapons, and assisted in binding together a series of alliances that played a vital role in bringing down the Soviet Union. The same flexibility can allow U.S. maritime strategy to shift once again and return to the more Mahanian idea of command of the seas, an idea that is essential to maintaining America's position as the preeminent power in the Pacific.

No less important, the same combination of projecting power, providing U.S. presence, extended deterrence, crisis response, and humanitarian assistance and disaster relief also complemented American foreign policy's aim of creating an international system that embraced and respected human rights, sovereignty, free markets, freedom of international navigation, and free trade. American seapower's flexibility and transoceanic reach allowed it to become the most visible representative and, where necessary, forceful guarantor of this system.

Flexibility, transoceanic reach, innovation, intellectual ferment, technological prowess, and of course leadership and the courage of its sailors did not materialize suddenly out of the ocean's depths. The qualities that describe the present-day U.S. Navy were incipient at its creation and developed as a result of reflection, practical experience, and national need into the form in which they appear today. But in essence, they can no more be separated from the early republic's security than they can from the United States and its allies' current security.

4

The Future of
American Seapower

THE ADVANCED COMPETENCE of American seapower remains very much intact. The seamanship and virtues of the sailors who brought the American fleet to its supreme position among the world's navies still exist. The longer and longer separations from their families that navy crews are asked to make today, as tasks mount without corresponding increases in numbers of ships, evidence resolve and dedication. The success of U.S.S. *Cole's* crew in saving their ship after suffering severe damage following

The aftermath of the terrorist attack on the U.S.S. Cole

an al-Qaeda suicide attack in the port of Aden in 2000 shows ingenuity, grit, and professional competence. Navy SEAL Lieutenant Mike Murphy, who received the Congressional Medal of Honor for continuing to fight after being wounded and exposing himself to enemy fire to call for support in Afghanistan and then died in the ensuing fight against much bigger Taliban forces, is a radiant and unsurpassed example of courage in the history of warfare. These officers and enlisted men are still very much a part of American seapower, but their numbers matter, and on that point the nation's increasing indebtedness presents a bleak picture of the future.

Despite a halting recovery from the economic downturn that began in 2007,[1] the Congressional Budget Office (CBO) projects that federal debt will amount to a total of $6.2 trillion for the decade that begins with 2011. This, says the CBO, will raise public debt from its 2007 level, 36 percent of gross domestic product (GDP), to 69 percent of GDP in 2020. The amount of interest that must be paid on what has been borrowed will also increase dramatically. According to the CBO, the interest on what the federal government owes will cost taxpayers $259 billion in 2012. The same source projects that this figure will expand to $778 billion in 2020. If the CBO is correct, the debt that the public holds will amount to 77 percent of GDP in 2023, a larger fraction than at any time since 1951 and almost precisely twice the forty-year average percentage of GDP that public debt occupies, 39 percent.[2] Economic predictions, especially those that look more than five years ahead, are notoriously subject to changes in policy, politics, and such important economic variables as inflation. But there is no getting around the large sums that were borrowed to stimulate the economy as the recession deepened. They have to be returned—with interest. If Americans remain as skittish as they are today about cutting such large budget items as Social Security, Medicare, Medicaid, and other legally mandated expenses, political pressure to reduce defense, whose size and growth is not written into law, will increase. In fact, the screw is already turning. In January 2011 Secretary of Defense Gates said that he would reduce defense spending by $78 billion over the next five years. This would have meant less than a 1 percent increase in the defense budget from 2011 to 2012 and resources in future budgets virtually constrained to inflation rates punctuated by no growth at all in the last of the five years for which the budget is projected. The Obama proposal to reduce the budget by more than twice as much per year for twelve years will have a much larger effect on the Defense Department as a whole and is certain to result in an actual reduction of forces. Even the *Washington Post*, which is commonly skeptical of defense spending, repeated then secretary Gates's caution that large defense cuts "would be disastrous in the world environment we see today." The *Post* added that "this is a warning that the administration and Congress cannot afford to disregard."[3] Secretary Gates and his successor, Leon Panetta, both argued that large defense cuts would seriously harm the nation's defenses. But the same reductions would not significantly reduce federal indebtedness, whose most potent cause is mandatory spending—entitlements—such as Medicare, Medicaid, and Social Security. Their growth since the 1970s has been by orders of magnitude, while defense budgets measured in constant 2012 dollars have barely risen, even including the sums spent on wars in Iraq and Afghanistan. As 2012 ended, entitlements amounted to 62 percent of the $3.6 trillion federal budget. Spending whose increase law does not mandate—known as discretionary spending—accounts for 36 percent of the federal budget, and of that defense represents one-half.[4] Even if defense were halved, the money saved would not be able to keep pace with the continued exponential growth in entitlements, much less the accumulation of federal debt. Or, as the Obama administration's secretary of defense, Leon Panetta, said in September 2011, "If you're serious about dealing with the deficit, don't go back to the discretionary account [which includes defense spending].

Pay attention to the two-thirds of the federal budget that is in large measure responsible for the size of the debt that we're dealing with."[5]

Preceding in time the administration's proposed defense cuts was a report of a bipartisan group that the White House appointed to recommend how best to balance the federal budget. The National Commission on Fiscal Responsibility and Reform delivered its findings in December 2010. The commission looked farther into the future than the CBO figures noted above. It agreed that annual interest on the U.S. debt could ascend into the neighborhood of $1 trillion in 2020 but estimated that this would amount to 90 percent of the GDP for the same year. If federal spending plus the accumulating debt and its servicing are left unaddressed, the commission foresees that the nation's financial obligations will exceed the total value of goods and services that the American economy produces, reaching 185 percent of GDP by 2035. Think about your personal finances again. How could rent or mortgage—to say nothing of any other expenses—be afforded if the annual interest on your credit card amounted to nearly twice your salary for the same year? Just as important, think about the results if the federal government decides that it has no choice but to borrow more money to pay back what it already owes. Massive borrowing will affect everyone who borrows. This includes those who want to refinance their homes, purchase new ones, obtain auto loans, use credit cards, start a new business, or grow an established one. Such borrowing would draw a giant, virtually impermeable curtain over the entire economy, choking innovation, stifling the ability to find capital, and crushing new jobs before they had a chance to be conceived. But if the large picture of indebtedness's cause and effect is too abstract, consider a snapshot: the U.S. federal budget deficit for fiscal year 2007 recorded its third consecutive annual reduction. It dropped to $163 billion.[6] Nearly three and a half years later the CBO reported a federal deficit for the month of February 2011 of $223 billion.[7] In other words, the federal deficit for the second month of 2011 was more than one-third higher than the total federal deficit for the entire fiscal year of 2007.

So the White House–appointed commission's anxiety about where all this leads is understandable. It warned that unless the federal debt is controlled, the U.S. government by 2025 will be able to pay for only Medicare, Medicaid, Social Security, and the interest on money it has already borrowed. This leaves out defense. The omission is what worried then chairman of the Joint Chiefs Admiral Mike Mullen in August 2010 when he told CNN that "the most significant threat to our national security is our debt."[8] Former director of Central Intelligence General Michael Hayden made the same point in January 2011. He said that the nation's economic situation is a threat to national security and that "while we really cannot afford defense budget cuts, we may have to have them anyway."[9] A year and a half later President Obama's second secretary of defense, Leon Panetta, offered a harder-edged assessment: "If sequester takes place it would be disastrous for our national defense," he told ABC's *This Week*.[10]

What then would be the source of money for defense? Borrowing at the level the United States has now reached resembles astrophysicists' descriptions of a black hole. The more that the black hole ingests, the greater its ability to attract and devour other matter. Gargantuan federal borrowing has the same gravitational effect. It absorbs otherwise productive sources of capital without producing any positive result.[11] Absent unexpected sources of earned income, the continued accretion of debt makes the problem worse and the solutions increasingly unpalatable. Besides pay cuts for, and reductions in, the Defense Department's civilian workforce, the national commission's recommendations on how to cut defense are as draconian as they are blind to the distinction between defending the nation and every other purpose to which public monies are put. The commission recommends that "Congress should . . . consider a 'BRAC commission'[12] for terminating major weapons systems appointed and headed by the Secretary of Defense, for trimming redundant or ineffective weapons from the Defense Department's inventory."[13]

This was an unfortunate and ill-informed recommendation. The most expensive major weapons system that is now in production is the F-35. This is the United States' next generation of tactical strike aircraft and, as its military description—the Joint Strike Fighter—indicates, will be used in different versions by the army, navy, air force, and marines. Here there is great expense, but where is redundancy? Does the United States need to stay ahead of others—such as the Russians and Chinese—who are also modernizing their aircraft to increase stealth, performance, and networking ability? Yes. The alternative is to surrender America's position as possessor of the world's most powerful and technologically advanced military aircraft. Does the F-35 qualify as a redundant or ineffective major weapon system? No one has said so. The navy uses planes that are modified to operate in the engine and frame-challenging environment of salty oceans. The Marine Corps would use a variant of the same plane that is designed to support marines in their unique mission of gaining a foothold under fire and to land and take off vertically from the ships that are part of an amphibious battle group. The air force's variant is intended to operate from secure airfields and support large numbers of army troops. No single plane could perform all these missions. Different variants of the same model can. Again, where is the redundancy?

Another example that fits the recommendations of the National Commission on Fiscal Responsibility and Reform on terminating major weapons systems is ballistic-missile defense. Is this redundant or ineffective? America's allies from Asia to the Persian Gulf to Europe don't think so. They welcome U.S. ships equipped with missiles able to shoot down such nuclear threats that can be lofted by North Korea and perhaps eventually by Iran in the tips of high-speed missiles, or perhaps someday by terrorist groups. Would the authors of the fiscal responsibility and reform report prefer that the United States return to the Cold War defense policy of mutual assured destruction to deter new and proliferating nuclear threats? This is unwise. Accidents, nuclear weapons borne by terrorist-launched missiles, or even nuclear material delivered by the same projectiles are far more likely to be stopped by an effective defense than by the threat of annihilation, especially when the attacker's location and connection to the state from which the weapon originated are unknown or unclear.

Moreover, the United States has consistently pared military programs where civilian and military leadership find good reason. The Bush administration canceled the army's new Comanche helicopter, arguing that defense resources would be more productively applied to preserving the helicopter fleet in being. The following administration pointed to the diminished likelihood of traditional land warfare waged between states that fielded thundering columns of heavily protected, large-gun bearers and troop transports and virtually eliminated the army's Future Combat System. The plan had lumped together in a large, multibillion-dollar program a host of new armored, mechanized, and infantry vehicles along with advanced networking ability and unmanned aerial and ground vehicles. Cuts in major defense programs do indeed occur, but the authors of the fiscal responsibility and reform report offered no evidence of the large-scale redundancies or ineffective programs they seek to eliminate—and with good reason. No such evidence exists. Returning again to the example of the F-35 fighter, some of the air force planes it will replace entered service thirty-four years ago. Others began their active service a year earlier. The navy aircraft that the F-35 is intended to replace flew first at almost exactly the same time as its sister services' fighters, and like them was not designed to be nearly invisible to enemy radars. An aging fleet of combat aircraft that lacks the technological superiority that other nations are building into their new aircraft, along with the ability to avoid increasingly sophisticated ground defenses, recapitulates nothing except America's traditional lead in and dependence on advanced weaponry as a large part of its strategy. Cost might conceivably be part of this debate. Redundancy has nothing to do with it.

As with any agency of the government through whose hands a large budget passes, efficiencies and improvement can always be found. The defense budget amounts to less than one-half of the federal spending that the president and Congress can decide without changing existing law. Called discretionary spending, this includes, in addition to the Defense Department, the budgets of such departments as Agriculture, Commerce, Health and Human Services, Housing and Urban Development, Labor, and Transportation. For the administration's projected 2012 budget, Medicare, Medicaid, and Social Security—the part of the budget that *would* require legislation to alter its increase—plus interest on the federal debt amounts to 90 percent more than discretionary spending. Balancing the immense current and projected federal deficit on the defense budget's spine is as impossible as it is reckless.

But the telling fact is that members of Congress, industry leaders, and budget experts are discussing such cuts as though defense were just another federal program. It is not. Excuses might be produced for believing that defense is no more than another claimant for federal largesse if the United States were a small state at extreme distance from great ones during a time of exceptional international calm, like New Zealand, for example, in the second half of the nineteenth century. But that is not the case today. The United States lives at the center of international politics. It stands the most to lose from the rise of a peer competitor, nuclear proliferation, prolonged instability in the world's large oil-producing states, a global breakdown in international norms, and the possibility of the United States' own debt-imposed inability to shape events, for example.

By comparison to such effects, the inability of the United States to begin construction of a high-speed rail system, as has been proposed by the Obama administration, matters little. Neither do federal programs for food safety or "transit-accessible housing," also proposed by the administration. As useful as such projects may be, the United States' future security in a dangerous world rests neither on their initiation nor sustainability. Still, the current administration counts defense as though it were a special candidate for budget reduction while other departments experience minor increases. The Transportation Department's budget, for example, is projected to grow from its fiscal year 2012 baseline request level of $72.5 billion to $74 billion in 2013, an increase of 2 percent. At the same time the Obama administration asked Congress for discretionary spending increases—from 2012 to 2013—in such other cabinet-level departments and agencies as Education, Energy, Commerce, Health and Human Services, Housing and Urban Development, Interior, State, and the U.S. Agency for International Development, Veterans Affairs, the Small Business Administration, and the Corporation for National and Community Service. More than speeches and declared policy, the budget is an accurate indicator of an administration's priorities. This administration, as noted, already intends to reduce the Defense Department's budget by $489 billion over a decade. A new defense spending review would precede the proposed cuts—and there is no way to guarantee that the cuts won't go deeper. With President Obama's re-election in 2012, large and even more consequential decreases in the Defense budget are likely.

Notions about future, bigger cuts are already in the air outside the government. Before they left Congress, Representatives Barney Frank (D-MA) and Ron Paul (R-TX) were among four members of Congress who asked several liberal, libertarian, and progressive research institutes as well as tax analysts and academics to recommend defense cuts "that would not compromise the essential security of the United States." They published their report in June 2010.[14] The sum of their recommendations would sharply curtail the United States' ability to project global power. In particular, the report recommends ending or delaying purchase of the next generation of U.S. strike fighters—the F-35—along with the refueling tankers that allow U.S. airpower to fly combat missions from the United States to virtually anywhere in the world without depending on foreign bases.

But nowhere is the report more effective in attempting to shatter U.S. global power than in its recommendation to reduce the size of the navy from its current level of 286 to 230 ships. Besides substantial decrements in large surface combatants, this would eliminate two aircraft carriers from the fleet. Their departure would end the United States' ability to keep three aircraft carriers continuously deployed around the world. It would also halve the number of littoral combat ships the United States currently plans to build and cut by more than one-third the size of the current U.S. submarine fleet. The report's justification for this self naval disarmament policy—about one hundred fewer ships than what the navy says it needs to carry out the missions it has been assigned by the Defense Department—is not that the ships in today's fleet are redundant, poorly tasked, ineffectively deployed, or unsuited to their tasks. The report notes that the U.S. Navy has more firepower than the next twenty largest navies combined. This observation is either aimed deliberately to support the diminution of America as a great power or it is ignorant. It fails to mention that none of those other navies, indeed no other navy, has the worldwide missions and responsibilities of the U.S. Navy. The large European and Asian navies have a limited ability to project power—as, for example, China, India, Japan, and France have demonstrated in their contributions to antipiracy patrols off the Somali coast. But, at least for now, these combat fleets' mission is the defense of the oceanic approaches to their homelands. For the most part they do not maintain a sustained presence in trouble spots around the world. A navy so constrained is what the authors of the report requested by Representatives Barney Frank and Ron Paul favor. They argue that a much smaller fleet would be confined to American waters and could be sent abroad when events require. It is true that a fleet reduced by one-third of its projected size would save money. It would also end the global presence of U.S. seapower, remove a powerful shield that assures allies and friends from the Persian Gulf to East Asia, and invite other powers to fill the vacuum left by departing U.S. force. The ratio of U.S. naval shipbuilding to the nation's gross domestic product is about 1:912. The current expense of defending American commerce, preserving the nation's global influence, and protecting U.S. security interests at a distance from our shores requires a minuscule portion of national wealth compared to the ill effects that can be anticipated as a result of substantially diminishing this power. "Filling the vacuum" in this case means turning over control of the world's littoral seas, and perhaps the oceans themselves, to another navy or to a combination of others. The report finds that "the link between generalized 'presence' [*sic*] and specific outcomes is too tenuous to warrant the cost."[15]

This claim, too, lacks empirical evidence. Can a public safety official be found—in America or anywhere else—who thinks that the link between monitoring deadly storms and protecting the people who live in their path is "too tenuous to warrant the cost"? The last decade of counterinsurgency warfare has taught the American military that protecting civilians in Iraq and Afghanistan is better accomplished by living among them, earning their trust, and gathering on-the-scene intelligence than by coming to the rescue when insurgents attack. While he was a senior U.S. military commander, would General Petraeus have agreed that the link between presence and providing security to a civilian population is "too tenuous to warrant the cost"? Would Emperor Hadrian imagine that the link between deploying legions from Judaea to as far north as Eboracum (York) and Rome's safety was "too tenuous to warrant the cost"? Could Rome have been more secure if its thirty legions were scattered about the midsection of the Italian peninsula and dispatched when word reached the capital of an attack on the empire's perimeter eight hundred miles away? In each case, the answer is no. Presence is expensive in dollars. Absence is exorbitantly expensive—in dollars, alliances, security, and diplomacy. It's the same with fire engines. They're expensive. But having so few that a chief must decide which alarms to respond to is much more costly. History offers no example of a maritime state whose rejection or abandonment of seapower and subsequently reduced oceanic presence improved its lot. As is discussed elsewhere in this work, China, England, the Netherlands, France, and Spain all rose and fell with the fortunes of their seapower. The fate of nations whose commerce and security are tied to the oceans is inseparable from their ability to command them.

The Frank/Paul report is less interesting for its recommendations than for its practical result. The Congressional Budget Office estimates that the federal deficit will reach $23 trillion over the next decade. The savings that the authors of the report envision amount to $1.1 trillion. The reduction of U.S. debt by about 4.7 percent in exchange for the crippling effect on the U.S. military that the Sustainable Defense Task Force recommends would be an extremely imprudent trade, although it is an exchange that, the ideology of Representative Paul's isolationism and Barney Frank's deeply skeptical view of U.S. power show, they are happily willing to make.

Still, as with the National Commission on Fiscal Responsibility and Reform's ideas, the prospect of uncontrollable debt threatens to throw an impenetrable fog bank over one of the U.S. Constitution's fundamental assumptions, that guaranteeing the nation's security is a primary condition of political liberty no less than balancing the powers of government.

A measure of the effect of the country's economic predicament on defense is that even without drastic proposals to throttle defense spending, American seapower is in trouble. Congress has traditionally asked the navy for a thirty-year picture of its shipbuilding plan. This picture offered the public a glimpse of how the navy would connect whatever strategic vision it had of the future with the pace of shipbuilding and spending, as well as the numbers and kinds of ships needed to turn the vision into facts. Because Congress relieved the navy of its obligation to offer

The two designs commissioned by the navy for the series of littoral combat ships. The Lockheed design is pictured above, the General Dynamics design below.

a long-term plan for shipbuilding, the fiscal year 2012 budget failed to include a thirty-year picture, as had its predecessors. Instead the navy offered five- and ten-year shipbuilding plans. These did not square with previous plans. The navy's new target size for the fleet is 320 or 321 ships. In 2011 the navy had planned to build seven littoral combat ships (LCSs) from 2012 to the end of 2016. The 2012 budget planned to build nineteen LCSs in the same period. The 2011 budget planned to construct eight LCSs from 2016 through 2021. The 2012 submission changed this figure to thirteen. The 2013 plan is to buy thirty-four LCSs over the next decade, as well as approximately fourteen Joint High Speed Vessels (JHSVs), light amphibious craft that operate swiftly in shallow waters using ramps to put Special Operations Forces, marines or army troops ashore. The additional JHSVs are in large measure responsible for the somewhat larger fleet at which the navy's 2012 budget aims. Buying more vessels in a compressed period of time usually results in economies of scale and savings. For the LCSs, it also allows the purchase of two different designs of the same vessel from competing shipbuilders, both of which ship designs the navy finds acceptable.

There is another result of purchasing these smaller combatants and amphibious vessels in quantity. They substantially increase the average number of ships that are built yearly—at least for the next ten years. This matters because the navy's average number of ships constructed annually has been steadily falling for several decades. In the 1980s the navy bought an average of 17.8 ships annually.[16] For the period from 1993 to 2000, that figure dropped to 6.8. For most of the first decade of the twenty-first century the average dipped to 5.8 ships yearly. Turning out more ships over the next five years brings up the averages to about eight, for a while. But, of course, there's a catch.

In addition to the LCSs are 19 logistics and support ships scheduled for construction over the next ten years. This means that of the 106 ships that the navy plans to construct over the next decade, 53 will be either relatively low-cost—that is, $700 million or much less per vessel—small combatants or support ships. The other 42 percent of new ships will be (two) aircraft carriers, destroyers, attack submarines, and other large combatants. The story does not end here.

In the opaque world that naval planners inhabit, the larger fleet that the navy says its missions require is not matched by plans to build the ships needed for a larger force. The navy's stated goal three decades hence is a 306-ship fleet. But its 2013 plan acknowledges a shortage of surface ships, amphibious ships, and submarines under the most optimistic but least realistic budget assumptions. No less important, financial constraint, not a calculation of threat or strategy, is responsible for the slow but unabated retreat from a more robust and larger future fleet.

The resulting vulnerabilities will manifest at a point in the future when such likely peer competitors as China, whose defense budget has increased by roughly 3.6 times in the past decade,[17] is likely to be making impressive strides in technology and sheer numbers. Potentially more serious, if one leaves aside the increase in smaller combatants and combat logistics and support vessels, the 2011 plan shrinks the number of powerful combatants in the fleet markedly. While the navy in 2009 was set on building 296 ships during the succeeding three decades, the 2011 plan shorts this to 276 by cutting one carrier, nine attack submarines, nineteen large surface combatants, and other lesser vessels. A smaller number of ships will be built and of them support vessels will represent a larger portion. One advantage of the tilt toward support ships is that they cost a fraction of combatants: the approximate ratio of support ship cost to combatant ship cost is 1:7.5. The future fleet may be better provided for with bullets than with guns to shoot them. The budget looks like a large pedestal supporting a small statue. While it is true that over the next five to ten years the fleet does appear to be recovering lost ground in size, the navy's thirty-year construction plans support neither the navy's stated requirement for even a very modest increase in ship numbers nor the minimal requirements to replace the combat ships built during the Reagan administration, whose effective service lives will end between now and 2040.

Moreover, once the comparatively cheaper LCS and logistics vessels join the fleet, keeping up the average number of ships built per year becomes impossible. The construction of ten large and sophisticated multibillion-dollar combatants each year is very expensive. Here, too, the numbers don't line up. The navy says that its 2011 thirty-year plan requires a yearly expense of $15.9 billion. The Congressional Budget Office estimated this figure at 19 percent higher—or $19 billion annually, a considerable difference even when money is flowing freely. And the navy includes neither the refueling of nuclear aircraft carriers nor ships' outfitting and postdelivery costs, an expense that the CBO says would increase the shipbuilding budget to $21 billion annually. Measured in constant (2010) dollars, the navy's budget estimates for shipbuilding fall $93 billion short of what CBO calculations—which *do* include inflation—predict the navy's shipbuilding plan will cost over the next three decades. Eric Labs, the CBO's senior analyst for naval forces and weapons, sums up the issue succinctly in his 2011 testimony: "The 2011 [Navy] plan would allow the Navy to reach its earlier 313-ship goal by 2020. However, the fleet would remain at or above that number for only seven years. After that, as older ships were retired faster than new ones were brought into service, the fleet would fall to a low of 288 ships in 2032 before increasing to 301 ships by 2040."[18]

But the naval shipwreck could occur much earlier. In an early February 2013 speech at Georgetown University in Washington, Secretary of Defense Leon Panetta said that if the Republican-controlled House, the Democrat-controlled Senate, and President Obama fail to avoid sequestration, "we're going to have to shrink our global naval operations with a reduction of as much as one-third in our western Pacific naval operations. This whole idea of trying to rebalance will be impacted."[19] This is an Olympic understatement. "Rebalancing" will be out of the question as large numbers of ships are kept in port to save on operating costs. Nor is this mere speculation. On the same day that Secretary Panetta warned about the effects of sequestration, he ordered the aircraft carrier USS Harry S. Truman not to deploy to the Persian Gulf because of "uncertainty surrounding the Pentagon's budget."[20] There is at least as much uncertainty about Iran's nuclear plans. Decreasing U.S. naval presence in the increasingly tense Persian Gulf tells the Iranian rulers that the U.S. is facing a crisis of intestinal fortitude. Regardless of the outcome, the prospect of sequestration has cast a shroud over the future of American seapower and confirms for all its portrait of straitened resources, contracting size, and slowly dissipating power.

5

America Adrift

AMERICAN SEAPOWER TODAY is a mixture of the nation's rise as a great power, the ideas of naval power that accompanied and propelled that rise, and the lore of U.S. maritime prowess as exemplified by what schoolchildren were once taught about Captain John Paul Jones ("I have not yet begun to fight"); Captain James Lawrence, commanding officer of U.S.S. *Chesapeake* ("Don't give up the ship"); and Admiral David Farragut ("Damn the torpedoes, full speed ahead"). Of the articulated ideas that materially advanced maritime strategy is central to national strategy, none is more important than the writings of Admiral Alfred Thayer Mahan. His argument that a sea-oriented state's greatness is built on a foundation of sea control, while sometimes poorly understood in the United States, exerts a powerful and robust influence in today's China, whose military planners listen with particular receptiveness to Mahan's arguments about the link between great power status and command of the seas.

U.S. military engagements over the past fifteen years have led to two results that threaten America's future security interests. First is the concentration of U.S. military forces in preparing for essentially counterinsurgency conflicts. America's armed forces already have an increasingly narrow counterinsurgency direction in their doctrine, training, and education. Their growing share of defense dollars supports this trend. Complementing a tilt toward unconventional warfare on land, the Defense Department has for years remained silent on the possibility of strategic rather than economic competition with China. This, too, is indicated by the Defense Department's budget and projected acquisitions, for example, the navy's difficulty in modernizing its surface fleet. Second, and more important: the United States has articulated no policy position that deliberately and carefully considers the strategic position of the United States vis-à-vis China. Certainly, U.S. national security planners understand China's booming economic growth, and its foreign direct investment in Africa, Europe, Latin America,[1] and the United States, among other indicators of Beijing's expanding intentions. But gone is the awareness—as demonstrated by strategic planning at the beginning of the Cold War—of how the United States once approached emerging competitor threats with careful strategic positioning. In January 2012 the Obama administration announced its intent to pivot U.S. resources to the Pacific. The strategic rationale is sound, but pivoting requires a fulcrum—namely, the continued presence of powerful U.S. forces in the region. If the defense budget is reduced by more than $1 trillion over the next decade—as is now expected—U.S. military power is certain to ebb. Lacking this fulcrum, "pivoting" will come to be understood as rhetoric rather than strategic planning.

The first approach to maintaining a strategic stronghold in the region is by assuring and protecting allies and by deterring Chinese expansion by sea—both of which are accomplished through maritime power. The question of strategic positioning is not a false alarm: recent developments in the navies of America's major regional allies—India, Australia, and Japan—are signs that they are preparing for two things: the threat of Chinese expansion by sea and the uncertainty of America's commitment in the region. Moreover, while China's intentions may be impenetrable, their capabilities as evidenced by their public declarations about denying the western Pacific to American military power, their impressive naval development, and their investment in cutting-edge antiaircraft carrier missiles is abundantly evident.

Thus, while U.S. policy makers have yet to articulate a comprehensive vision of China as both an economic and a strategic competitor, the actions of American allies in the region suggest their awareness of a coming threat. They are in the midst of arming themselves through a recent and clearly intentioned accumulation of naval power.

In fact, the most telling evidence that a fundamental shift in American grand strategy is under way is best provided by the Asian states that border China. They have considered America's engagement in the Middle East dating back to Desert Shield and placed it alongside the United States' diminishing presence in Asia. Their actions bespeak anxiety. American leaders say the right things about the center of power and wealth moving east, but Asian leaders ask: Do the Americans back up their words with action? Singapore's great statesman and former prime minister Lee Kuan Yew, closed a speech in Washington in 2009 by reminding Americans that their "core interest requires that [the United States] remain the superpower in the Pacific."[2] Admiral Robert Willard, then commander of the U.S. Pacific Command, offered a parallel view. He told an audience in Seoul that China's military growth had exceeded the expectations of most U.S. intelligence estimates over the past decade and said specifically that "our regional partners are somewhat uncertain about [U.S. estimates and China's military growth]."[3] Other states in the region are unsure that the United States will listen to Lee. They are acting consistently with Admiral Willard's characterization of their uncertainty.

In November 2010 Vietnam's prime minister said that Russia had committed $2.2 billion to rebuild and repair port facilities at Cam Ranh Bay and that Vietnam is looking to India and Russia for deals that would allow their vessels access to the rebuilt port for naval resupply and repairs. Major U.S. allies in the region may find Vietnam's offer one that they cannot refuse. Early in October 2010 Vietnam agreed to a substantial increase in its submarine fleet with the purchase of a half dozen Russian-built Kilo-class attack submarines, which will give Vietnam an extended-range naval capacity it had previously lacked altogether.

At the end of October in the same year, Japan's Defense Ministry leaked that plans were under consideration to increase Japan's submarine fleet by more than 37 percent over the next four years. A professor of international relations at Waseda University said that Japan needs to balance Chinese naval growth and pointed to "a sense of insecurity" as additional justification, an implicit concern that the continuity of U.S. presence is in question.[4]

The previous month India's air chief marshal said that he had begun to base fighter jets in the country's northeast; the army is adding two new mountain divisions in the same area, as well as an artillery brigade in Arunachal Pradesh, the country's northeasternmost state. Also in the autumn of 2010 the Indian defense minister called for increased operational contact with the region's littoral states to strengthen interoperability and professional ties. Developing a more robust defense together with other friendly states in the region fits intelligently into the Indians' larger effort to extend their naval reach as indicated, for example, by the ten stealth frigates that New Delhi plans to build over the next decade. Calling them frigates is an understatement. They displace 6,000 tons, roughly equal in displacement of large U.S. destroyers.

Noting the need for a "capacity to do more when required," a 2009 Australian government white paper confirmed the government's intent to double the size of the navy's submarine force as well as to make significant increases in their surface fleet. The Australian electorate, as former prime minister John Howard's national security adviser noted in a Washington speech delivered in October 2010, is alarmed about the solidity of American commitment in the region and strongly supports the defense increases. Less than a year later, Australian leadership sensibly decided against putting too many strategic eggs in a single basket. In April 2011, Prime Minister Julia Gillard said that she had discussed greater military cooperation with Chinese president Hu Jintao and that more PLAN (People's Liberation Army Navy) ships would be welcomed to Australian ports as well as increased defense exercises between the two countries.[5] If other countries in the area—and the distance between Australia's north coast and China's south is about the same as from New York to Dublin— begin to doubt U.S. staying power in the region, the small hedging of bets represented by the Australian government's decision modestly to increase military cooperation with China will become a strategic stampede.

Lee Kuan Yew and his fellow leaders in the region see the growing problems with American seapower's inability to modernize, prevent a continued evanescence of fleet size and capability, or retain industrial capacity, plus the coming budget troubles, as evidence that parallels America's focus on conducting and preparing for counterinsurgency operations in the Middle East and Central Asia. Together these two facts do indeed constitute a shift in American grand strategy. The shift may not be intentional, but it doesn't have to be to be real. U.S. leaders see competition with China as based in economic competition and assured by each country's commercial investment in the other. American political leaders of both political parties repeat this often. The Defense Department's silence on the possibility of strategic, rather than economic, competition with China is another compelling example of the asymmetry between the two nations' views of each other. Chinese leaders' public statements about denying American power access to the western Pacific show that China's leaders do not see America as American leaders see China.

The Navy's continually diminishing fleet is consistent with the entire U.S. government's purblind view of China as a potential threat. Current budgets as well as the likelihood of additional deep defense cuts underscore American seapower weakness. The current cost of new ship construction is $10.9 billion. But the Navy reported that it needed an average of $16.8 billion annually to reach its desired fleet size, while the CBO said that the amount required would be $20 billion. Whichever estimate is right, the increase is huge, even in belt-*loosening* times.[6] The CBO has projected that at current ship costs and funding plans, the navy will shrink to slightly more than 200 ships in a little more than twenty-five years. Lack of resources is responsible for the possible reduction by twenty-five thousand personnel in the next few years. The service has cut scores of thousands of personnel since 2004. The U.S. seaborne logistics fleet, which is critical for maintaining a U.S. presence at the other end of the Pacific, is shrinking and aging. If the United States does not have the military capacity to continue a grand strategy based importantly on sea-based forces, then American grand strategy will crumble.

The last place to look for proof of this change is in the United States' public statements. The U.S. government's public foreign policy and national security strategic documents are, in fact, lists of threats and goals. They commonly lack priorities and always fail to express how a particular administration will get from where it is to where it wants to go. But even if official policy over time is not united by deliberate strategy, there are patterns—and they matter.

In 1989, the United States invaded Panama to remove the drug lord–cum–military dictator Antonio Noriega. Since then, twenty-four years have passed. Throughout the period U.S. forces have been in combat in the Balkans, twice in Iraq, and in Afghanistan. All of these campaigns have been essentially land-based, transforming Americans' idea of military force from the traditional balance of sea and land strengths. Such balance has undergirded American foreign policy over the past century to countering insurgencies, training others to do the same, constabulary operations, and nation building. These ground-based competencies reflect and reinforce the United States' unarticulated shift toward a national security strategy that is essentially continental but, more important, a change in Americans' self-understanding that is coming to look like a grand Whac-A-Mole game. Jihadist threats emerge from holes and as quickly as the force is applied to counter them, other threats surface from different directions. The Arab rising that began in Tunisia during the winter of 2011 ignited a rebellion in neighboring Libya that resulted in the use of American force to protect civilians—and then flared up again in the fall of 2012 when terrorists killed the U.S. ambassador to Libya and three other Americans. The same unrest had previously caught fire in Yemen, where U.S. military attention was already on alert to the possibility that Yemen and nations in the nearby Horn of Africa would be added to the list of disintegrating states that al-Qaeda and its sister organizations could use as bases for terror. These have become candidates for interjecting increased American land forces.

The political arguments against such uses of American force are well enough known: the United States has become the world's police; democracy cannot and should not be built by force; the regimes American arms support are unworthy of the sacrifice the U.S. military is asked to make, and so on. But the shift in the United States' grand strategy, which has heretofore reflected the nation's geographic position and natural strength as a maritime power, has gone virtually unnoticed. In the past, Americans have conceived of seapower as the foundation of presence that would keep distant conflict from approaching the homeland, and U.S. policy looked to honor alliances with states that surrounded a threat as the natural extension to project American influence. This idea of grand strategy has been gradually replaced with another: the appearance of coalitions and allies is desirable and useful, but America will supply the preponderance of boots on the ground or, as has increasingly been the case, drone strikes against terror chieftains that fail to produce potentially valuable intelligence while avoiding the issue of where and under what circumstances enemy combatants should be incarcerated. The Obama administration in particular sees multilateral action not only as a strategic goal but as moral justification for the use of American force. However, similar to the approach of its immediate predecessors, the Obama administration's approach has been to lean heavily toward land engagements. The shift is a profound departure from the once unified vision of American grand strategy dating back to the nation's beginning.

Grand strategy is the set of objectives that unite a nation's foreign and military policies at any single moment and give a coherent view over a long period of time to how a state protects itself and ensures its interests. Since it became a major world power early in the twentieth century, the United States has paralleled Britain's centuries-old maritime grand strategy. British policy used seapower to secure the sea lines on which its trade and eventually its colonial empire depended, to support and reassure its continental allies, and to protect itself from waterborne assault. Complementing its maritime strategy was the long-standing effort to preserve security by building continental alliances and coalitions—and contributing ground forces only where necessary—to prevent the emergence of a dominant European power that might enlarge to challenge Britain at sea.

In the early eighteenth century, the possibility of a single monarch over Spain and France offered just such a possibility. Britain crafted an alliance with the Dutch, several German principalities, Prussia, and Portugal to prevent the rise of a continental hegemon along with what would have been a profound upset in the European balance of power. At the same time, British seapower preyed on the sea lines of communication over which New World gold passed to Spain, and on French possessions in the Caribbean that provided material support for Louis XIV's war effort. Exhausted, the combatants negotiated separate agreements under the Treaty of Utrecht, which averted the effective union of France and Spain.

A century later, France again sought continental hegemony, this time under Napoleon. English policy makers resisted anew. Alliances and coalitions with continental powers nibbled at, and then destroyed, French power on land. But seapower was key. It maintained Britain's ability to transport troops and conduct commerce and eventually destroyed the French and Spanish combined fleet along with Napoleon's ability to invade England. British grand strategy repeated its earlier success in preventing the rise of a single power that sought to dominate the European continent.

American grand strategy is also shaped importantly by geography. As demonstrated in the historical sketch of chapter 3 the U.S.'s fundamentally maritime conception took root in the wars against the Barbary pirates, the War of 1812, and the riverine and coastal encirclement that helped choke the Confederacy. The war against Spain severed the last European power's foothold in the Western Hemisphere and simultaneously acquired an American interest in and responsibility for island possessions—the Philippines—at the far side of the Pacific. In allowing American seapower to shift smoothly and strategically between the Atlantic and Pacific, the Panama Canal acknowledged the United States' increasing interest in the entire breadth of great oceans on both its coasts. Theodore Roosevelt's other major seagoing accomplishment, the construction and round-the-world deployment of a large U.S. battle fleet, underlined the same idea: that the world's oceans provided strategic defense in-depth for America's increasingly global interests.

U.S. policy during World War I rested as much on safe transit of a large number of American troops and a huge amount of logistical support through the Atlantic's U-boat-patrolled seas as it did on a coalition strategy with Allied forces on the ground in the northern European plain.

For reasons different from Woodrow Wilson's, Franklin Roosevelt saw peril in the threat that Germany would rule Europe. But the dovetailing relationship between sea and land power remained central to American grand strategy. The United States would supply the tools Winston Churchill asked for, but they must travel safely over water first.

The danger that a single power would control the European continent remained after the Nazis disappeared. The U.S.S.R.'s battlements reached unto the border of divided Germany. Its reserve rested in large numbers among the other satellite nations of Central and Eastern Europe. Again, U.S. grand strategy aimed to prevent a single hostile power from dominating the continent. NATO was a coalition of continental democratic states that stood between the Soviets and the waters surrounding the European peninsula. America's allies would be assured of goods and trust as the United States resupplied them with secure seaborne supplies and ground troops. At the same time, U.S. naval combatants would whittle down Moscow's submarine-borne strategic reserve and provide diversionary assaults on the flanks of the large Soviet ground force if it struck westward.

Maritime power would not itself break the enemy's back in a conflict, but it would hobble, divert, frustrate, and provide the life blood of resistance to prevent the necessity of a second D-Day or, far more complicated and expensive, the need for another return to Europe, this time from an American base.

Through alliances and coalitions buttressed and reinforced by maritime power, American grand strategy for a century has aimed to prevent the rise of a dangerous peer competitor on a distant continent. Seaborne power has supported this strategy by responding to crises, even those that did not directly engage opponents' interest. It has supported coalitions and alliances through presence and by helping to deter nuclear exchanges. Perhaps most important, seapower by its large transoceanic role has protected freedom of navigation and acted as representative as well as occasional enforcer of such standards as respect for sovereignty and nonaggression that serve America's broadest interest in a peaceful international order.

Several major policy changes since the end of the Cold War show that this fundamental idea of grand strategy has shifted. The invasion of Iraq in 2002 and the continuing war in Afghanistan are continental struggles in which no threat of a rising peer competitor exists. Allies were called on and coalitions formed. Naval power was and is being used in the war against the Taliban. It was deployed against the Libyan ruler Mu'ammar Gadhafi's military in the spring of 2011. But the appearances do not alter the reality. U.S. grand strategy has loosed the moorings of its previous understanding that significant hegemony in either of the world's two most important continents, Europe and Asia, constitutes a perilous threat to U.S. security, and that partnership with the states that separate these threats from the world's major oceans offers the first and surest way to protect America's interest in preventing danger from approaching any closer.

The change in direction of U.S. strategy is more than a political and geographic refocus. America's armed forces are transforming and reinventing themselves to concentrate on the type of warfare they have experienced in the Middle East. Under the current and previous administration, the Defense Department is changing itself into a large counterinsurgency operation, just as the British did after World War I when Britain's political leaders decided to emphasize imperial defense. This was a deliberate choice made at the expense of the far more costly preparations required to reshape their military by exploiting advances in air and armor—and their combined use—against the possibility of renewed major warfare on the Continent. Hitler took a different and more effective course, as was demonstrated in the Blitzkrieg's early successes in Poland, Belgium, and France.

Secretary of Defense Gates's fiscal year 2011 budget emphasized "rebalancing the force," an expression of the Pentagon's shift in the direction of counterinsurgency operations and thus an expansion in America's direct or indirect continental engagement. The Department of Defense (DoD) budget lists as examples "more robust funding" for helicopters and aircrews, Special Operations personnel and their equipment, increases in electronic warfare capabilities, and the purchase and deployment of more unmanned vehicles. Major conventional weapons systems, such as the air force's F-22 fifth-generation fighter—which would have been the most effective instrument to pierce China's increasingly sophisticated air defense system—or the building of a new class of navy destroyers and cruisers have been abbreviated or just canceled. Investments that could have been made at the beginning of this decade in underwater unmanned vehicles that would greatly expand the fleet's combat effectiveness were not. The U.S. aerial refueling fleet is adumbrated and old. Without these aircraft, long-distance strikes in the famously vast Pacific theater are difficult, if not impossible. The maiden flight of the Boeing's KC-135 Stratotanker, similar in outward appearance to the Boeing 707, took place two months before Dwight Eisenhower was elected to his second term. The last new KC-135 was delivered to the air force in 1964, the same year that Congress passed the Gulf of Tonkin Resolution that authorized President Johnson to prevent attacks against U.S. forces in Vietnam.[7] Defense Department efforts to replace the aging tanker fleet produced dispute, scandal, and corporate protest from 2002 to 2010. In 2011, nearly a decade after the effort began to build a plane that is essential to the United States' ability to project airpower around the globe, the Defense Department awarded the $35 billion contract to the Boeing Company.

Promotion policy has paralleled acquisition policy's taste for counterinsurgent warfare. In 2008, General David Petraeus was brought back from Iraq to head the board that selects army officers for promotion from colonel to brigadier general. Nearly half of those selected for promotion had been or would serve in the Middle Eastern wars. This is not surprising since the United States has been at war there, but it is clear indication that the army sees future warfare as an image of today's conflict projected onto a larger and more distant mirror. Absent from the Defense Department's calculation about the nation's strategic future are questions about whether Americans will tolerate a chain of small wars justified by preventing states from failing, denying safe haven to terrorists, increasing greater regional security, and promoting democracy.

Also absent is China. The Quadrennial Defense Review (QDR) that the Obama administration published early in 2010 mentions China's rise and its large population twice. The same document notes that China is making substantial investments in its military, "which could enable it to play a more substantial and constructive role in international affairs."[8] Otherwise the QDR, which is supposed to survey the nation's defenses and set its future course, is silent about the possibility of strategic competition with Asia's largest state, whose oft-declared intent is to deny the United States access to the western Pacific.[9]

The loss of balance between maritime and continental strategy that was formerly the distinguishing characteristic of effective American security strategy occurred without legislative debate, serious discussion within the highest circles of government, or public understanding. The balanced strategy that previously characterized America's broadest foreign and national security policies was consistent with, and rested upon, America's traditional democratic strength in promoting a world order that encourages political liberty, expanding commerce based on free enterprise, and such international norms as respect for sovereignty and untroubled transit through international waters. The rise of a dominant power in Asia threatens these goals at least as much as the contest for European or Eurasian hegemony once did. China's mercantilist economy, based on exports and sustained by the manipulation of currency that also helps support nonproducing state-owned industries; its increased assertiveness with smaller neighbors over sovereignty questions in the surrounding seas; its growing nationalism; and its increasingly powerful navy all demonstrate an ambition that appears to seek Asian hegemony.

The consequences for America would be profound. The network of U.S. alliances with democratic Asian states like Japan, the Republic of Korea, and whatever was left of Taiwan would splinter as these and other smaller Asian states sought economic, diplomatic, and military accommodation with China. Denied access to the region, the United States would lose its century-old status as a major Pacific power along with the bases from which it can now project air and amphibious force as well as support naval operations throughout the region. China's capitalism-on-an-authoritarian-leash economic and political system would become the model of governance and regional intercourse. Japan's quest for regional superiority extended to Australia in 1942. Australia's proximity to some of the narrow Indonesian straits through which oil passes from the Middle East to East Asia and Australia's leverage with Indonesia suggest that China would be as interested as Japan had been in influencing the Australian island continent. The weight of Chinese influence borne by its uncontested naval power would reach far and the continued diminution of the U.S. Navy that was importantly responsible for the extension of Chinese power would find itself equally impotent in shielding India. With Asia's huge population—about half the world's—and growing wealth, the loss of status as the major Pacific power would spell the end of America's position as a great international force.

Jihadism in Afghanistan or Yemen or anywhere else does not present the same danger. Indeed the jihadists, like their Arab nationalist, pan-Arab predecessors, are likely to collapse under their own weight and be replaced by some other trend in the Middle East's procession of ideologies. But when the costs of supporting combat operations in the Middle East reach close to one-third of the entire annual defense budget, as they have in recent years; and when Congressional Budget Office predictions of American seapower show a significant decline in the future size of the U.S. combat fleet; and as other conventional forces dedicated to the western Pacific are increasingly supplanted by the Defense Department's emphasis on counterinsurgency, America's traditional and effective balanced grand strategy is at precisely the same serious risk as the nation's staying power in Asia.

Restoring Strategic Balance

A U.S. exit from large-scale military engagement in fighting jihadists coupled with policy that seeks to shift the debate within

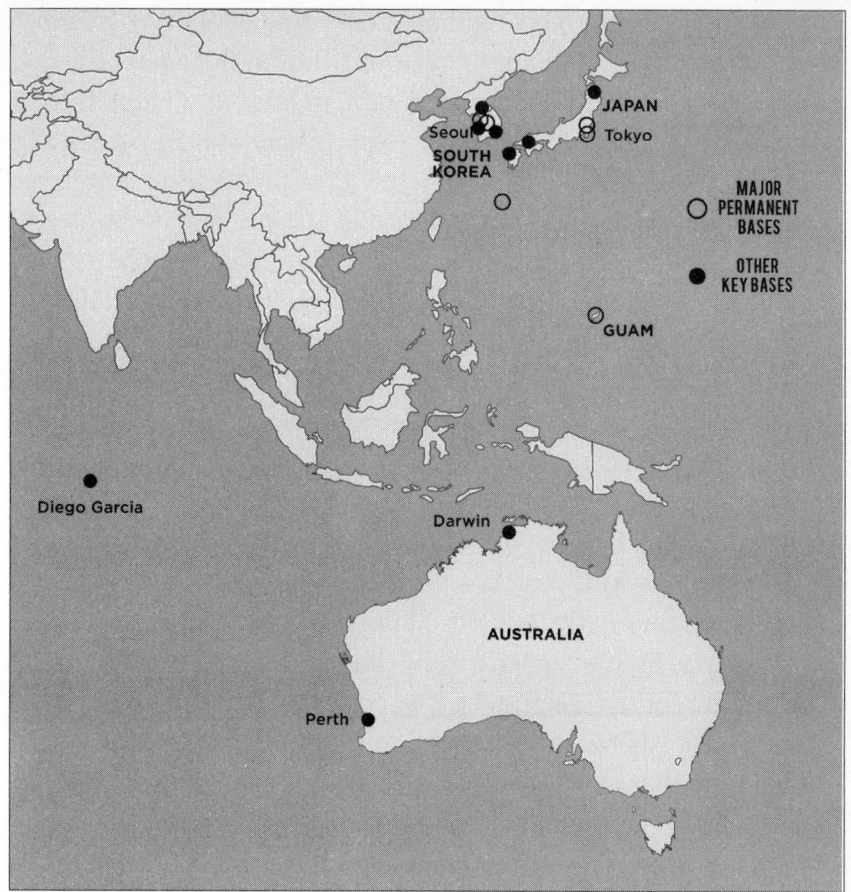

The location of the major U.S. naval bases in Asia and the South Pacific

the Islamic world as the United States selectively captures or kills violent radical leadership or degrades their ability to use failed states as bases to attack the West is one way of balancing U.S. grand strategy and restoring its complementary relationship between maritime power and continental alliance. The Central Asian Turkic-speaking states that border Afghanistan, for example, have at least as large an interest as the United States does in preventing Islamists from returning to power in Kabul. Assistance to those states, selective employment of U.S. Special Operations

Forces, and strikes from unmanned air vehicles (UAVs) may not utterly destroy the Taliban. But current U.S. policy is not headed in this direction. And the cost in blood, money, and focus cannot be compared to the opportunity costs that are being forgone in Asia and the Pacific as the United States prosecutes expensive wars that have yet to meet the first test of successful counterinsurgency strategy: the ability to control the defended state's borders. In NATO members' loss of confidence that the Afghanistan mission will succeed as measured in conventional terms of victory and defeat, U.S. policy also lacks the minimal demands of a coalition strategy: dedicated allies who share the brunt of the fighting. Insofar as significant U.S. military ground forces are dedicated to the effort, the continued armed pursuit of al-Qaeda and its imitators has become a strategic diversion. President Obama has insisted that al-Qaeda is a violent organization, but in denying the fundamentally radical Islamist dogma that is central to the jihadists, he disengages from the ideological battlefield on which gains could be achieved that could well diminish the need for force. The successful eradication of jihadists ad seriatim and by force is a distant prospect. The likelihood of mounting expense and increasing domestic political apathy—absent another large and lethal terrorist incident—is more reasonable to expect. Domestic political apathy will increase public skepticism about the general usefulness and application of American power as it specifically distracts attention away from the longer-term threat of challenges in Asia.

Domestic politics is also an obstacle to setting U.S. grand strategy back on a course where seapower and continental engagement support each other in a balance that maintains America's global position. Republicans still enjoy the political benefit of having steadfastly opposed the Soviets and supported military action generally since the 1960s when the two political parties drew apart in their idea about using American force. Republicans think of, and represent themselves as, the party of strength and want to continue to be seen this way. Disengaging from world-wide military efforts to prevent failed states from falling into the hands of jihadists risks being seen by the electorate as less strong and could open deep divisions within the Republican Party. Democrats' decades-long doubts about the use of American force and opposition to major weapons systems contributes to the public's skepticism about the Democrats' foreign policy credentials generally and national security policy specifically. Candidate Obama avoided the appearance of weakness on foreign policy by balancing his opposition to the Iraq War with support for the one in Afghanistan.

The polarization within and between the political parties complicates rational debate on the merits of a particular war, and grand strategy is not a subject that candidates from either party are likely to see votes in. In recent years the American electorate has increasingly examined presidential candidates more on the basis of voters' private concerns, ones that just graze broad public interests—tax policy and moral issues, for example—rather than take on questions of strategy. Nevertheless, important differences separate candidates for national office and are rooted in fundamentally different strategic conceptions of American security. Still, debate over Iraq and Afghanistan concentrated more clearly on the cost of war than on American actions' link to broad national strategy. In large measure this points to the electorate's remove from the virtues of public life as demonstrated, for example, by the strategic national debate Franklin Roosevelt undertook in his 1941 State of the Union address. FDR offered at once a history lesson in American defense and a reminder of the importance to the United States of the "armed defense of democratic existence (that) is now being waged on four continents." No more. National strategies that look into the future are challenging to articulate and difficult to implement in democracies, many of whose citizens have become gradually accustomed to considering their private interest in the government's largesse above the nation's long-term strategic interests. Apportioning responsibility is not the point here, but appeals for political support that rest on the federal government's munificence reduce the nation's ability to pay for its defense as they avoid essential debate over strategic direction.

Persistent national failure to consider these large questions gives the imprimatur of experience and usage to the United States' drift toward regarding failed states and jihadists as major threats to national security. They may indeed be, but there is no national consensus on this, much less a serious deliberation at the highest level of government. What has eluded the United States since the decade between when China's rise became common knowledge and the attacks of September 2001 is a public debate over future threats to U.S. security and how best to meet them. As one direct result, the question of what *is* American foreign policy and how grand strategy will advance it is increasingly difficult to answer.

The problems of a decreasing U.S. fleet—which should also be addressed if balance is to be restored to U.S. grand strategy— is just as perplexing. Chairman of the Joint Chiefs Admiral Mike Mullen told a "Tribute to the Troops" breakfast in June 2010 that "our national debt is our biggest security threat," repeating a point he had been stressing that entire summer: U.S. taxpayers will be paying $1 trillion in debt service in 2020.[10] Admiral Mullen's point is serious.

One of the most likely sources of reducing the debt is to cut defense spending. The National Debt Commission's preliminary report released in early November 2010—and noted earlier— recommended, among other cuts, reducing U.S. military forces in Europe and Asia by one-third, reducing defense procurement by 15 percent of its current level, and substantial reductions in existing defense programs that focus on marine and navy acquisitions.[11] An administration that resists the temptation to decrease the debt by cutting defense spending will have more resources to rebuild a fleet, which today is less than half the size it was in the

Reagan administration and needs an increase in number of vessels by at least 14 percent to reach the levels that navy leadership says are needed to accomplish the missions they have been directed to execute. The alternative—to cut large defense expenses, like ships—accelerates the decline of American seapower, unintentionally adding strategic weight to Beijing's naval buildup and, more important, to China's rise to dominance in Asia. Politicians have not faced this basic question of strategy.

More than two decades after the end of the Cold War, a genuine national debate over the purpose and direction of American foreign policy would benefit the United States. But even if a path forward becomes clear, the strategy needed to implement it could be daunting. Seapower and the industrial base required to supply it are far more expensive to replace than to sustain. A significant loss in naval combatants and the means and experience to produce them takes decades to overcome, time that would permit an opponent to solidify his gains. The size of the U.S. fleet is important because a shrinking navy will lose its ability to be seen and to threaten or apply force around the world with resulting loss in the global perception of the United States as a great power. Public debate over fleet size and purpose may not reverse current shrinkage, but the absence of such a national discussion smoothes the silent course toward America's decline as a power to be reckoned with. The effect is that long-term interests are crowded out by discussion of immediate needs or private expectations of the government. This slowly moves the electorate away from political engagement. Critical arguments such as those that explain and favor the preservation of the industrial base needed to support the nation's defense are pushed out by arguments over corporate profit and the unfair advantage of lobbyists. Stoking the fires of democratic resentment leaves more serious concerns in ashes.

This drift underscores the importance of leadership that is willing to engage in a national debate about broad American strategy. A debate could help return balance to national security priorities. But even if such an exchange produced bipartisan agreement, large hurdles remain. Political correctness within the military services, for example, is a serious challenge to important decisions about the nation's large strategic direction. To prevent bureaucratic wars among the military services, the defense budget has for years been divided equally. This would not change if all U.S. forces ceased combat operations overnight. But tripartite equality was not always the rule. As American grand strategy once made deliberate choices, the division of the defense budget once reflected them. In fiscal year 1958, when the Eisenhower administration placed its hopes for strategic deterrence primarily in the Strategic Air Command, the air force received 48 percent of the budget. The navy's portion was almost 29 percent and the army fell to 21 percent, down by nearly a half from its 39 percent share during the Korean War.[12]

When large-scale U.S. participation in the Middle Eastern wars ends, a division of the defense budget consistent with strategy that aims to maintain a balance of power in Asia—including not least the United States' stabilizing presence there—will be needed to fortify the military services best situated to the task. If "strategy" has any meaning, it must always choose among competing claims and place informed bets on the most pressing and farseeing ones. Bureaucratic politics often overrides such choices. So, the contentment of the three military services is purchased by the equal division of the defense budget among them. But such contentment is not a greater good than an allocation of resources that sustains America's disinterested power in Asia and prevents the continued rise of a rival regional hegemon. If the United States cannot make such strategic decisions under the burden of increasingly straitened national resources, it may no longer be capable of providing international leadership, much less the nation's own security.

Paying for strategic restructuring can be assisted not only by a more strategic division of resources but by reducing the number of DoD's multiplying, centrally run defense agencies that employ thousands upon thousands of employees. The Defense Logistics Agency, for example, which purchases food, fuel, medical supplies, and a host of other items from spare parts to uniforms, employs twenty-six thousand people, or three thousand more than the number of Pentagon employees. The Defense Contract and Audit Agency operates more than three hundred field offices and has four thousand employees. The Defense Finance and Accounting Service sends out paychecks and travel reimbursements and employs twelve thousand people. Another ten thousand work at the Defense Contract Management Agency. The Defense Commissary Agency, which sells groceries and household supplies to the military, has six thousand employees. That's fifty-eight thousand employees, or over one-fourth the size of the Marine Corps. And this is not an exhaustive list of defense agencies. There are many more and the Obama administration has proposed to add thirty-thousand employees to provide more oversight of the military's acquisition system. Congress created many of the large, centrally run agencies. Congressional action to return responsibility for some of these important functions to the military services and allow others to be contracted out would save billions as the cost of salaries, benefits, and pensions are reckoned over entire careers.

Similar savings would result from greater internal discipline within the military services. World War II's military, at a very conservative estimate, reached seven times the size of today's. In World War II the entire Washington headquarters of the U.S. military was located in the 662,598-square-foot Old Executive Office Building—now called the Eisenhower Building—just west of the White House. The Pentagon has about ten times the square footage of the Eisenhower Building. The Defense Department is bloated, overcentralized, and unaccountable, as only a huge agency with multiple overlapping jurisdictions can be. Decentralization, flattened management structures, and the return of responsibility and accountability to the military services would also save enormous sums as DoD shed its resemblance to the committees that were responsible for economic planning in the Soviet Union. If there is to be a return of responsibility to the military services it will need teeth, specifically in the form of relieving officers where necessary. Even before World War II this was standard procedure in the U.S. military. Today, fitness reports make the psalmists' praise of the Almighty look faint. Relieving senior officers for professional incompetence or failure is unheard of—in the field or on staffs. If effective management is to be restored to the Pentagon reward for merit and punishment for non- or poor performance are necessary.

Effective strategic restructuring also requires more U.S. attention to alliance management. China is surrounded by states that, like the United States, wish to avoid another cold war and hope for a less aggressive neighbor with whom relations are better characterized by economic interests than fear. But the China's recent record provides scant hope for more tranquil relations. The September 2010 collision between Chinese and Japanese vessels in the Senkaku Islands was immediately followed by China's suspension of rare earth sales to Japan. China's first-ever live-fire military exercises in Tibet near the Indian border in October of the same year didn't smooth any waters. Neither did Chinese foreign minister Yang Jiechi's repetition to Secretary of State Hillary Clinton in September 2012 that "China has sovereignty over the islands of the South China Sea and the adjacent waters," that is, international waters.[13] Equally unhelpful was China's May 2012 seizure of two Vietnamese fishing boats along with fourteen crew members in the disputed Spratly Islands.[14] These incidents paint an imaginable portrait of how Asia is likely to look if Chinese hegemony is established.

The United States has not ignored the prospect of Chinese ambitions, but its responses are better described in the form of speeches than action. Secretaries Clinton and Gates both used visits to Hanoi in 2010 as platforms to argue that resolving these disputes between China and its neighbors is an American interest. This is sensible policy. But whether it is sufficient remains to be seen. Senior American officials began to discuss the so-called

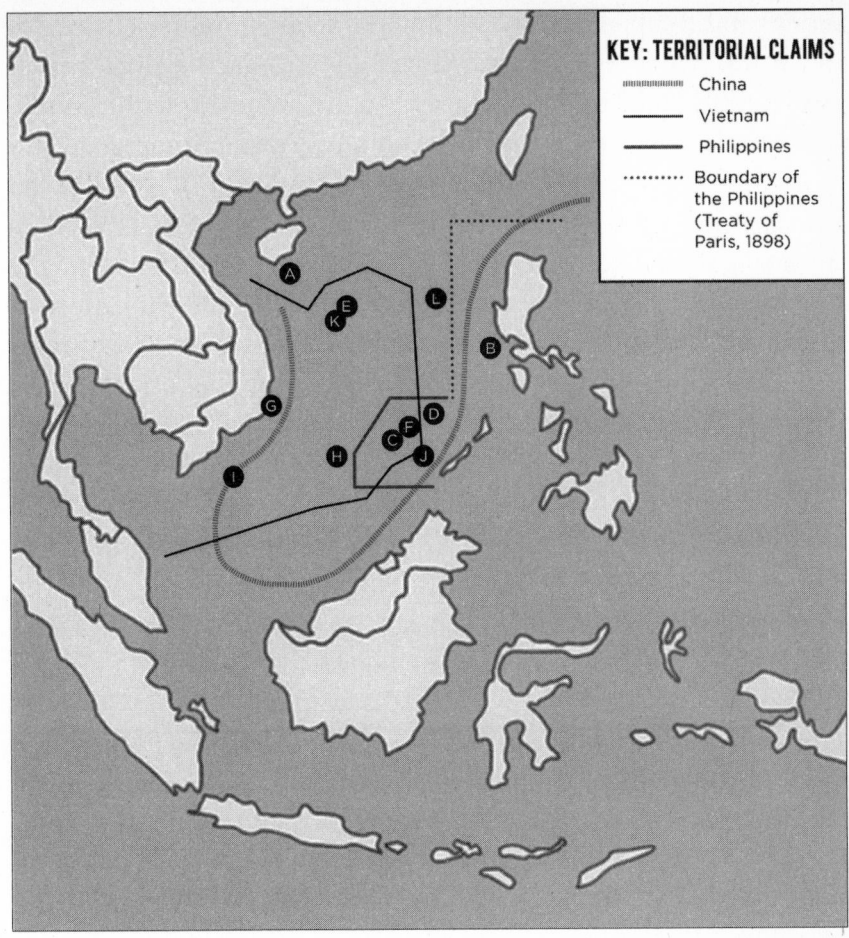

In recent years, China has been involved in an increasing number of territorial disputes in the South China Sea. The lines denote the claims of various countries and the dots, lettered A-L, mark the spot of aggressive incidents in which China has been involved.

pivot to Asia, that is, away from engagement in the Middle East in the spring of 2012. Again the idea is sensible. But the execution depends no less on diplomacy than persuasive military deterrence. With the defense cuts already in place and those that sequestration may trigger, it is extraordinarily difficult to see how American seapower in the western Pacific will be strengthened unless at the expense of the nation's strategic presence elsewhere in a world, where events are calling for it with increasing urgency.

Beijing's ability to resolve the many regional territorial disputes in its own favor depends importantly on superior naval and amphibious power. The same force supported by land-based naval aviation and antiship ballistic missiles threatens U.S. bases in the western Pacific and U.S. naval presence throughout the region, especially if the American combat fleet continues to diminish. Diverting China from its naval ambitions would reassure the region and distract China's rulers from the influence and power that command of the seas and possession of a large navy offers. Strengthening ties between India and the United States advances this goal, not only through military cooperation but by supporting New Delhi's quest for permanent membership in the UN Security Council. So would closer association with the Uighur Muslims in China's Xinjiang provinces whose dissatisfaction with the local Han Chinese population occupied Beijing's attention in the summer of 2009. The mutually suspicious relations between Russia and China offer U.S. policy the same opportunity to divert China toward its continental west and away from its oceanic east. The United States is seen in the region as an advocate of balance, stability, respect for sovereignty, freedom of navigation, and security. America is seen by its democratic friends in the region as an advocate of political liberty. China's recent actions have reinforced the views of its neighbors that it stands for all the opposites. Should not U.S. policy exploit this correct difference in regional perceptions to the fullest?

Domestic policy is always linked to foreign policy, sometimes subtly, but not so today. As America's indebtedness increases along with its servicing, there will be less to spend on the military. This raises the importance of strategy. The United States can no longer do everything it would like to do, nor has there ever been a time when such a goal could be attained. Choice has always been demanded. It still is, but more so. The policies that have led the United States deeper and deeper into the Middle East play to American weakness, which is intolerance for extended military commitments that produce doubtful results. Current policy would keep the United States in the Middle East for an unknown length of time. It is inconsistent with America's traditional reliance on continental alliances supported by maritime power and incompatible with America's long-successful grand strategy of thwarting a dominant power on the world's great landmasses.

Strategic restructure requires a departure from Afghanistan and an end to America's essentially ground action that seeks the unachievable goal of denying jihadists access to collapsing or collapsed states. Special operations forces, limited use of airpower, contemporary advances in unmanned military technology, cooperative vigilance with the intelligence and security services of friendly governments, rejuvenated public diplomacy, and such measures as maritime security operations are best suited to destroy jihadist networks, assassinate their leaders, and foil their worst schemes.

U.S. maritime power and presence play to the nation's strength, the sparing and selective use of force that resolves or prevents crises, demonstrates resolve, and supports allies united by the shared objective of avoiding conflict by assuring a balance of power. A return to America's most basic strategic principles necessitates an imbalance in how the U.S. defense budget is divided, a radical change in managing the nation's defense assets, more assertive alliance management, the recognition of China's growing naval reach as a serious threat, and the reinvigoration of U.S. maritime strength. This will not only secure peace in Asia. It will preserve America's status as the world's indispensable power.

6

China and the Coming Threats to Dominance

T HE MIDDLE KINGDOM, as China has called itself for millennia, is a cultural, not a geographic, self-description. Chinese civilization is as ancient as it is accomplished, and it has long been at the center of cultural and technological development. Chinese artisans were crafting wine vessels, weapons, bells, and belt hooks of surpassing intricacy and beauty thousands of years before the pyramids were built. Chinese naval skill including navigation and shipbuilding often predated similar technology in the West. China was a great naval power in the early part of the fifteenth century, at whose end Columbus landed in the New World. The British biochemist and historian Joseph Needham's extraordinarily detailed multivolume work *Science and Civilization in China* dates the appearance of the magnetic compass for use in seagoing navigation to 1090, approximately a century before its first use for the same purpose in the West.[1] The Chinese scholar and inventor Su Song worked in the eleventh century. His celestial atlas divides the skies according to regular movements of the moon with stars projected onto a cylinder in relation to the North Star.[2] This performed a similar function as, and preceded by approximately five centuries, the Flemish astronomer Gerard Mercator's projection of a terrestrial map onto a cylinder, which permits ship pilots to set straight-line courses that intersect each succeeding meridian at the same angle, thus simplifying navigation.

Chinese developments in ship technology paralleled their navigational achievements. Chinese vessels had started to use fixed axial rudders for steering rather than long oars lugged to and fro at a ship's stern as early as the beginning of the twelfth century.[3] Three centuries later the first pictures of axial rudders appear in Persian and European nautical drawings. China also pioneered multiple masts. Needham notes the surprise of thirteenth-century Europeans when they first saw five-masted Chinese seagoing junks and dates European shipbuilders' introduction of multiple masts to the fifteenth century.[4] Chinese innovation reached from masthead to keel. Marco Polo's late thirteenth-century description of Chinese blue-water merchant ships included his account of the city that is called Quanzhou in Fujian province.

> Some ships, namely those which are larger, have besides quite 13 holds, that is, divisions, on the inside, made with strong planks fitted together, so that if by accident that the ship is staved in any place, namely that either it strikes on a rock, or a whale-fish striking against it in search of food staves it in . . . And then the water entering through the hole runs to the bilge, which never remains occupied with any things. And then the sailors find out where the ship is staved, and then the hold which answers to the break is emptied into others, for the water cannot pass from one hold to another, so strongly are they shut in; and then they repair the ship there, and put back there the goods which had been taken out.[5]

The description continues and explains in detail the internal and external caulking, nails, and iron pins that Chinese naval architects used to build watertight compartments that would save a ship whose hull had been pierced.

One decade short of five hundred years later, another letter

from a famous author offers his views on the design of mail pack-
ets to be built for routes between the United States and France.

> As these vessels are not to be laden with goods, their holds
> may without inconvenience be divided into separate apart-
> ments after the Chinese manner, and each of these apart-
> ments caulked tight so as to keep out water. In which case if
> a leak should happen in one apartment . . . This being known
> would be a great encouragement to passengers . . .

Benjamin Franklin penned this letter to his friend M. St. Jean de
Crèvecoeur in 1787. At the end of the following decade, the British
admiralty ordered the design and building of six of a new class of
vessels "with partitions contributing to strength, and securing the
ship against foundering, as practiced by the Chinese of the present
day."[6] Sir Samuel Bentham, naval architect, inventor, and brother
of the philosopher Jeremy Bentham, had visited the Russian town
of Kyathka and traveled to nearby China in the early 1780s. In
China, he learned about watertight compartments for ships. The
commission to build the British ships was awarded to Bentham
whose wife, in a mid-nineteenth-century biography of her hus-
band, said that watertight compartments were "no invention of
General Bentham's" but rather "practiced by the Chinese of the
present day, as well as by the ancients."

Chinese ships were also larger than their Western counter-
parts constructed at the same or a later date. Christopher Columbus's flagship, *Santa Maria*, is estimated at between 200 and 300
tons. Marco Polo describes Chinese river vessels in the thirteenth
century that were twice this size. Needham observes that the
effective limit for the largest wooden-hulled ships built in
the West—about 3,100 tons—was reached in the mid-nineteenth
century, but that Chinese vessels had come quite close to this size,
about 2,500 tons, in the first half of the fifteenth century when
Ming Dynasty treasure ships ventured far beyond China's coastal
waters.[7]

A statue of Admiral Zheng He in Nanjing

Vessels' seaworthiness, endurance, and their masters' ability to navigate safely over long distances are fair measures of maritime excellence. The large Chinese ships of the early fifteenth century were most famously commanded by Zheng He (1371–1433), a eunuch from Yunnan province in southwestern China whose surname at birth, Ma, suggests that his family was Muslim.

When the Ming army defeated the Mongol rulers of Yunnan in 1382, Zheng He was captured, castrated, and dispatched to Beijing to join the household of the man who would twenty years later become the third Ming ruler. Zheng He abundantly demonstrated military skill and loyalty to his master before, during, and after the struggle for succession that followed the death of the first Ming emperor, Hongwu. Hongwu had a King Lear–like problem: Which of his three sons should inherit the imperial throne? Hongwu's answer to the problem of fractious and competing male offspring was to name his grandson, Jianwen, as heir. Upon ascending the throne the grandson sought unsuccessfully to prevent challenges from the princes who had been passed over. Zheng He's patron defeated Jianwen, seized power in 1402, and became known thereafter as the Yongle emperor.

The Yongle emperor was as active in exercising power as he was in gaining it. He initiated a war to conquer Vietnam, a string of campaigns to subdue Mongolia, the construction of Beijing's Forbidden City as the imperial capital, and a series of large naval expeditions to the south and west of China whose command he gave to Zheng He. His seven voyages began in 1405 and ended in 1433. They took him and his armada as far south as today's Indonesia, through the Malacca Straits, to the northern most reaches of the Bay of Bengal, down India's east coast to Ceylon, and up the subcontinent's west coast to the Strait of Hormuz at the mouth of today's Persian Gulf, to the Bab el Mandeb, and the Horn of Africa.

The armada's ships were large and many. A Chinese writer of the late sixteenth century figures that Zheng He's *smallest* class of large ships was between 158 and 186 feet in overall length and between 60 and 68 feet in beam. This would compare favorably with such early nineteenth-century behemoths as Lord Nelson's flagship, H.M.S. *Victory*, with a length of 186 feet and beam of 51 feet.[8] Relying on Marco Polo's accounts of draft as well as the ships' records of the ports they visited and how far upstream they were able to navigate large rivers, the largest of Zheng He's treasure ships measured between 385 and 440 feet in overall length and 157 and 180 feet in beam, with a displacement of between 19,000 and 25,000 tons.[9] By comparison Nelson's *Victory* displaced 3,500 tons and the U.S. Navy's 610-foot-long amphibious assault landing ship U.S.S. *Gunston Hall* displaces 16,500 tons with a full load-out. Comparisons to amphibious ships of today are apt. The large ships of Zheng He's fleet were manned by six hundred sailors and four hundred marines. The armadas sailed with forty to sixty large ships and another two hundred smaller vessels, all of which together carried about twenty-seven thousand souls. The fleet could impress or, if desired, apply power. It did both.

Western writers of the twentieth century saw in Zheng He's voyages "the clear desire to impress upon foreign countries even beyond the limits of the known world the idea of China as the leading political and cultural power."[10] Similarly, Western writers found that the large fleet sailed to gain experience threading Southeast Asia's convoluted archipelagos, offering presents to open or reinforce diplomatic relations, expanding knowledge about the natural world, and—it is admitted—gaining military experience, "although the duties of the troops were primarily ceremonial."[11]

Chinese leaders echo this hagiographic picture of Zheng He. Observing PLAN's sixtieth anniversary, a senior Chinese naval officer wrote in 2009:

> The Chinese people actively put the notion of a harmonious ocean into practice . . . More than 600 years ago Zheng He, the famous navigator of the Ming dynasty, led the then world's strongest fleets, to sail to the western seas seven times, reaching as far as the Red Sea and the eastern coast of Africa, and visiting more than 30 countries and regions. They did not sign any unequal treaty, did not claim any territory, and did not bring back even one slave. They wiped out pirates for the countries along their route, broadly dissemi-

nated benevolence to friendly nations, brought China's tea, silk, cloth, chinaware, and Eastern civilization to the countries they visited, brought back other people's trust and friendship toward the Chinese nation, and created a world-level example of peaceful and friendly maritime exchanges.[12]

The Chinese news agency agrees. To mark the six hundredth anniversary of Zheng He's first voyage, the Chinese vice minister of communications declared that "during his seven voyages to the West, Zheng He treated other countries with friendship and respect instead of occupying a single piece of land, establishing a fortress or seizing any treasure."[13]

There is some truth to the current Chinese account. Some. But the large historical picture is missing from their story. Zheng He's master, the Yongle emperor, should not be confused with Mohandas Gandhi. He extended Chinese power where he could and paid special attention to the lands south of China. Early in his reign the autonomous region of Yunnan, bordered by today's Burma, Laos, and Vietnam, was colonized by force or its threat. Looking farther south, the Ming emperor used military forces transported from China by sea to invade the northern half of today's Vietnam in 1406, which within a year was folded into China as its fourteenth province, although not before what may have been an immense slaughter.[14] Colonization followed immediately.

The Yunnan and Vietnam invasions allowed the Ming Dynasty uninterrupted land access to the Indo-Chinese peninsula. Zheng He as well as a host of other eunuchs led voyages to the stubby crescent of island- and archipelago-dotted oceanic swaths that begin in today's South China Sea and curve through the Indonesian barrier islands into the Indian Ocean. The exceptional size of the vessels, their number, and their large complement of military officers and men delivered a clear and deliberate message. The Yongle emperor was powerful and entitled to the highest respect. He was the Son of Heaven and the deference shown to him traced an earthly shadow of the heavenly order. A tributary system represented this order, which was a temporal manifestation of the hierarchical system that established where each of the region's greater and lesser powers stood. This model influenced trade, diplomacy, and power relationships as far as China could reach. Strengthening and extending the tributary system increased China's influence. Under the tributary system itself, foreign representatives would visit China with gifts, which were acknowledged by return gifts that signified imperial recognition of the international order. At the top sat China's emperor, attended by bejeweled retainers, enthroned in splendor, and closest to heaven. Naval power exhibited daunting force, demonstrated presence, and broadened imperial influence by enlarging the geographic orbit of China's tributary system. But the calculations on which tribute receiver and tribute offerer established their place in the large scheme of things were not always economic, commercial, or founded on the enormous difference in power between China and other Asian kingdoms or polities. Zheng He also used direct military force.

The first voyage of Zheng He's armada took it to the port city of Qui Nhon, the capital of what was then the dominion of Champa, which is today the southern half of Vietnam. However, at the beginning of the fifteenth century it was a Hindu kingdom and a rival to the part of Vietnam that China had taken by force within a year of Zheng He's arrival.[15] The appearance of so large a naval force in a friendly realm directly adjacent to one that was the object of Ming ambition and military force demonstrates a solid grasp of seapower's ability at once to shore up useful partnerships and warn unruly neighbors. From here the fleet crossed the South China Sea to the Sumatran city of Palembang, which was the base of a pirate fleet ideally situated to prey on traffic between East Asia and the Indian Ocean. Different from a true seaport, like San Francisco or Hong Kong, whose docks jut into bays within sight of the ocean itself, Palembang is separated from the sea by several dozen miles of delta and river. It is accessible by the smaller, shallow-draft vessels that were part of Zheng He's fleet. These he used in moving upstream the military forces that put five thousand pirates to the sword. Their leader he sent back to China for execution.[16] A Chinese expatriate, Shi Jinqing, was appointed to head what appears to be a Chinese colony established to sustain the order that Zheng He's defeat of the pirates enforced. The Ming Dynasty solidified its presence in Southeast Asia.

In the same year, 1407, and on the second of his seven voyages, Zheng He called at Java and took sides in the civil conflict of a kingdom whose previous ruler had challenged China's at this critical maritime juncture of Southeast Asia. One hundred and seventy of his men were killed and the Ming government demanded compensation in gold. The same communication invited the Javanese king to reflect on the unhappy fate of northern Vietnam as he considered the Ming demand.[17]

Zheng He's third voyage also confronted a strategically located kingdom—Ceylon—ruled by a sovereign who was insufficiently respectful of Ming power. The Chinese commander arrived at the island with an impressive fleet of sturdy ships, great and small, landed a large contingent of armed men on the island, assaulted the capital, took prisoner the impertinent king along with his household, and shipped them back to China.

The fourth voyage also unmasked Ming power at a key node along the route that connects China with the Middle East and Africa. Zheng He called at the northern part of Sumatra along the wide mouth of the Malacca Strait, possibly on his return from Hormuz in today's Persian Gulf. There he turned his attention to an opponent of the local king who favored, and was favored by, China. The unruly subject, one Sekandar, whose exclusion from official Ming recognition angered him, was caught and sent to China where he was dispatched in a more sanguinary manner.[18]

The Yongle emperor's strategy of imperial expansion—consolidate continental power to the north and extend the tributary system that extended Chinese influence to the maritime south and west—is not a mirror likeness of the Ottomans. The

Ottomans faced down competitors in Anatolia to their east and then turned their attention west to European conquest—but the Ottomans took things one at a time. The Yongle emperor moved on both fronts at once. However, the strategic visions of the two great empires are close enough: provide security and expand by increasing strategic depth.

China's tributary system is a far cry from Alfred Thayer Mahan's idea of sea control exercised over intercontinental distance by means of a self-sustaining mixture of economic power, commercial dominance, and internal lines of communication that provide lifeblood to ports where great fleets are resupplied and from which they sally forth to command the seas. But there are resemblances. Both the tributary system and the succeeding European maritime powers whose oceanic dominance is Mahan's subject served a kind of world order. Mahan looks upon Rome's strong control of the central Mediterranean and weaker but still potent grip on Carthage's ability to transport supplies by sea to the Spanish base of its land operations against Rome as decisive in the Punic Wars. When Hasdrubal, late to reinforce his brother Hannibal because of Roman sea control, was defeated in northern Italy, Hannibal is said to have remarked that "Rome would now be mistress of the world."[19] Rome's appearance in Mahan's preface sketches his overarching view of peerless seapower, and Hannibal's lamentation on his defeat sums it well: Rome's mastery breathed life into a world system that it led, organized, and held together, the Pax Romana.

Chinese policy hoped that a Pax Ming would establish its position as the preeminent realm of a vast geographic area. Zheng He sought to secure that status in the maritime regions to China's south and west. In meting out force more sparingly than Rome, he would be regarded as a practitioner of what some of today's strategists call "soft" power. But the contemporary distinction between hard and soft power would have been perplexing to leaders who regarded power as a whole made up of parts, each of whose utility is determined by its ability to accomplish a given task. Zheng

He meted out force where he judged it necessary. Supporting the tributary system, awing the kingdoms of the swelling Indo-Pacific expanses with their gargantuan vessels and large fleets, and using force anchored the Middle Kingdom's supreme position. Contemporary China's conventional view of Zheng He as an explorer and pioneer naturalist—the latter for shipping giraffes and elephants back to China on his final voyage—affirms current Chinese leadership's widely disseminated view that the old roots of Chinese seapower are essentially and profoundly benign. But these accounts are longer on political purpose than historical accuracy. According to the court records of the Yongle emperor's grandson, the Xuande emperor, the animals were tribute offered in several ports of call.[20] Moreover, as the scholar J. V. G. Mills has observed, "Zheng He did not discover anything which had not been known to Indonesians, Indians, or Arabs for over a thousand years."[21] The Chinese weren't far behind these seafaring peoples. Chinese merchant vessels had been plying most of the same oceanic routes where Zheng He sailed for centuries.

By the time Zheng He died, early in the fourth decade of the fifteenth century, China had abandoned the Yongle emperor's maritime ambitions. The emperor's war in Vietnam had become as expensive as it proved incapable of successful conclusion. Expeditions to subdue the Mongolians shifted the Ming strategic focus toward continental defense. The same military needs increased the financial burden on the treasury as did construction of the new capital at Beijing. Japanese pirates who could descend on China's coasts called into question the value of a great oceanic fleet that was largely useless in protecting the Middle Kingdom's own coastline. In the bitter disputes of palace politics, civil service officials fought with the eunuchs, who were more closely tied to, and personally identified with, particular emperors. The civil service saw and framed the argument in terms of the prohibitive cost of a great fleet. Other civil servants hearkened back to the old Hongwu emperor's wariness that a merchant fleet paired with its necessary naval protection must be purchased at the expense of an effective defense against piracy. The civil servants won. Chinese naval power began a retreat punctuated by devastating naval defeats beginning in the mid nineteenth century to British, French, and then Japanese naval squadrons. Ming seapower receded into the past. The past elongated into more than five and a half centuries, during which China's decline as a great power can be measured by its inability to defend its coasts, its failure to protect vital internal lines of commerce, and its surrender of territory to foreign powers. But the Ming fleet and its distant sojourns remain in memory as proof of China's ability to build a large, awe-inspiring fleet that could show the flag from the West Pacific through Southeast Asia and its strategic choke points, to the subcontinent, the Middle East, and Africa's east coast. They remind China and its knowing observers today that the maritime lanes that slice across this large arc of the earth's surface are as suited for trade as they are to project military power, exert influence, enforce the subordination of lesser states, and establish regional hegemony. Zheng He did not return to Chinese consciousness as a source of national pride in the twentieth century because he brought back elephants and giraffes. He occupies his current position of admiration because he embodies an energetic, vigorous, ambitious, and successful China that its neighbors had good reason to look upon with awe.

China as a Modern Naval Power

The naval force that Communist China set out to build was more a triumph of ideology than an exercise in practicality. The Korean War's tilt toward ground action reinforced Mao's idea of a military whose virtue lay in size and absorption of Communist notions as understood by Mao himself. The navy may have been more than a side dish, but not much more. Republic of China patrol craft preyed on People's Republic shipping, descended on coastal facilities, and raised the possibility of returning to the mainland by sea. The Soviets helped China out with naval advisers and some old vessels. But relations between China and the U.S.S.R. lapsed at about the same time that the results of Moscow's large military buildup became visible. If the expansion of the Soviet Pacific fleet worried Chinese military planners, the Cultural Revolution's zealous embrace of Mao Tse-tung thought froze naval and strategic thought into incapacity. The People's Liberation Army Navy—an oxymoronic term that is still used and points back toward the Maoist notion of ground forces' superiority—remained an old coastal fleet, except for the development and introduction into the fleet of nuclear-powered attack and ballistic missile–carrying submarines from 1970 to 1991.[22] This was an impressive technological achievement for a large state on the cusp of modernity. China's navy labored mightily and at constant and mortal risk to build nuclear-powered vessels. Valves and steam generators leaked radiation that endangered the crew. Corrosion, defective pumps, and malfunctioning main reduction gears compounded the dangers of radiation.[23] Indeed, an assistant secretary of the navy returned from a visit to China in the mid-1980s and astonished a group of senior American naval civilian officials repeating a question that had been put to him by a senior officer with responsibility for China's submarine forces. "We place our entire nuclear-powered submarine crews in the hospital for a 30-day observation period immediately upon returning from a deployment: do you do the same with your crews?"[24] Of course the answer was, and is, no. But this was as remarkable a demonstration of frankness as it was an admission of obstacles that remained in the way of China's nuclear-powered submarine program.

Deng Xiaoping's succession as supreme leader in 1978 began in earnest the modernization of China's military that continues today, but he saw no reason to change the navy from a coastal force. The United States was the dominant naval power in the Pacific and could be counted on if the Soviet navy growled, or worse. The Nixon-Kissinger understanding with China retained its glow. In the 1980s the strategic landscape shifted. The Soviet

Union disappeared. China's economy—in particular the part of it located on or near the Pacific coast—began to record double-digit annual increases. Raw materials arrived by sea and finished products were delivered to global customers by sea. The measurements of this commerce are astonishing.

Chinese shipyards manufactured 220,000 deadweight tons of commercial ships—cargo vessels—in 1980, the early years of Deng's time in office. Deadweight tonnage measures the weight that a ship can safely transport. This includes fuel, potable water, ballast, cargo—whether new cars or naval aircraft—crew, and such necessities as food. Sixteen years later, the PRC's annual production of deadweight tonnage exceeded 13 million tons. The 2006 total represents a sixtyfold increase over the earlier figure. The 2010 figure was expected to reach 20 million tons and the value of China's seagoing commerce borne in Chinese-owned and -operated vessels was predicted to amount to $1 trillion in 2020.[25] The increasing level of output is at least as impressive as the absolute annual tonnage. By comparison, for example, the deadweight tonnage of America's entire aircraft carrier fleet amounts to nearly one-quarter of a million tons. Alfred Thayer Mahan's encapsulation of the fundamentals of seapower remains timely in describing China's maritime progress. "The necessity of a navy, in the restricted sense of the word, springs, therefore, from the existence of a peaceful shipping, and disappears with it . . ."[26] In loosening the strictures on its people's entrepreneurial gifts and building a merchant fleet to help conduct its commerce, China placed the horse before—or at least, alongside—the cart. Economic development preceded and provided the wherewithal for China's growing carrying fleet, and from that fleet—as Mahan put it—sprang "the necessity of a navy." Again, Mahan: "If sea power be really based upon a peaceful and extensive commerce, aptitude for commercial pursuits must be a distinguishing feature of the nations that have at one time or another been great upon the sea. History almost without exception affirms this that this is true. Save the Romans, there is no marked instance to the contrary."[27]

China and the Coming Threats

Mahan built his case for seapower not on the keels of cannon-bearing battleships but on merchant shipping, markets, and national talent for commerce.[28] The Chinese continue to demonstrate aptitude for commercial pursuits. The last year in which China's economy contracted was 1976, the year Mao died. Deng Xiaoping solidified his position as leader of all China two years later. At that time, as measured in current dollars, China's gross domestic product (GDP) amounted to $148 billion, about 2 percent higher than the same figure for the Netherlands. For the next four years, China averaged single-digit increases in the growth of its economy. In 1980, GDP rose into the double-digits and has maintained an average yearly increase of 10 percent since then.[29] In 1998 the Chinese economy broke the trillion-dollar ceiling of GDP and eleven years later—the last year for which complete figures are available—had virtually quintupled this amount.[30] Also during the three decades from 1980 to the end of the third millennium's first decade, per capita GDP, the figure obtained when dividing the total value of a country's goods and services by its population, multiplied by a factor of about 27—from $250 to $6,827.[31] Trade figures mirror this sudden accumulation of wealth. In the first decade of the twenty-first century U.S. imports of Chinese products more than tripled—from $102 billion to $364 billion.[32] U.S. exports to China more than quadrupled, although at a lower total value—from $19 billion to $92 billion.[33] After Canada and Mexico, China—and including or excluding Hong Kong—is the United States' largest export market.[34] This commerce, as does virtually all of China's major trade, travels by sea.

China fits what Mahan called the changeless conditions of seapower. It has a large coastline and increasing lines of internal communication. Its population is the largest in the world. It is building a huge merchant fleet to carry its shipping to and from the rest of the world where markets abound. Its people are famously enterprising. And it is constructing a navy to protect its multiplying interest in the sea as a source of future national wealth and greatness.

Certitude about what long-range strategy China's leaders seek with their expanding navy remains elusive. But the PLAN's modernization and growth over the years suggest several complementary objectives. Taiwan and the possibility of its declared independence remain a perceived threat. Politically, a Taiwan declaration of independence is an invitation to unrest for often dissatisfied minorities from Tibet to Muslims in China's far west, as well as a potential recapitulation of historic dangers to mainland rule that have come from the same island. Strategically, Taiwan is close to the geographic center of the chain of islands that extend from the Kurile Islands through Japan along the Ryuku Islands to Taiwan and then south to the Philippines, Indonesia, Borneo, and ending in a minor Indonesian archipelago that hooks north toward Vietnam. Much of this land barrier is friendly or allied to the United States and one of the world's largest navies—Japan's —is located to the barrier's northern end. To the west of the first island chain is mainland China and the seas known as the East and the South China Sea whose control is essential for access to China's ports and the movement of Chinese combatants within and beyond coastal waters. Being able to steam through the same international waters also allows a potential adversary to threaten Chinese targets along and beyond the Pacific coast and support the security of such U.S. allies and partners as Japan, South Korea, and the Philippines. In addition to its political troublesomeness, Taiwan possesses nearly as much potential for strategic irritation. China's military development over the past decade reflects this irritant. The number of the PLAN's amphibious vessels has increased by approximately 28 percent. These ships would likely be essential to any serious military attempt to take Taiwan by force. The PRC has also been adding scores of missiles to launch sites directly across the Strait of Taiwan in close proximity to their assumed target in recent years. They are intended no less to intimidate Taiwan than to destroy such targets as the command and control facilities that Taipei would use to defend its population if attacked. Since 2000 the PLAN has been modernizing its submarine fleet. This has included adding five

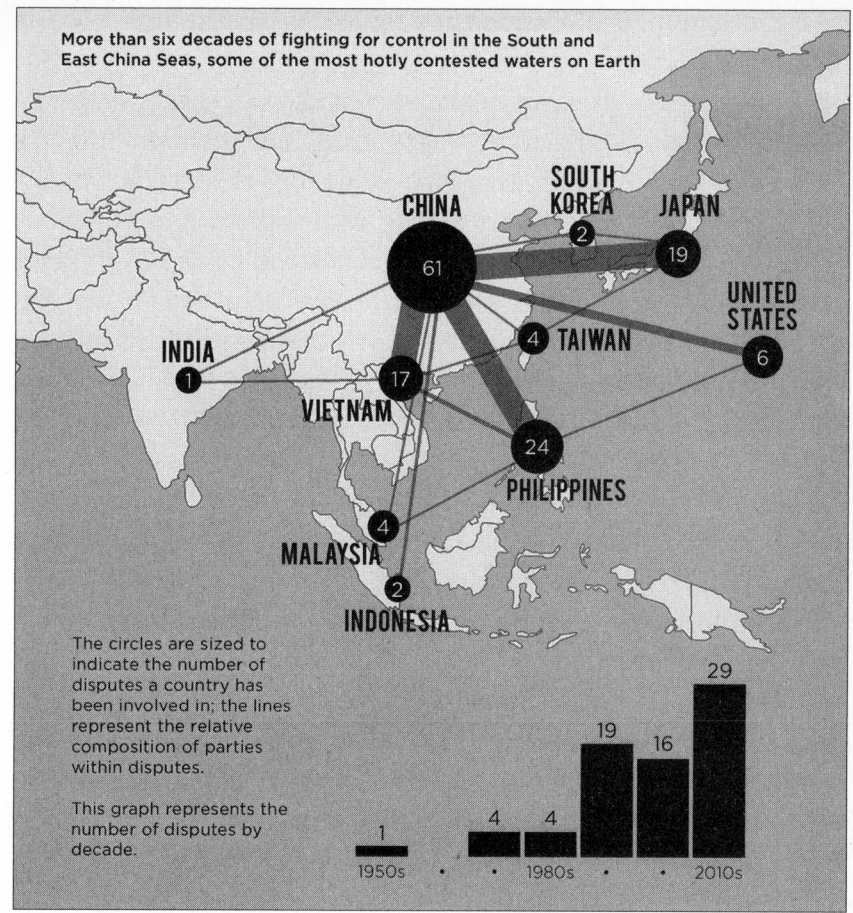

More than six decades of fighting for control in the South and East China Seas, some of the most hotly contested waters on Earth

The circles are sized to indicate the number of disputes a country has been involved in; the lines represent the relative composition of parties within disputes.

This graph represents the number of disputes by decade.

China's aggressiveness toward its neighbors has increased dramatically in recent years, as this map shows.

new classes of diesel-electric and nuclear-powered boats.[35] Nuclear-powered submarines are designed to remain submerged for long periods during which they can patrol over long distances. Diesel-electric boats have shorter ranges, cost less than nuclear-powered submarines, and are quieter. Both could be used to blockade Taiwan and—added to Chinese missiles and amphibious vessels—hold American military power at bay long enough to complicate or frustrate American efforts to aid Taipei if hostilities with the PRC broke out.

But although Chinese rulers for years have routinely used diplomatic pressure, military threats, and political leverage to isolate Taiwan, there is scant evidence that China's strategic worldview is restricted to resolving cross-strait tensions in their favor. Throughout much of his tour as commander of the U.S. Pacific Command, Admiral Robert F. Willard warned publicly and repeatedly that China is developing an aircraft carrier. For example, he told the House Armed Services Committee in January 2010 that a former and unfinished Soviet *Kuznetsov*-class carrier known as the *Varyag*, which China bought in 1998, had been undergoing renovations since 1998. Admiral Willard said, "I expect this carrier to become operational around 2012, and will likely be used to develop basic carrier skills."[36] On August 9, 2011, *Xinhua*, China's state-run news agency reported that China's aircraft carrier platform had begun its sea trials.[37] Thus China took its first operational step toward projecting naval air power globally.

China is separated from Taiwan by approximately one hundred miles of ocean. Aircraft carriers are expensive—as are the planes that fly from their decks. The Chinese air force already has 490 combat aircraft based at locations from which they could reach Taiwan without being refueled and, according to the U.S. Defense Department, "has the airfield capacity to expand that number by hundreds."[38] Aircraft carriers' military virtue is their ability to project combat power at long distances from their home-ports. China has no more need for an aircraft carrier to use air-power against Taiwan than the Allies did in 1944 when they invaded Normandy from across the English Channel. China is unlikely to stop at building a single carrier. The 2009 U.S. Defense Department report on China's military power predicted that "the PLA Navy is considering building multiple carriers by 2020."[39] The Defense Department repeated the identical assessment the following year. The PLAN's announcement that it seeks more than two thousand additional personnel with Ph.D.s in the next five years may not prove the existence of a Chinese aircraft carrier program.[40] But such proof is hardly needed. China's defense minister, Chen Bingde, stated publicly in June 2011 that the PLAN would launch and begin testing its first aircraft carrier later in the same year.[41] All of this adds convincing evidence of the large investment that China's navy is putting into modernizing its forces. And the statement of PLA National Defense University professor Zhang Zhaozhong that an aircraft carrier fits into the size of a surface vessel for which the new Ph.D.s will be recruited reasonably supports the same conclusion: China's transition to a blue-water fleet includes aircraft carriers.

A fleet of aircraft carriers is not merely the means for a great power with wealth and advanced technical skills to impress the international community—as Zheng He did. It also allows its possessor to project combat power at large distances. Japan used aircraft carriers to attack Hawaii, Midway, and at the Battle of Leyte Gulf where U.S. naval forces successfully contested the Imperial Japanese Navy's hold over the Philippine island chain that separated Japan from the sources of its Southeast Asian strategic supplies—such as oil. Combat air power could endanger Japan and South Korea and pin down U.S. naval forces in the mid-Pacific that would be required to defend Hawaii against possible attack. Carrier-borne aviation would be useful to China in a conflict where possession of the first island chain might again be key to holding U.S. naval forces at bay. Carrier planes would be valuable in providing air support for invading amphibious forces, reducing the defenses of states in the region such as the Philippines or Vietnam, which would be critical in a contest for control of the South China Sea. Farther west are the long archipelagos that separate the South China Sea from the monsoon-driven expanses of the Indian Ocean. Through its northern reaches pass the sea lines that connect Middle Eastern oil with Europe, the United States, and East Asia. Carrier-based aircraft could oppose India's freedom of naval action and merchant shipping in the seas around India and far to the south. The same power could threaten Indian naval bases or assist in hunting for submarines and surface ships whose mission was to slice Chinese shipping lanes in the event of hostilities.

Primarily, although by no means exclusively to secure these shipping lanes, a naval base including underground pens for nuclear-powered ballistic missile–carrying submarines on China's Hainan Island first reported by *Jane's Intelligence Review* in the spring of 2008[42] is one of the so-called string of pearls that Beijing has fixed its attention on securing as a means of sustained presence throughout the Indian Ocean. Others include large investments in Sittwe in Burma, Chittagong in Bangladesh, Hambantota in Sri Lanka, Gwadar in Pakistan, and the port of Lamu in Kenya. To India this may look less like a string of pearls than a noose. In whichever nautical direction Indian defense experts gaze, they now see growing Chinese presence and access to strategic port facilities. Dr. Srikanth Kondapalli, a professor of Chinese studies at Jawaharlal University in New Delhi, told the BBC in May 2010, "This is not a fear, this is a fact."[43] The bases China is helping to build increase Chinese access to the entire region, facilitate trade, and could also be used to reprovision and repair naval vessels, thus expanding and strengthening the PLAN's reach. If hostilities were to occur in the region, aircraft carriers would also demonstrate their worth by helping to deter or, if need be, by engaging an opposing naval force. The watchful reader may also have noted the geographic congruence of the bases today's China is seeking to establish and the ports at which Zheng He called almost six centuries ago. A great power's strategic interests may come and go. Geography doesn't. On six of his seven voyages Zheng He called at a Vietnamese port that is 300 miles south of China's naval base on Hainan Island. He put in at Chittagong and Sri Lanka, precisely where China seeks maritime access today. And his travels took him to Hormuz, about 350 miles west of China's investment in the Pakistani port of Gwadar. He or his squadrons thrice visited Mogadishu, about 400 miles north of the Kenyan port China will help Kenya build. Any navy whose purposes include the security of its nation's seaborne commerce share with that commerce a need for the refueling, provisioning, repairs, and diplomatic succor that bases offer.

China sees this, too. All signs point to the likelihood that China will build an aircraft carrier fleet with the ability to project power over long distances. Such vessels along with their escorts, aided by the remote and strategically situated shore facilities that China is now engaged in acquiring, point to a national interest in achieving status as a great seapower that far transcends the intimidation or subjugation of Taiwan. China's several deployments of surface combatants along with a supply ship to the Gulf of Aden indicate the same attention to developing the practical experience to operate a long way from home waters. These deployments, which support the international antipiracy mission off the Horn of Africa, began in 2008 and continue today. In fact, the PLAN is showing up around the world. In 2007, a naval task force completed an eighty-six-day cruise through three oceans including port calls at four European states. The U.S. Defense Department 2009 annual report on Chinese military power stated that "such voyages both within and beyond Asia" have been steadily increasing since 2002.[44] Naval ship visits familiarize officers and crew with the distinct characteristics of foreign waters and ports as they support diplomatic relations and subtly remind both host and visitor of the latter's ability to conduct operations in the area. In 2011, two of China's guided missile frigates docked at Durban in South Africa. The visit continued the two countries' recent naval exchanges and is consistent with China's large and growing economic interest in Africa in general and South Africa in particular. An article that appeared five months earlier in the *Christian Science Monitor*'s *Africa Monitor* quoted China's vice minister of commerce, Gao Hucheng, who observed that "the African continent's biggest economy is China's number one source of African iron, copper, manganese, chrome, and diamonds."[45] Also in 2011 Chinese naval vessels called at Dar es Salaam in Tanzania where trade with China increased by almost 50 percent in the first nine months of 2009. China has been investing in Tanzanian agriculture, pharmaceuticals, and of course mining, which—like South Africa—produces iron and diamonds as well as gold. Africa has large and untapped mineral reserves that Chinese leaders see as critical to future economic growth and expansion into exports of increased technological sophistication. Naval diplomacy extends the fleet's experienced reach to a transoceanic plane, establishes the Chinese flag as a fixture in foreign ports, and supports the friendly diplomatic relations that help seal deals. These broad strategic maritime objectives far surpass the subsuming of Taiwan. "Today Taiwan, tomorrow the world" may be overstating broad China's national objectives, but while the existence of such grand objectives remains unspoken, every shred of evidence suggests that Beijing's goals do not stop in Taipei.

Nor is demonstrating China's broad goals limited to Africa. Following their participation in antipiracy operations off the east African coast in 2010, a Chinese naval detachment arrived in Piraeus. The timing was propitious. It followed by three months European banking officials' agreement on a plan to bail out Greece, whose socialist government had spent itself into a debt crisis that required large financial transfusions to avoid government default. Two months after the naval visit, China's Communist government was in a good position to offer assistance. Premier Wen Jiabao flew to Athens and announced plans to double the volume of its annual trade with Greece and a specific proposal to provide Greece with a credit of $5 billion toward the purchase of merchant ships built in China. A comprehensive list of recent similar anecdotes that illustrate the effort to spread naval presence over a widening geographic area in tandem with diplomatic and commercial interests would bore and exhaust. But the point is as straightforward as it is consistent with the ideas of Alfred Thayer Mahan. Genuine seapower does not exist as a disembodied concatenation of armed vessels, intelligence, communications, and the related competencies necessary to launch and sustain great armadas. Rather it is an almost live organism nourished by commerce, animated by a large merchant fleet, sheltered by bases, and fortified by naval power itself. China understands this. Massive increases in the building of merchant shipping, sustained and large annual increases in national wealth as the result of exports, steady successful expansion of access to port facilities from coastal waters to the end of the Indian Ocean, and naval modernization all attest to China's understanding.

Chinese naval modernization is particularly troublesome for the United States. It has taken unexpected tactical shapes with unanticipated strategic consequences. Foremost among these is the development of a weapon that does not exist in the U.S. arsenal, the antiship ballistic missile or ASBM. Ballistic missiles fly at hypersonic speeds and are usually aimed at a fixed land target, for example, a port, a silo that contains a nuclear weapon, or, under the most lethal circumstances, the population of a city. The DF-21 is a solid propellant medium-range missile that is estimated to travel at ten times the speed of sound, or about 7,680 miles per hour or a little more than 2 miles per second.[46] Its range is alternately estimated at between fifteen hundred and two thousand kilometers—or between almost 1,000 and 1,240 miles.[47] Satellites and what the U.S. Defense Department calls "a sophisticated command-and-control system"[48] are supposed to allow the missile to be maneuvered in the final descending stage of its flight. The maneuverability would allow the DF-21 to hit a large ship under way, specifically a U.S. aircraft carrier. Because neither the warplanes aboard U.S. aircraft carriers today nor those that will begin to replace them in the foreseeable future have enough range to fly a round-trip mission of 2,000 miles, U.S. carriers must come within range of the DF-21 if they are to launch aircraft that can reach targets within Chinese coastal waters or the mainland itself. One alternative is that the navy would refuse to endanger so large and expensive a vessel and keep it out of range of the Chinese missile, thus nullifying the advantage of U.S. naval aviation's striking power. This would successfully accomplish China's goal of denying sea access to the United States' biggest and most lethal combat vessels to large sections of the western Pacific.

The DF-21 antiship ballistic missiles pose a grave potential threat to U.S. naval dominance in the region.

China's efforts to limit or end U.S. naval presence in the western Pacific do not end with a single weapons system. The Defense Department's 2004 report on Chinese military power noted the "development of an antiradiation SAM (surface-to-air missile) most likely to target AWACS (advanced warning and control system) aircraft and standoff jamming platforms."[49] The weapon turns the idea of the successful U.S. high-speed antiradiation missile (HARM) on its head. The HARM missile is carried by fighter aircraft and uses the emissions of enemy radars as a homing beam to find and destroy the transmitting antennae. U.S. carrier–borne aircraft used HARM missiles to destroy Libyan antennae that would have helped Libyan missiles down attacking American planes in the 1986 strikes against Colonel Gadhafi's forces. The same missiles proved useful in suppressing Saddam

Hussein's air defenses in Operation Desert Storm. The Chinese missile to which the Defense Department's 2004 report referred would be launched from the surface. It would use as its homing beam the radiation from U.S. command and control planes whose radars are instrumental in relaying the vital information that U.S. and allied aircraft need to find and destroy enemy aircraft. Like the Chinese ASBM whose target is the source of potential strike aircraft—that is, the carrier itself—Chinese missiles that are able to destroy U.S. and allied command and control planes, when placed aboard PLAN vessels, aim at the heart of American air superiority, the ability to see and understand the battlefield, in this case, airspace. Denying U.S. forces this critical information adds to the PLAN's ability to proscribe effective U.S. access to the air-sea belt that girds China's coasts.

Beneath that belt lie the depths of Asia's littoral seas and a potential for submarine warfare whose closest parallel is the European navy-to-navy contests of the sail and cannon centuries. Without a defense against the ASBM, the previous access of U.S. naval airpower in the region is at risk, as may someday be most U.S. surface naval combatants. Antisatellite warfare—which China successfully demonstrated by launching a missile to destroy one of its old satellites in January 2007—aimed at disrupting or eliminating the system of networks that U.S. naval forces depend on to communicate tactical information. Missiles that could blind what aircraft the United States and its allies are able to put into the skies put at risk traditional U.S. air superiority.

But as air superiority, while necessary, is rarely sufficient to accomplish key political or military objectives in a conflict, neither is it enough by itself to deny access to a potential enemy. China currently fields over a hundred missile boats.[50] Eighty of them—known as the Houbei class—are new and stealthy. They have been put to sea since 2004. Displacing 225 tons, these high-speed catamaran-hull craft can dart about launching one or several of their eight antiship cruise missiles with a range of 160 kilometers (one hundred miles). The number of these small, fast, new, hard-to-see combat vessels is likely to rise to 100,[51] or a little more than one-third as many combatants as exist in the U.S. fleet today. Of course, 225-ton small combatants do not compare to American destroyers or aircraft carriers. But the number of Chinese missile boats is impressive, and not only because a large portion of them can be concentrated in seas adjacent to China. By comparison, America's global responsibilities disperse the U.S. Navy around the globe and prevent the concentration of force in the western Pacific. However, so large a fleet of small Chinese fighting ships also serves a larger purpose. China should not be compared to the Lilliputians since its navy is one of the world's largest, but while it has come a long way in a short time, the PLAN is still inferior in most respects to the U.S. Navy. The trend—theirs toward greater size and the United States' toward a smaller force—should be the cause of American and allied concern.

But in the meantime the comparison of China's strategy to that of Gulliver's Lilliputians is apt. Equal or greater force can be countered by concentrating a large quantity of smaller forces—just as a smaller fighter can deflect the powerful thrust of a much larger martial arts opponent by parrying him off balance. Combinations of several different means of simultaneous attack could seriously challenge a U.S. battle group. Chinese strategic thinkers call for exactly such coordinated attacks from different quarters: a combination of antiship ballistic missiles, submarines, ground-based aircraft that can target U.S. surface ships with cruise missiles from a distance, and fast-moving small vessels that can launch a host of low-flying antiship cruise missiles would test all the defenses of an American battle group—at once. And the Chinese instruments of attack would not only be more numerous than those of their American opponents. They would be cheaper and more dispensable. China can afford to lose missile boats, like the Houbei. They are small, relatively inexpensive, and have sacrificed traditional self-defenses for the speed to get out of harm's way. As in a land battle, units of a huge army that are lost in action or incapacitated can be replaced by plenty of others.

The fate of the PLAN in a contest with the U.S. Navy is unlikely to be determined by any single Chinese missile, ship, or aircraft system. China's objective is to offset current U.S. strength with an array of weapons whose range Chinese planners are deliberately extending and for which the antiship ballistic missile's long-distance range is emblematic. In destructive tandem with the ASBMs are fourth-generation land-based Chinese aircraft, the Soviet Su-27, which possess the capability to reach targets one thousand kilometers (about six hundred miles) distant. The missile could pressure the U.S. Navy by threatening to sink or incapacitate large American ships—carriers or large amphibious vessels—so that the U.S. high command will neither risk coming to Taiwan's aid nor position American naval forces where they can threaten China's access to the Pacific. The aircraft when armed with antiship missiles will complement China's ability to challenge the U.S. Navy. The submarine picture is no brighter. In a 2009 report the Office of Naval Intelligence estimated the number of Chinese submarines at sixty-two and anticipated that this will rise to about 75 boats before the end of this decade.[52] At the same point in the future, the U.S. Navy anticipates that its submarine fleet will number sixty-six boats and then decrease to fifty-four boats in 2030, coming to rest at about sixty-one boats in 2042.[53] The numbers fail to draw a good likeness. Unless there are large changes in policy, the United States' intent to remain a transoceanic force with submarines as well as surface ships on duty around the globe invalidates a simple comparison of numbers. China may concentrate its forces in its nearby waters. If the United States chooses to follow suit, such policy must come at the expense of its naval presence throughout the world. And, again, submarines differ in kind and capacity. Many of China's diesel-electric boats are quieter and more difficult to detect than the United States' nuclear-propelled submarines. Moreover, submarines are but one of several weapons that Chinese doctrine emphasizes must be employed in concert to keep American seapower at a safe distance from the Asian landmass and its seas.

This concert might deny U.S. seapower the access to the western Pacific that restored peace to that part of the ocean at the end of World War II and has been essential to its preservation thereafter. If the center of such a conflict were Taiwan, the United States' inability or prolonged delay in bringing naval force to bear would be China's victory.

If the increase in naval forces in the region—Australia, Japan, South Korea, and India are all building larger navies—set off an accident or incident that led to conflict, or if a probing of American resolve outside the Taiwan Strait spun out of control, the balance of naval forces would still be important, but not likely more important than the ideas about the use of naval force that determine how each side prosecutes such a conflict. Think of the footage that is most often seen on televisions around the world when American seapower is used in anger today and over the past twenty years. The pictures show large missiles riding a pillar of fire and smoke as they disappear into the night. Or there are images of aircraft catapulted off the decks of the navy's great ships. The target of these attacks are all land-based, an enemy's command and control facilities or his power generation grid or other strategic infrastructure. Then imagine the same images from World War II: U.S. destroyers launching depth charges at enemy submarines: battleships, cruisers, and planes from U.S. carriers engaging ships of the Imperial Japanese Fleet in large and decisive naval battles where command of the seas would determine who controlled the highway of islands and archipelagos that led to Japan. The U.S. Navy of World War II thought about and prepared for combat to support amphibious operations as well as to defeat other naval forces at sea. The U.S. Navy of today is more focused on applying naval power in direct support of essentially land operations such as Operation Desert Storm, Operation Iraqi Freedom, and Operation Enduring Freedom, the name for U.S. participation in the war in Afghanistan. There is a profound difference between naval power aimed at projecting power ashore and naval power that focuses on destroying an enemy's seapower.

To offer one example, the former must possess robust amphibious and supporting, covering force. It uses submarines to protect surface combatants that can project power inland, striking at fixed land targets and eroding enemy infrastructure. The latter is more likely to see in amphibious forces a means of securing logistics bases that assist in expanding the area of sea control and in submarines an instrument of actively destroying enemy shipping. If the shift in American grand strategy toward continental engagement continues, the likelihood is that U.S. seapower will find itself increasingly preoccupied with applying power from sea to land, not preparing to defeat another naval force at sea. The growth of China's navy threatens to turn this American grand strategy into a grand strategic mistake.

If for no other reason, the nuclear missiles that both China and the United States possess are a strong reason for both countries to avoid even conventional attacks against targets on each other's homeland. But there are other compelling reasons. Naval action ultimately is aimed at producing results on land, and the intended result in such a conflict would be at a minimum to preserve the continental relationships that now exist within Asia and between the Asian and American landmasses. The corollary of this truth is that a land war with China is not a winning proposition.

This argues strongly for restricting any conflict with China to the ocean and preventing it from jumping to land. Specifically, the best result that U.S. policy could achieve in a conflict with China is a preservation of the status quo. U.S. alliances with its Asian and regional allies would remain in place, buttressed by successful common action and perhaps enlarged to include other states that dread Chinese hegemony. American seapower would turn back a serious armed threat and demonstrate again its ability to keep and, if needed, restore peace in the western Pacific and East Asia. Chinese leadership would conclude that future challenges to American seapower would be as destructively futile as the first. And the United States would retain its position as the world's preeminent power. A conflict with China, however it began, must be kept at sea.

This will require work. American seapower has been conceived of, and trained to, apply force to the shore "From the Sea," as two separate public statements of naval purpose crafted since the end of the Cold War have argued and used as their title. The rise of the PLAN to date and the likelihood of its future growth in size, power, and reach are a warning that defeating a hostile force at sea ought again to be an important U.S. naval objective. Putting most of China's navy out of business either by disabling or sinking it without attacking land targets would help restrict a possible conflict at sea, avoid escalation on land, interrupt oceangoing commerce, disrupt the flow of strategic supplies to China, and help assure the unconstrained flow of communications between the United States and its Asian and regional allies. War, of course, is not what China or America wants. The task of avoiding one is eased by maintaining American naval dominance in a form that Chinese leadership has no interest in challenging. The most important step toward preserving America's seapower is one that occurs in the mind. It may already have been taken. Admiral Michael Mullen, then chairman of the Joint Chiefs of Staff, said in mid-2010, "I have moved from being curious to being genuinely concerned" about China's military capabilities.[54]

Mullen had every reason. China, as Zheng He's voyages show, marshaled great fleets and sent them forth when European vessels were at an inferior stage of development. Zheng He's master, the Ming emperor, had a clear idea of cementing Chinese influence over a broad maritime dominion. Neither Chinese naval competence nor the idea of a Chinese international order established by awe-inspiring naval power is new. What's new is the importance to the entire world of the growing economic activity in the littoral area that the crescent from Shanghai to the Persian Gulf comprehends, including the supply of oil that emerges from the latter. Also new, in relative terms, is the existence of a great power—the United States—whose beneficent application of power has more often than not combined self-interest with a broader concern for an international order that seeks the liberal goals of nonintervention, peace, free markets, untroubled access to international sea and air routes, democratic governance, and stability. The world order that China's leaders see is not the same. Its support for Iran's nuclear program would help initiate a nuclear arms contest in the Middle East and allow it to support terror on a global scale with little fear of retaliation.

China's declaration that the international waters of the South China Sea represent a "core interest" raises the same question that Colonel Gadhafi's inclusion of the Gulf of Sidra into Libyan territorial waters did in 1986. And China did not merely claim nearby international waters as its own. At a conference in late June 2011, an Australian academic[55] noted the increasing number of incidents at sea between China and its southern neighbors that had taken place since the beginning of the year. These incidents included firing at a Filipino fishing vessel, accosting a Filipino oil exploration ship, violations of Filipino airspace and territorial waters, as well as unauthorized construction in Filipino waters. Vietnam was also the object of Chinese aggression. Two incidents where Chinese vessels cut the cables of Vietnamese seismic survey ships and cyber attacks against Vietnam were some of the provocations the Australian professor noted. These acts suggest belligerency rather than the "peaceful rise" that Chinese leaders have claimed is their international objective. They do not exhaust the list of Chinese misbehavior. China's blockage of the sale of rare earth minerals (used, for example, in the refining of oil and the manufacture of flat-screen TVs, iPods, and laser-guided weapons) to Japan and other countries, including the United States, can be read as anything from economic nationalism to old-fashioned mercantilism to a heavy-handed attempt to drive up world prices while encouraging companies that depend on such minerals to locate plants in China. Free trade this isn't. But restricting international sales of rare earth minerals is a good indication of the kind of international order that might accompany an ascendant or triumphant China: trade gradually tilts away from its role as an engine of prosperity toward a weapon of national economic or diplomatic interest. China's economic interest in African minerals pursued regardless of their partner state's human rights violations, for instance Sudan's policy in Darfur, is another example of a vision of world order that is essentially illiberal. In this vision, wealth is as much a zero-sum game as power. Each is finite and can only accrete at the expense of another. A state in such a world may grow great not by helping to create the conditions for expanding global wealth and by balancing power, but by accumulating wealth—necessarily at the expense of others—and by getting and employing power to secure hegemony. China and the United States' vision of world order are opposed—and in terms of force, nowhere more so than in the waters of the Indo-Pacific region. It is difficult to see how these conflicting visions can easily be reconciled.

There is no reason that the United States and China must be enemies. The trade between the two states and China's large holdings of U.S. government debt argue in favor of normal relations and the normal give-and-take of occasionally conflicting economic and diplomatic interests. This is well understood in the United States. China is equally aware of its interest in a dependable U.S. market for its products and the stability that is a condition of its continued prosperity. But Chinese leadership possesses an understanding of strategic competition with the United States that finds little or no parallel among most American leaders. It is, for example, highly unlikely that a senior American military officer would publicly discuss the circumstances in which the United States would use nuclear weapons against China. A different idea holds in China. In 2005, a Chinese major general, Zhu Chengu, told a gathering of foreign journalists that "if the Americans draw their missiles and precision-guided ammunition on to the target zone on Chinese territory, I think we will have to respond with nuclear weapons."[56] The remark is not only notable for its frankness but also for its contradiction of China's policy of no first use of nuclear weapons. It also suggests the expanding role of China's military in the state's policy-making organs. So does the timing of the PLA air force's first test of its new fifth-generation stealth fighter plane, the J-20. The test occurred while U.S. Secretary of Defense Gates visited Beijing in January 2011 seeking to improve the defense relationship between the two countries, and it seems to have caught the highest-ranking Chinese civilian officials by surprise.[57] When the U.S. Navy SEALs killed Osama bin Laden early in the morning of May 2, 2011, the director of the military channel at China Central Television (CCTV), Zhang Xin, declared that "single-handedly confronting the world's sole superpower, the United States, . . . bin Laden is the greatest national hero in the Arab world," a significantly different view than that expressed by the civilian-run Foreign Ministry, which called bin Laden's death "a positive development of the international anti-terrorism effort."[58] Military officers whose influence over important national security policy is on the rise is consistent with the more assertive Chinese behavior in the region of recent years mentioned above: declaring virtual sovereignty over international waters; harassing naval and merchant shipping; increasing presence in distant ports; surfacing a PLAN submarine close to the American aircraft carrier U.S.S. *Kitty Hawk*; warning the United States not to hold naval exercises in the international waters between South Korea and China. The list is a long one and continues. The sum of these actions cannot be dismissed as coincidental, accidental, or purposeless. There is no other seapower presence in the region to equal the United States' in magnitude and force—or the esteem of most states for its peaceable intent. China has embarked on a policy of probing and challenging the most visible manifestation of U.S. power in the region, the U.S. Navy. But while the navy is the immediate object of strategic competition, it is a stand-in for the United States.

American policy makers rarely acknowledge this strategic competition. U.S. naval officials may speak about China's development of an antiship ballistic missile, but they do not discuss

China as a possible strategic competitor. They do not justify their budgets before Congress as necessary for the preservation of American power in a region where it is being challenged. Administration officials fail to respond to Chinese provocations in kind. They answer China's accusation that scheduled exercises between the United States and South Korean navies are provocative by delaying them for months.[59]

In sum, the signs point to a change in power in the western Pacific. U.S. naval power has diminished substantially over recent decades and promises to wane more in the decades ahead. At the same time, the American government's financial situation appears incapable of summoning the modest resources needed to increase the fleet. American political leadership for the most part fails to acknowledge that a state of strategic competition exists between China and the United States and persists in the hope that trade and economic connections will trump all else. A grand American strategy aimed at preserving its position in the western Pacific may exist on some shelf but lies there utterly inchoate. China is modernizing its fleet with the avowed intent of denying the western Pacific to American naval forces and—as Beijing's aircraft carrier program demonstrates—projecting naval power at great distances, most likely into the Indian Ocean and Gulf of Aden through which its imported oil travels, as well as to the site of its mounting investments in strategic minerals, Africa's east coast. Its leaders feel the geopolitical winds at their backs as they claim, contest, harass, and threaten. The web of logistic support they are crafting is as far-reaching as the Ming admiral's remotest peregrination. The stage could be set for a transfer of naval power from the United States to China that recapitulates the one that occurred when Great Britain surrendered its naval dominance to the United States. Except that this time the recipient will not share the same values as the one who preceded.

7

What Is Lost Can Never Be Regained

WHATEVER THE RELATION between seapower and great power status, one fact is unassailable. Great powers come and go, but they are not the same ones. Athens had her day and it set. So did Rome, Venice, France, Holland, and Spain. In no instance did the seapower of any eclipsed state return. In no instance did her great power status return. Britain today is a good example. Its Royal Navy is made up of six destroyers and thirteen frigates[1] as well as six attack submarines and four ballistic-missile submarines. The number of British warships that had to be sacrificed to build two new aircraft carriers chopped the size of the fleet virtually in half. Large and unanticipated increases in the cost of the American-built fighter-bombers that would have flown from her decks raised precipitously the expense of the new carriers and resulted in a return to the American fighter-bomber that, while more affordable, lacks the range of the model that the U.S. Navy will use. A new Type 45 destroyer was designed as a replacement to the aging Sheffield class that dates from the 1960s. An all-purpose combatant, it will defend against ship-killing missiles and submarines and carry a powerful gun for use against shore targets and surface ships. But Britain's straitened finances will reduce the original purchase by half—from twelve to six. The Royal Navy has not been as small as it is today since the approximately forty-ship fleet in being when

Henry VIII died in 1547.[2] As with the United States, the UK government routinely spends more than it takes in. Borrowing to make up the difference has accumulated a national debt of over £1 trillion, or about $1.6 trillion, small by comparison to what America owes but equally restrictive in what monies are left for defense. Defense budget cuts over the past two decades have halved the percent of GDP the UK spends on defense. The likelihood that the Royal Navy will return to anything approaching its former strength is as remote as the chances of Britain's return to the great power status she achieved in the nineteenth century. Because of the many different purposes to which seapower can be put, shrinkage necessarily means disappearing national power.

Because of its intimate connection with protecting commerce and the flexible uses to which it has been put throughout history—everything from defeating other navies, to applying force to the shore, to blockades, to amphibious landings, fighting pirates, quelling nascent crises, and serving humanitarian purposes—seapower is an exceptionally flexible instrument of military power. States whose leaders understood this have generally prospered. Where this understanding vanished or where states have proved incapable of maintaining seapower, the consequences have usually been dire. Athens is the best ancient example.

The Athenian playwright Aeschylus was born around 525 BC, a quarter century before the Persian conquest of Greece began and in which he participated at Marathon and at the naval battle of Salamis. Unlike Thomas Jefferson's tombstone, which mentions his authorship of the Declaration of Independence but omits his two terms as president, Aeschylus's tomb passes over his remarkable literary achievements and speaks only of his participation in the wars against Persia:

> This tomb hides the dust of Aeschylus, an Athenian,
> Son of Euphorion who died in wheat-bearing Gela;
> Marathon declares his valor
> And so do the long-haired Medes who knew it well.

Persia's western frontier at the beginning of the war reached the Mediterranean where it washes modern-day Turkey's shores. Under its king, Darius, the first Persian invasion was turned back at the Battle of Marathon in 490. Darius's son, Xerxes, led a second large invasion twelve years later. A large army crossed the Hellespont accompanied by an equally impressive naval force assembled to provide supplies, assist in moving troops, and maintain communications with the Persians' land base in Asia. During this second major invasion the Spartan king Leonidas, commanding a small force of his own and allied units, held back the entire Persian army at a narrow coastal pass between steep mountains immediately to the south and the straits that separate the long island of Euboea from the Greek mainland. The Athenian-led naval coalition also suffered a defeat in the same straits of Artemisium. The Greek commanders' intent to stop the Persian force before it could move south along the Aegean's eastern coast toward the Peloponnese had failed. The Greek fleet retreated to the strait of Salamis near the end of the Attic Peninsula and by the stratagems and deceptions of its commander, Themistocles, succeeded in engaging the numerically far superior Persian fleet in the narrow waters of the strait where the Persian navy's large size probably worked against it. The naval battle of Salamis demoralized the Persian force and was followed by Greek coalition victories at Plataea and Mycale, thus ending the Persian threat to Greece. Athens's naval prowess was decisive in turning back the Persian invaders and the alliance known as the Delian League—named after Delos, the island on which the alliance was formalized—established itself to avoid a third Persian invasion and came eventually under Athenian control. The alliance was composed of coastal areas of the northern and eastern Aegean, the islands large and small that lie between Asia Minor and Greece, and a handful of polities on the east coast of the southern Adriatic Sea. As the original NATO alliance was composed of states that bordered the Atlantic or its adjoining waters, the Delian League was an association of city-states, islands, and littoral areas that bordered the sea or were set in it.

Almost within sight of the Aegean, Athens's livelihood, commerce, and security rode on the sea. By the beginning of the Peloponnesian War in 431 BC, she was the Mediterranean's great naval power. In the midst of a dispute between two Greek city-states, one that ultimately precipitated the Peloponnesian War, an emissary from the smaller power argued for alliance with Athens, noting that the combination of the two polities' navies would strengthen both. "Yourselves excepted, we are the greatest naval power in Hellas."[3] In fact, Athenian policy in this dispute—which turned violent—turned importantly on calculations of the consequences for Athens's naval power. But initial Athenian strategy in the war against Sparta is the most persuasive testament to the breadth and reach of Athens's naval power. The great Athenian statesman Pericles argued effectively at the beginning of the Peloponnesian War for a strategy of deterrence. He advised his fellow citizens to withdraw from their lands and farms outside Athens's defensive walls and allow the superior Spartan armies to pillage and burn while remaining safely behind the city's fortifications. Pericles argued that Athens's superior naval skill and fleet could keep the city supplied with both finances from its tributaries and food and other necessities; that it was as foolish to take on Sparta at the point of its greatest strength—its highly disciplined soldiery—as it was prudent to base Athenian strategy on its greatest strength, naval power. War would come, Pericles saw. However, showing the Spartans that Athens could not be taken by storm but would survive by the efforts of its navy must persuade Sparta that war was futile. Sparta would be deterred by realizing that its military objective was beyond reach. Thucydides holds that Pericles' strategic insight was correct but tempers his endorsement of the naval strategy with the observation that it rested on the great man's ability to shape public opinion in the Athenian democracy. Arguments over whether Athens's dominant seapower, employed as Pericles advised, could have prevented the war from continuing for twenty-six years have not been resolved.

As the war progressed, both of the competing hostile powers sought to develop competencies in each other's strength. In the end Sparta defeated Athens, although not without Persian help. The defeat was naval and hearkens back to Pericles' advice about the maritime source of Athens's strength. Sparta ultimately defeated the Athenian fleet in the enclosed water of the Marmara Sea between the Mediterranean and the Black Sea. This cut off Athens from its profitable trade in the Black Sea and depleted the city's wealth sufficiently to end the war. If there had ever been any question in the minds of the Athenian high command after Pericles' death that naval power was key to Athens's strength, Sparta's victorious commander, Lysander, had no such doubt. The terms of the peace that he imposed stripped Athens of her Aegean empire, the fleet she had used to maintain it, and the long walls that had protected her access to the nearby port city of Piraeus. After a quarter century, Athenian freedom and her fleet, as well as an association of allies, would be restored, but the remaining glory of Greece vanished in more internecine quarrels that ended in Persian and eventually Macedonian domination. The disappearance of decisive seapower and an empire finished Athens as a great power.

Close to the western edge of the Balkan Peninsula, another great seapower learned similar lessons nearly seventeen centuries later. As Germanic tribes challenged Roman rule at the head of the Adriatic, and the empire's capital moved east to Byzantium, Venice, its bargemen, and the immediately neighboring lagoon areas stayed under Constantinople's control. The early Venetians traded fish and salt within the lagoon and along the rivers that fed it. The Lombard invasion of Byzantine Italy in the sixth century sent a stream of refugees east who looked for safety in the lagoon's islands. Lombard attempts to envelop the watery region were as unsuccessful as that of Charlemagne, who saw the strategic position that Venice occupied as a geographic pivot between Europe and the East, but failed to capture the island city-state. The lumber business became profitable, as did the slave trade that

Christian authorities in the ninth century still countenanced. Venice increasingly turned her attention to the sea. Seapower was needed to protect commerce. The Venetians used it against pirates who darted out from the islands of the Dalmatian Coast. Venice partnered with the fading Byzantine navy against Arab seaborne raiders off the coast of southern Italy and built large ships to secure the approaches to the lagoon itself when Saracens threatened in the ninth century. When the Normans, who had established a firm presence in Italy's south, began to subdue the Byzantine Empire's western dominions, Emperor Alexius I turned to the Venetian navy. It performed with courage and imagination, the reward for which was increasingly favorable trade terms and eventual responsibility for the Byzantines' naval defense.[4]

If Alfred Thayer Mahan had not chosen to look at global seapower, he would have pointed to Venice as an example of how commercial and naval interest intertwine and support each other. Venice thrived as her commerce grew and her navy's reach and power expanded to protect the growing trade. The Crusades, beginning with the first one at the end of the eleventh century, supplied additional commercial opportunities as Venetian merchant ships supplied Christian attackers who were reinforcing and extending their holdings in the Holy Land and were duly rewarded with trade concessions. Venice's naval forces moved into the eastern Mediterranean and added to the state's wealth by sweeping the seas of Muslim challengers, plundering Muslim shipping, and then turning on Byzantine seaborne trade after losing the commercial privileges gained previously.

The Venetian Senate and elected doge used their wealth and power to fortify the city's seapower, specifically to establish bases along her trade routes to Constantinople and the Black Sea. Today's Greek island of Corfu, just below the mouth of the Adriatic, became a Venetian possession in the thirteenth century. Other key ports were purchased subsequently, from the Adriatic itself to the Peloponnese—then called Morea—into the eastern Aegean. Indeed a map of Venice's Aegean possessions including

Crete looks like a string of glass beads encircling modern-day Greece. This made sense. Galleys required rowers. Rowers took up space, always at a premium aboard ships. Food and water from land bases freed up cargo space on merchant ships and room for combatants who would board enemy ships in battle. The Venetian bead strategy offered another advantage. It gave Venice high lookout points to observe seagoing traffic and harbors below from which naval squadrons could sally as Ottoman naval power increased. Mahan would not assemble his thoughts on seapower for another six centuries, but La Serenissima's rulers understood, just as the American admiral did, that merchant fleets produced wealth whose partial diversion to naval force was a wise investment that allowed each to prosper.

To Venice's eventual undoing, this understanding never took root among the general populous. The fifteenth-century contests of Italy's warring cities distracted Venice from maintaining her seapower and drained her finances while a powerful challenge to stability in the eastern Mediterranean, the Ottomans, destroyed the Byzantine Empire and captured the gleaming emerald in its crown, Constantinople. Venice virtually looked the other way as the Ottoman Empire's gaze shifted to Europe and its naval power grew. Like the Athenians, the Venetians forgot that seapower was the source of their wealth, worldly position, and strength. The naval empire she had begun building three centuries earlier regarded holdings on land as an aid to seapower. As Venice declined, territory became an object itself and alliances and continental warfare the means of increasing expansion on land. To make matters worse, the land forces and commanders Venice turned to for continental warfare were mercenaries. They cost the city its good financial condition as the change in focus toward land depleted Venice's reserve of experienced naval officers and seamen.

The struggle for dominant power in northern Italy seesawed, and French and German invasions loosened Venice's grip over the lands she had gained. Ottoman and Spanish seapower at the eastern and western extremes of the Mediterranean took full advantage. The Ottomans developed from a coastal force into a raiding one that paralleled in tactics their Ghazi predecessors, and eventually sought successfully to project naval power across the entire Mediterranean. By the end of the sixteenth century the Ottoman Empire reached from the north end of the Adriatic's east coast down to the tip of the Balkan Peninsula. It reached up the Black Sea north of Crimea—through Turkey, of course—and wound south along the eastern shore of the Mediterranean. It had dug in across North Africa to Morocco's border with today's Algeria. Ottoman territory also included much of today's Lebanon, Syria, and Iraq as well as the productive section of Egypt, the entire length of the Red Sea's eastern coast, and the Persian Gulf's west coast as far south as Qatar. The Ottomans controlled most of the Mediterranean's littoral areas, the great cities of the Middle East, and most of the fertile lands that bordered the Black Sea as well as the strategic waterways that connect the Mediterranean with the Indian Ocean. Venice found that she could no longer shape events and wield influence alone. Alliances became a necessity, as did accommodation to the interests of allies. The famous sea battle of Lepanto in 1571 pitted an alliance of Venice, the Papal States, and Spain commanded by the half brother of the Spanish king Philip against the Ottomans. The proximate cause of the battle was Ottoman atrocities committed in defeating the Venetian-held garrison on Cyprus. This galvanized the heretofore fractious Christian naval powers. They challenged the Ottoman navy and won at Lepanto. Venice's outsized contribution to the victorious fleet, however, failed to enlist the alliance in retaking Cyprus. The Ottomans' conquest of the island stood, and more of Venice's strategically indispensable real estate disappeared as a result of her incapacity to do as she pleased.

The next century—the seventeenth—ended the contraction of Venice's naval empire, but not before losing almost all of Crete to the Ottomans in a war that lasted twenty-four years. Venetian holdings were confined to a strip of Dalmatian coastline and Corfu, the well-situated island at the mouth of the Adriatic from which naval power could preserve the strategic depth that protected Venice itself. At her height Venice had been a seapower whose trade was protected by force from the Black Sea to Northern Europe in the early fourteenth century. Her distraction by land warfare and misapprehension that commerce with the Ottomans would overshadow their imperial ambition reduced this great power to guarding her seaward approaches. In the end this protection also failed as La Serenissima's finances crumbled under heavy debt and she sought refuge in a neutrality among the warring powers of northern Europe that she could not enforce. The Napoleonic Wars finished off Venice as a power, although the city retained its position as the Adriatic's most important port and shipbuilding center.[5] Seapower, the complementary and mutually reinforcing mix of waterborne commerce and protective naval force together with geography and an enterprising population, may not guarantee a state great power status. But seapower once lost—and where it proved instrumental in a state's rise to greatness—has no example in history of recovery. Andrea Gritti governed Venice from the age of sixty-eight until his death at eighty-three. Titian's 1540 portrait shows him in his late years as doge. Even as an old man he is formidable. The eyes glower. They penetrate with a discernment and will that would make an enemy think that this is not the right day to attack Venetians. Gritti wears the doge's gourd-shaped crown banded in gold cloth. His outer garment is the same glittering material. It is a picture of wealth and majesty earned by mind and determination. Gritti's widespread fingers clutch the arm of the throne on which he sits like an eagle's talons. Idealized it may have been, but this was Venice at her height. The city today is a gorgeous theme park for tourists. The self-inflicted loss of seapower brought her down.

Venice had been the hinge of trade between northern Europe and Asia. Wine, furs, wool, and precious metals crossed over the Alps into Venice. Spices, silk, slaves, and cotton arrived from

Asia at the head of the Adriatic through various overland and sea routes. Portuguese mariners' discovery of a sea route to India around the Cape of Good Hope at the end of the fifteenth century occurred at roughly the same time that Venice lost her strategic focus on the sea. Moreover, it was easier to ship goods in northern Europe's large deep-bottomed hulls directly from point of embarkation to destination than to transport them overland and across seas with repeated interruptions to load cargoes on and off ships and wagons or caravans. Within a century Dutch and English seapower helped begin the colonization of India, had filled the vacuum left by the Mediterranean naval powers' decline, and were recasting the world's economic and military shape. Mahan argues that the sea itself was the foundation of the Dutch republic's wealth. Fish were caught, cured, consumed at home, and sold at a substantial profit as Venice tottered and Western European commerce bounded forward with the discovery of the Americas and a new trade route to Asia.[6] From pickled fish, Holland's seagoing empire sprang. Merchant ships were built. "The wheat and naval stores of the Baltic, the trade of Spain with her colonies in the New World, the wines of France, and the French coasting trade were . . . transported in Dutch shipping. . . . Favored by their geographical position, intermediate between the Baltic, France, and the Mediterranean, and at the mouth of the German rivers, they quickly absorbed nearly all the carrying-trade of Europe."[7]

Even cornering Europe's carrying trade was not enough to satisfy the material resources for which this small state with one-quarter of its land below sea level reached. By the seventeenth century Dutch merchant ships called at ports from New Amsterdam to Nagasaki and from Russian ports on the White Sea to Cape Town. Dutch trading settlements dotted the Indo-Pacific from India to Malaysia to Indonesia to Taiwan. Until Matthew Perry's 1854 success in securing the Convention of Kanagawa, the Dutch had been the only Europeans who had been permitted to trade in Japan, to which they had been sailing since 1639. The Dutch East India Company (VOC) held a monopoly on cloves, mace, and nutmeg from the Indonesian Spice Islands (Moluccas) and cinnamon from Ceylon. This growing global commerce sufficiently energized Dutch commercial interests that when the possibility of peace arose with the Portuguese in 1640, the VOC insisted that any truce be restricted so that they could continue their profitable conquest of Portugal's diminishing Asian possessions. VOC directors argued that peace with Portugal in Asia would imperil Dutch trade along with the commercial empire's increasing number of ships and the industrial base that produced them. These arguments were nothing if not consistent. An early seventeenth-century Dutch colonial governor of Batavia (Jakarta today) told the VOC's directors that "we cannot carry on trade without war nor war without trade."[8] The Dutch, however, like the Venetian traders they supplanted, were uninterested in imperial rule as a means of extending their dominion or establishing Dutch rule and culture around the globe. The United Provinces looked neither back to Rome as the seat of a universal polity nor forward to England as a global power on which the sun never set. The Dutch saw the sea as a boundless highway sparkling with natural resources and well-situated trading centers whose wealth supplied the deficiencies of their dike-girded realm. With her navy to defend her merchant shipping, seapower transformed the Lowlands into a shining gilded enterprise.

At the beginning of Louis XIV's reign in 1643, the Dutch merchant fleet alone numbered ten thousand ships and 168,000 seamen, this in a land of 260,000 souls. Dutch ships carried all the trade between America and Spain and between America and France. The total value of merchandise carried in Dutch bottoms amounted to a billion French francs.[9] This put the Dutch in much the same position as a corporation whose large cash reserves make it a lumbering target for takeover. England, notwithstanding the United Provinces' aid in turning back the Spanish Armada, regarded the Dutch as an economic and seagoing competitor. Shared religion, similar political systems, and proximity did not suppress competition. They spurred it. And the two states' economic and seapower positions were opposite. The Dutch were an economic giant with global geographic reach whose merchant ships far eclipsed in number their naval protectors. At the mid-point of the seventeenth century, English trade was relatively small compared to her powerful and growing navy. The English navy could prey on the rich traffic that shunted between the Netherlands and the distant sources of their wealth. At the same time, the Dutch navy was too small to defend the same lines of communication from the English war fleet whose commerce-protection responsibility was minimal. With war in the air, a Dutch ambassador returned from England noting that "the English are about to attack a mountain of gold; we are about to attack a mountain of iron."[10]

The conflict marked the beginning of the end of Dutch naval supremacy. Disunity among the formerly united provinces of the Netherlands contributed to naval unpreparedness. Reluctance to bear the expense of maintaining the combat fleet and overweening confidence bred by prior victories over the inferior Spanish navy accentuated the Dutch predicament. Defeat followed defeat and trade suffered grievously. Two years before the war began, customs receipts recorded by the Amsterdam Admiralty amounted to two million florins. One year after the war started, this income had been reduced by two-thirds.[11] The balance of naval power see-sawed between England and the Netherlands as the seventeenth century entered its seventh decade and Dutch overseas trade largely recovered from its earlier setbacks. But a new danger in the form of Louis XIV's ambition to rule the continent turned the Netherlands' attention landward, and at enormous cost as the Dutch raised armies to fight alongside the English against the Sun King. Public borrowing paid for large additions to the republic's land forces, which increased from 45,000 to 75,000 men while another 42,000 soldiers were hired from German Protestant princi-palities. By 1708, Dutch ground forces dwarfed those of the British in their alliance against Louis XIV. The Dutch fielded 119,000 troops to the 70,000 that England committed to the continent.[12]

Despite their majority representation in the field, the republic ceded command of the coalition to a British commander and reinforced this implicit act of subordination with malingering. The irresolution of the Dutch high command is best described in Winston Churchill's history of his illustrious ancestor, John Churchill, the first Duke of Marlborough. Churchill commanded the English-Dutch coalition in attempts to destroy French forces in Flanders, yet Dutch hesitation, obfuscation, and reluctance repeatedly frustrated the campaign. Such obstacles to decisive military engagement mirrored the political disunity, loss of industry and trade as a result of neighboring states' tariffs, and consequent rise of competing states' economies that the Netherlands experienced as its power waned in the late seventeenth and early eighteenth centuries. Dutch manufacturing, trade, shipping, and fishing crumbled. As the historical author J. Ellis Barker put it, "The Netherlands ceased to be the workshop of the world, and even their own workshop, for the Dutch became dependent on manufactured articles made abroad."[13] Captains of industry and trade were replaced by directors of financial houses whose personal wealth burgeoned while the state eventually learned the impossibility of flourishing on the work of foreigners.

Equally important, the expensive land conflict against France sapped resources, which might otherwise have been spent on maintaining the Dutch navy. Commercial misfortunes reinforced and reflected naval decline. The fishing industry that had been the seed of Dutch prosperity withered. In the late sixteenth century three thousand Dutch boats harvested and salted away the northern waters' catch. By 1765 the Dutch fishing fleet had shrunk to two hundred.[14] In tandem with the loss of Dutch merchant marine and naval vessels went what had once been the large and thriving industrial base needed to build ships. It migrated to England and France. In his 1778 work, *La Richesse de la Hollande*, the French author Jacques Accarias de Sérionne recorded that "during the last 30 years more than a hundred sawmills have been pulled down in Zaandam, the center of the

Dutch shipbuilding industry, and during the last three years a larger quantity of sawn timber has been imported into Holland than a hundred sawmills could furnish."[15] Prussia invaded the Netherlands in 1787 and the armies of revolutionary France replaced the Prussians in 1795 seizing what was left of the Dutch navy. The wealth and might of the Dutch began and ended at sea. Seapower in its commercial form raised up the United Provinces and infused them with the wherewithal to enlarge. Expansion created a vast commercial and trading empire that enriched and defended the republic's continued growth, which rested on control of the seas. Internecine political strife shattered the purposeful leadership that had marshaled the Dutch people's energies. They dissipated in an unwise concentration on continental power at the expense of sustained seapower. Commerce and seapower contracted. Industrial power and an economy based on manufactures were replaced by financiers and banking houses. Capital surpluses that had been amassed in the previous (the seventeenth) century enriched foreign competitors as they were lent out abroad at the lowest interest rates in Europe. The state weakened, was swallowed, and became a client state of revolutionary France. The naval Battle of Camperdown between the Royal Navy and the Dutch was one of the many contests in which England sought to limit or end revolutionary France's ability to use the seas that enveloped the widening French hold on Europe. It would be the last major Dutch naval engagement. The Royal Navy won a resounding victory by sinking, putting out of action, or capturing most of the Dutch fleet. The golden age of the Dutch had ended years before, never to be resurrected. Camperdown was an exclamation mark.

England's downfall as a seapower and the virtually simultaneous waning of its economic strength and status as a great world power trace mingling paths along a double helix whose similarity to the Netherlands was noticed as early as the twentieth century's dawn. Joseph Chamberlain, father of Neville and previously secretary of state for the Colonies and president of the Board of Trade, observed in 1906:

We are richer—there is no doubt that we are richer than we were ten years ago, or fifty years ago . . . but what of other nations? Take the case of Spain. I think in the case of Spain, and I am certain in the case of Holland, that there is more acquired wealth in these countries today than there was in the palmiest times of their history; but that is all. In spite of the growth of their wealth they have fallen from high estate. The scepter they once wielded so proudly has passed into other hands and can never return to them. They may be richer, but they are poorer in what constitutes the greatness of a nation, and they count for nothing in the future opinion of the world.[16]

Chamberlain saw that industrial strength as measured in the sinews of the shipbuilding industry of the time—iron and steel manufacturing, as well as shipyards themselves—were diminishing relative to American and German growth in the same industries. Chamberlain made his comment in 1904, but in fact the United States had surpassed Britain in iron and steel production before 1890, at least a decade and a half earlier.[17] Comparisons of British to American and German manufacturing as a whole from 1870 to 1913 give a broader and grimmer picture. As a portion of world production, German manufacturing during this period increased by 18 percent. America's share of world production increased by nearly 54 percent. Britain's *declined* by nearly the same amount, 56 percent.[18]

While Britain's relative industrial strength—and thus the base on which her military power rested—decreased, public spending that had remained stable after the Napoleonic Wars began to rise. "As the working classes got the vote—in 1867, but especially in 1884–5—it became only too obvious that they would demand—and receive—substantial public intervention for greater welfare," wrote the British intellectual Eric Hobsbawm.[19] During the 1870s national spending amounted to approximately £66 million a year. By 1895 all this changed. Government spending that year exceeded £100 million. A Treasury Department official observed:

> Some of the services which the State has undertaken are in their nature services of automatic growth, notably educational services; while the tendency of responsible as well as irresponsible persons is to saddle the State with further undertakings which must be accompanied with heavy cost to the taxpayer. Agriculturalists are pressing to be further relieved from the burden of local rates; school teachers are demanding pensions; the working classes are demanding some provisions for old age—a claim which, if it be freely satisfied, may mean a boundless subsidy from the State.[20]

Then as the twentieth century opened, Britain found herself in a land war that dwarfed the cost of previous challenges to the empire. The Indian Rebellion of 1857 lasted seven months before the British were able to contain it. Its financial burden did not register. When in 1899 the descendants of Dutch settlers balked at the prospect of British rule and the increasing presence of British settlers who flocked to South Africa's gold mines, which in 1900 were producing one-fourth of the world's gold,[21] the Boer War began. It lasted until 1902. During the war's first year, monies spent on the army more than doubled over the previous year's peacetime expense, and then doubled again in the war's final two years. The national budget for 1901–1902 doubled from its 1895 level. As deficits began to accumulate, the government increased income taxes, imposed new import duties, and borrowed. Contributions to a government fund—the Sinking Fund—established to retire national debt, were interrupted. Keynesian notions that national indebtedness might in fact be a kind of blessing had yet to triumph. Shakespeare's Polonius better expressed British statesmen's idea of financial responsibility: "Neither a borrower nor a lender be." Sound fiscal governance must keep the lid on what the government borrowed—or took from its citizens in the form of taxes—and what it lent, or in this case paid out to sustain the state. Yale's Professor Aaron Friedberg argues that Adam Smith and John Stuart Mills's arguments in favor of minimal government taxation and spending retained their hold over statesmen's ideas. As British spending rose precipitously, along with the taxation and borrowing required to sustain them, so did anxiety about the outcome of this deflection from what was regarded as safe and wise. The government's ability to tax had reached the limit beyond which additional impositions would harm the economy. Spending must be decreased. And political leaders proved as unable to imagine a world order altered by the evanescence of British seapower as they were insistent on co-opting political pressures for what the above-mentioned Treasury official described as a "boundless subsidy" and which would be called today nondiscretionary spending. The army and navy were included in spending cuts.

And with profound effect. At the moment that military spending was to be included in spending reductions, the fleets of other states were increasing. The United States, Germany, and Japan were becoming not only large naval powers but modern ones. As early as 1878, France had embarked on a naval armament program that matched England's in cost.[22] Russia and Italy were also adding significantly to their naval strength. The great power—Britain—had not started to diminish but measured against potential rivals or some combination of them; the Royal Navy started to look less foreboding. Domestic political alarm bells began to ring and British leadership answered them with the assurance that building a navy twice the size of the next two largest potentially competing fleets—after the Royal Navy— would assure continued command of the seas. A larger-than-the-next-two naval force had a comforting sound to it, but scanty strategic justification. France and Russia were seen as the two competitors most likely to join forces, but this could no more be predicted than that a third might join them. More important, Great Britain's naval task was to keep open the sea-lanes that England used to maintain communications with an empire on which the sun did not set. Her navy must span the globe in breadth and changing degrees of naval power. France had aspired to but possessed no such empire. Russia continued to ooze outward on land from its center in Moscow. Also, Ottoman control of the narrows of the Dardanelles and the long northern Russian winter that hemmed in its northern fleet vessels were powerful obstacles to a French-Russian combined fleet. But if they could join, or if Germany offered a threat in European waters while rising powers outside Europe challenged the Royal Navy around the world, the equal-or-greater-than-the-two-next-powerful-navy solution would founder.

Uncertainty about Britain's naval supremacy grew as the fleets of European and non-European navies—those of Japan and the United States—increased. From 1898 to 1906 Britain's battleship fleet increased by 31 percent. During the same period the battleship fleets of France, Germany, Italy, Japan, Russia, and the United States grew by 41 percent. At the midpoint of the twentieth century's first decade, Great Britain maintained the world's largest battleship fleet with sixty-one ships. But other European powers plus the United States and Japan now operated a total of 112 battlewagons. Yet the idea that security lay in maintaining a fleet at least as powerful as the two European navies closest in size to Britain's held. And so did the numbers. Despite the growth of other fleets, London deliberately preserved its lead over the next two largest European states, France and Russia, which were seen as the most likely opposing coalition. The problem was that the relative and absolute rise of non-European fleets risked the global dominance that Britain had enjoyed for much of the nineteenth century. Events deepened the uncertainty. The expensive Boer War raised questions about the ability to protect supply lines that extended nearly six thousand miles from Portsmouth to Cape Town. The 1898 Fashoda incident with France over imperial reach in Africa ended satisfactorily from London's perspective but served to remind that French naval power could become a challenge.

Resources raised the strategic dilemma: as naval powers from Asia to Europe to North America emerged, which British interests must be defended first? In the mid-1890s Washington and London had argued over Venezuelan borders, a dispute more pinned to American interpretation of the Monroe Doctrine than the demarcation of Venezuela and neighboring British Guiana. With other crises pressing, Britain deferred to the United States. At about the same time the British high command grasped that the continuing American naval buildup virtually guaranteed numerical superiority over Royal Navy ships that guarded the approaches to Vancouver. Lord Lansdowne observed: "We have already committed ourselves in regard to our Navy to the Doctrine that for every ship of war constructed by certain foreign Powers we should construct another. It is hard to say where this doctrine may lead us. If we include the United States among the Powers, whose progress in naval matters is to be met by a similar rejoinder on our part, our Naval Estimates are likely to be a curiosity before we are much older."[23]

The two-European-power standard was already expensive to sustain. Lord Lansdowne, secretary of state for war, saw jagged financial shoals ahead if Britain tried to keep apace of American naval armament. America swiftly defeated Spain the following year and established a strong naval presence in the Caribbean and at the western end of the Pacific. Combined with the prospect of the Panama Canal—which allowed the American fleet to shift strategic weight between the Atlantic and the Pacific—British political and military leadership became convinced that the balance of naval power in home waters was strategically more important than retaining dominance in the North American littoral. Were the American fleet to become one of the two largest after Britain's, it would not be included in the two-power standard. Unopposed, the United States would rule the waves that lapped America's shores.

Retreat under the weight of rising competitors and a self-restriction on building enough ships to keep pace also ended

British naval dominance in the Far East. European contestants for Chinese holdings upped their naval ante challenging Royal Navy preeminence in East Asia and pushing Japan to develop naval power as insurance against a fate like China's. British naval power ebbed. French and Russian power flowed, as did Japan's naval mass. The colonial outposts at Hong Kong, Singapore, Australia, Malaya, and India still flew the Union Jack. But the oceanic sinews that tied them to the mother country had visibly frayed and the thrumming sounds of Britain's global factory grew fainter. Japan's intercession could break a naval deadlock between the European powers. Alliance with Japan would even up the stakes in the Far East and relieve Britain of the need to equal or surpass a combined French and Russian effort. And the prospect of a large German navy now offered reason to worry about keeping a third European fleet at bay in the event of serious trouble. Dominating the Far East's seas was an ocean too far. A partner was necessary. Britain and Japan signed a mutual defense pact at the beginning of 1902. Britain had embarked on a resource-driven repositioning that emphasized the shift of naval forces from its imperial perimeters toward the seas that surround the European peninsula. At the same time, the two-power standard was retained as a measure of the nation's ability to command not only Europe's seas but all those over which Britain's links with its undiminished empire must sail. Thus the two-power standard was an ignoble misrepresentation. It appeared to preserve the Royal Navy's transoceanic dominance while in fact Britain had greatly constricted the international area over which it ruled the waves, by its treaty with Japan and acknowledgment of American naval dominion in the Western Hemisphere.

Professor Friedberg rightly noted that the issue of pulling back the geographic scope of British seapower was neither thoroughly considered by the government nor argued in public. Britain's leaders, both civilian and military, as well as its populace, slept confident that the two-power standard secured both nation and empire against all naval threats. The idea that Nelson's devastating 1805 victory over the combined French and Spanish fleet had so powerfully reinforced—that British sea-power was as motile and internationally ubiquitous as it was unassailable—remained unshaken in the nation's mind, although the facts had changed. The Royal Navy was shrinking relative to the rise of a third European fleet—the kaiser's. And it was shrinking relative to the growing power of the American and Japanese fleets.

Technology would never overcome the lightening relative weight of total British combat tonnage. British capital ships in 1905 were built faster, more heavily armed, and equipped with more accurate guns than their potential enemies. Steam turbines were substituted for reciprocating engines. Commanding officers' quarters were moved from their former stately elegance at the ship's stern toward the bridge from which the ship would be fought. And the shape of hulls was transformed to reduce drag, thus allowing savings in weight gained by slightly cutting back the size of engines. The weight saved was transferred to increases in vessels' armor.[24] Technology is one of several variables that measure a fleet's strength. Others include ship type, leadership, and strategy. These are important and often pivotal. But examples of major seapowers that have experienced absolute or relative losses of fleet size over a sustained period without losing their seaborne preeminence do not exist.

For a city-state, a nation that sits astride the sea, or one surrounded by it and depends on command of the sea-lanes and key oceanic choke points for wealth and security, the loss of seapower is a one-way ticket to insignificance or, at best, loss of stature. Impotence at sea arrives in different forms, but it has the same effect. Athens built a powerful empire in and around the Aegean based on trade and the shared need to defend against Persia. When confronted by a land power, Sparta, she forgot the seapower that was the foundation of her wealth and security, and stumbled, never to stand up again. The Venetians, too, were distracted by land power and the Queen of the Adriatic became a minor courtier who was no more able to effect her will at sea than on land. Political disunity, overweening and undeserved confidence that past naval accomplishments would assure future naval success, intense competition from an ambitious England, a preoccupation with French continental forces that perhaps could not have been avoided, and a diminution of wealth that followed such other misfortunes as the inability to defend her shipping ended forever Dutch seapower and her so-called Golden Age.

Comparisons to the United States' experience today are inescapable. America has been using force continuously in the Middle East since 1991, to drive the Iraqis from Kuwait, to keep much of the Iraqi air force on the ground in the aftermath, to remove the Taliban, to destroy Saddam Hussein, to fight a shadow war against terrorists from Yemen to the mountains and valleys of northern Pakistan, and to continue to fight against the Taliban in Afghanistan. In 2007, the Congressional Budget Office estimated that the cost of the war to remove Saddam Hussein and the cost of the war in Afghanistan including interest on monies borrowed could reach $2.4 trillion from 2001 to 2017.[25] Whatever the sum, it is large, and at the same time China has greatly increased its naval buildup. The U.S. experience recapitulates that of other great seapowers that have been diverted by costly land wars at the same time that rising competitors sought and gained strategic advantage in seapower. Venice and the Netherlands were distracted respectively—and expensively—by the warring Italian city-states and by France. But the greater threat to Venice came from the Ottomans, who sharpened the Venetians' economic decline by seizing the string of naval bases on which La Serenissima's commerce and security were based. However, another seapower, England, turned out to be more dangerous than France to the Netherlands' status as a great power. More important, the United Provinces' declining economy diminished the economic base that might have supported a more robust economy capable of protecting its seapower.

But no example is at once both less like and more like America's than England's. As Britain found the Boer War far more expensive than it had anticipated, so has the United States, beginning with the war to liberate Kuwait and including not only subsequent military campaigns in the same region, but the as yet unreckoned expense of defending against and attacking terror worldwide, adding an additional super-layer of national intelligence bureaucracy and large federal disbursements to local law enforcement authorities, to name a few. As the Boer War coincided with increased social spending, America's defense expenses coincided with substantial tax cuts. Economists will continue to disagree about whether or to what extent significantly increased government expenses combined with significantly decreased tax rates affected the American economy. But there can be no dispute that both early twentieth-century Britain and America a little over a century later were feeling seriously pinched. One consequence for Britain was simultaneously to reduce military expenses and commitments. She effectively withdrew her naval presence from the Western Hemisphere and from the Far East, hoping that goodwill in the former and a treaty in the latter would substitute for presence, the ability to project power, and the security of her communications with the empire. In the Western Hemisphere, Great Britain's bet turned out to be sound. But the point not to be overlooked is that Britain's retreat from a transoceanic global naval power proved irreversible. A straight and virtually uninterrupted line connects the early twentieth-century end of Britain's worldwide naval presence with the nation's general decline and specifically with the shriveled Royal Navy that exists today, a force wholly devoid of the means to hunt submarines using land-based aircraft and composed of fifty-six midsize and smaller surface combat vessels as well as attack and ballistic-missile submarines.[26] This is about the same size as the English fleet at the end of Henry VIII's reign and approximately one-sixteenth the size of the Royal Navy[27] when Vice Admiral Nelson trounced the French-Spanish fleet off the Spanish coast at Trafalgar in 1805. And the current situation is likely to worsen. A group of senior retired British flag and general officers warned in a September 2011 United Kingdom National Defence Association report that "an effective [naval] force of one part-time carrier, maybe 5 attack submarines, and perhaps 12 frigates is hardly likely to deter much . . ."[28] The same report, drily attesting that British leadership's occasionally interrupted reluctance to spend on national defense hearkens back to pre–World War II days, observes that "had funds the [Neville] Chamberlain government belatedly spent on defence gone instead on new hospitals we would have had the finest health service in Nazi-occupied Europe."[29] Britain's decline as a great power began well over a century ago with the redistribution of its naval forces away from their global reach. The best that can be imagined for the UK's status as an international power is to stanch the hemorrhaging.

But the resemblances between British seapower then and American seapower now do not end with similarly straitened financial resources. Britain's two-power standard hid a darkening strategic picture with an easy-to-understand but illusory mathematical shield. Its brightness deflected the truth that British seapower would no longer cover the world. The United States possesses no parallel formula. But there are plenty of ideas that would save money while producing a similar decline of American naval presence. A Center for Naval Analysis report noted that surging forces—rather than maintaining a consistent forward presence—was an option in the face of costs that threaten to become politically unsustainable. The recent strategic report written at the request of Representatives Barney Frank and Ron Paul recommends wholesale cuts in the U.S. forward presence in Asia. To take the place left by these cuts, says the report, we should "rely on our incomparable capacities for rapid deployment to flexibly send more troops and assets . . . if and when needed."[30]

This is strategic gobbledygook. Hitler completed the invasion of Poland in a little over five weeks, and that was almost three-quarters of a century ago. Naval and amphibious forces take weeks to amass and additional time to cross the Pacific. The

United States' rapid deployment ability remains strong, but unlike in science fiction, cannot travel at the speed of light. Its men and equipment—especially in large quantities—are restricted by the laws of physics, laws that are especially inconvenient in crossing the Pacific's vast emptinesses. Distant and dispersed force may be useful in a slowly accreting crisis. But in a sudden and deadly emergency such as a volley of ballistic missiles followed by a naval and amphibious attack across the hundred miles that separate mainland China from Taiwan, no substitute exists for forward-based force. Potential enemies know this and can be depended on to act accordingly.

Yet the strategic follies persist. A paper published by the New America Foundation and written by an NAF fellow and a Harvard researcher in 2011 suggests that the United States would not only reduce its defense costs but enhance global maritime security if it were to "scale down the reach of its international activities and force presence."[31] Specifically, the report recommends changing its posture in the Pacific and Indian Oceans by transitioning to "an over the horizon presence centering on Diego Garcia, Guam and the Second Island Chain."[32] Other recommendations include reducing the size and capabilities of American forces in the region by withdrawing advanced fighter aircraft, aircraft carriers, multimission guided missile destroyers, and littoral combat ships in exchange for an increase in purely defensive hardware such as air and ballistic-missile defenses and antisubmarine craft.[33] The authors' logic rests on two points. The first is what they call the "free rider problem." They argue that the United States needlessly picks up the slack for other states in the region. If U.S. allies in the area would contribute according to their capability in providing maritime security, Washington would be relieved of significant expense.[34] Just as harmful, it is claimed, the U.S. presence not only raises American taxpayer costs but actually generates "spirals of insecurity," which the forward presence of the U.S. Navy accelerates and intensifies. For example, the authors suggest that the continuation of the United

States' more-than-half-century presence in the western Pacific impels China to invest in maritime force and assume a more confrontational stance toward the United States.[35] If this argument holds, an American curtailment of its seapower in the Indo-Pacific would improve the area's security and lead to greater regional cooperation.[36]

It's a nice wish. But facts speak otherwise. Territorial disputes over islands, seabed mining rights, and territorial waters in the South China Sea and adjacent waters, for example, would not result from a diminished U.S. maritime presence. In fact the United States is the only power in the region without such a claim and can take an active, effective role in helping to resolve regional disputes using diplomacy supported by naval force in reserve. Like other recommendations to curtail U.S. force, this one would decrease federal spending over the short term. It would also encourage others to fill the vacuum left by departing American power. The most likely power to replace the United States is China. The report's understanding of basic strategy is as skewed as its view of history. The authors cite as an appropriate model for the United States the British Empire's decision in 1902 to withdraw from the Far East in exchange for an alliance with Japan.[37] The report claims that the British "successfully utilized the Japanese Empire to preserve Britain's Far East interests over 1902–1920 while improving relations with the United States and Russia."[38] This makes no sense. London's alliance with Tokyo worked for a while. It was followed by Japan's brutal invasion of Manchuria and eventually its attack on Pearl Harbor.

Britain's slow retreat from the supreme power it enjoyed in the nineteenth century did not make the world safer. History offers no evidence that a benevolent power's retreat adds to either regional or global safety. The repositioning of England's powerful navy away from its far-flung stations did not add to global security despite its continued ability to deploy forces around the world albeit from a reduced position. England maintained an empire with bases—for example in Singapore, both coasts of Canada, and the Caribbean—which could supply and harbor surged naval forces. But crimes can be committed and criminals can reap the benefits long before opposing forces can be dispatched halfway across the globe. The notion that surge forces can substitute for an immediate or nearly immediate armed response or preemptive strike is our self-deception to match that portion of Britain's two-power standard of the twentieth century's first decade that maintained the fiction of Britain's continued transoceanic dominance. Adding to this self-deception is our willful disregard that our navy has diminished in size by half since the end of the Cold War, our near metaphysical certainty that the economic relationship between the United States and China will always transcend power struggles, and a similar confidence that we will always leave Chinese military technology in the dust. The last of these is a particularly unreflective notion. It fails to acknowledge, for example, that anyone who had suggested as recently as twenty years ago that China might within a generation be able to use ballistic missiles to strike an American aircraft carrier under way in the Pacific would be thought daft. In sum, all but a handful of British leaders were aware that the strategic reach of her seapower had shrunk. The two-power standard helped preclude meaningful debate in political circles or the media, and the public clung to their opinion of British seapower's omnipresence and omnipotence despite the broad strategic changes that foreshadowed the end of the empire and Britain's position as a superpower. Britain then—like the United States today—avoided public debate about the scope and breath of its seapower as the relative size of potential competitors waxed, imperiling both. Finally, the difference between British seapower's decline and the predicament of U.S. seapower today is at least as striking as the similarity. As noted earlier, the international order that Britain had championed fell to the United States to preserve. At the time of the transfer the two states shared the same fundamental political and economic values.

U.S. command of the seas represented no substantive change in large principles from Britain's. A shift in dominant seapower—even if it was restricted to the Indo-Pacific—from the United States to China would have the most profound affect on international order.

8

Can America Still Manufacture Its Own Weapons?

NAVAL VESSELS HAVE ALWAYS BEEN among the more complex human machines. The sea is violent by nature and naval combat is violent by artifice. Good design and skilled construction can reduce these dangers, especially those that combat presents. The contemporary naval rail gun is a good example. When developed and deployed to the fleet, it will use an electromagnetic impulse to shoot at very high speed—between 1.25 and 1.5 miles per second—a round that will have a range of between fifty and one hundred miles.[1] Besides the rail gun's ability to increase its ship's distance from hostile fire—the current five-inch naval gun has a range of thirteen nautical miles—the rail gun projectile means that ships will no longer be required to plan for space to carry either gunpowder or armed shells and will be spared the danger that accompanies the volatile compounds of traditional ammunition. The kinetic energy of the new projectile is sufficient alone to cause greater damage to a target than a conventional round of similar weight that contains high explosives. New and better technology, however, is not an unmixed blessing: before a single gun is put aboard a ship, the navy is likely to have spent nearly a half billion dollars to develop the rail gun.[2]

Shipbuilders of antiquity faced many of the same problems

that challenge naval architects and builders today, for example, the need to balance size and volume against maneuverability and offensive capability and the need to contain costs. Scholars debate over Rome's naval activity before the Punic Wars but agree that the conflicts with Carthage forced the republic to learn not only how to fight major engagements at sea but how to build the ships needed to win them. Over this there is also scholarly disagreement. Should the ancient historian Polybius, who claims that the Roman navy was built on the pattern of a Carthaginian warship that had fallen into Roman hands,[3] be believed? The same author explains that when Romans saw how the Carthaginian fleet could tip the balance of power in Sicily by coastal raiding despite Rome's iron grasp of the strategic island's interior, the republic for the first time decided to build a fleet. But their shipwrights had never constructed large vessels intended for fleet actions. There was no question of sufficient technological resources for such an enterprise. Rome had none at all.[4] In contemporary terms, Rome lacked an industrial base, the supporting shore institutions that in those times designed ships, harvested timber, manufactured cordage, wove the cloth for sails, and fitted all the parts together into warships.

The United States today does not face the same problem. Knowledge of shipbuilding remains part of American manufacturing. But accelerating cost, an aging workforce, reduced orders for warships, and an uncertain future risk the nation's future ability to turn out sufficient numbers of vessels at affordable prices and profitably enough to keep shipbuilding companies alive. Indeed, the destabilization of the American shipbuilding industrial base is causing the cost of warships to outpace the rate of inflation. All sources suggest that the navy's reduced procurement of ships over the past twenty years has caused the industry to contract, lay off workers, and in general to become less reliable. This has driven up the cost of labor and the cost of construction materials. The fewer ships the navy buys, the less lucrative the industry is for skilled workers. As the cost of labor rises, shipbuilders are increasingly pressed to attract and train qualified personnel. The negative trends reinforce one another. As younger workers are dissuaded from seeking employment or remaining in the industry by the prospects of sporadic employment, those who remain—the existing workers—age. The cycle is self-defeating. Paying older workers increases overhead costs and makes it increasingly expensive to invest in the training and education of a younger workforce. The destabilization of the industrial base also causes costs to rise since many of the materials and products that go into building navy ships are not useful for other purposes. Since the navy is buying far fewer ships now than it did in the 1980s, many shipyards are forced to rely on a single source for necessary materials. With a virtual monopoly on these products, the suppliers have in large part the ability to name their price. The inefficient manner in which the shipyards acquire these materials drives up labor and overhead costs.

The solution lies in stabilizing the American shipbuilding industry. This means that the navy must either increase its orders of ships or discipline the changes it requires of shipbuilders once orders have been placed and vessels are under construction. Buying and stockpiling spare parts for ships that are already in service and whose need for regular maintenance and repair is well known would also help provide stability for the American shipbuilding industry. Repeal of the Jones Act of 1920 would breathe life into the ailing U.S. shipping industry with positive benefits to the navy. The Jones Act restricts ocean-borne transportation between American ports to American-owned companies, ships, and crews. Under the law, shipping rates, along with the cost of American shipbuilding, are protected against the competition. This competition would generate lower costs, affordable technological innovation, and the modernization to attract foreign bidders for the American carrying trade and foreign purchasers for American vessels. Imagine what Boeing would look like if it never had to compete against other American manufacturers, to say nothing of Airbus. A 2001 Department of Commerce study found that the United States builds about 1 percent of the world's large commercial ships. Repeal of the Jones Act would strengthen the industrial base the United States needs to maintain a robust workforce for naval shipbuilding. It would also create new American jobs, spur marine technology, and help build a competitive American merchant fleet as a strategic alternative to China's burgeoning merchant marine fleet. A protracted and major international conflict in which the United States must depend on Chinese hulls to sustain its economy, transport critical war matériel, and communicate with overseas allies would place the United States at a greater strategic disadvantage than we knew during the Revolutionary War. If American designers, engineers, and skilled workers can build the world's finest airliners, there is no reason why America cannot similarly lead the world's shipbuilding industry. But the industrial base on which U.S. security directly rests must be reinvigorated.

In a presentation delivered at the Naval Postgraduate School in Monterey, California, David Berteau, the senior adviser and director of the Defense-Industrial Initiatives at the Center for Strategic and International Studies, identified the "chronic underutilization of capacity" of major shipyards as one of the main threats to the "affordability" of navy Ships.[5] Joe Carnevale, adviser to the Shipbuilders Council of America, reached a similar conclusion.[6] He attributed the rising cost of ships over the past decade to "low quantity orders" on the part of the navy.[7] In a study conducted on the subject in 2006, the Rand Corporation concluded that the rising costs of building ships is the result of a combination of unsteady U.S. government procurement rates and a "monopsony relationship" between the government and the shipbuilders.[8] In a monopsony a single purchaser is faced with a host of sellers. Because there is so little American shipbuilding outside of what the navy purchases, U.S. firms are at the commercial mercy of that fraction of the navy budget devoted to buying ships. A 2005 Government Accountability Office (GAD) report attributed cost increases in shipbuilding to instability in the entire industry, the difficulty in recruiting and training qualified personnel, high rates of skilled personnel turnover, and the ship-builders' dependence on a rapidly shrinking supplier base.

The navy's reduced rate of procurement of ships makes it more difficult and more expensive to hire shipbuilders. The Rand study notes that throughout the 1990s American shipyards attempted to enter into the world of commercial shipbuilding to compensate for the sudden decrease in contracts with the U.S. Navy that followed the Cold War. The attempt failed. American shipbuilders were simply unable to compete with well-established foreign shipyards. Between the industry's inability to compete and the government's anemic demand for naval vessels, shipbuilders have found it increasingly difficult to attract qualified workers. The Rand study noted that the industry is faced with two problems with labor: an aging workforce and a young, or "green," workforce. As workers who possess substantial experience in the industry are approaching the age of retirement, they become a growing source of overhead costs, especially health care.[9] The Rand study also notes that a "green" workforce offers shipbuilders very little return from their investment. Shipbuilding is tough work, and shipbuilders have learned that it is too expensive to train new workers who find the navy's unreliable demand for ships discouraging and will jump at the chance for more stable employment. A 2005 *Defense Industry Daily* article reached a similar conclusion, finding that a combination of shipbuilding "competition from low wage countries, and the process of budget projections and reductions in military requirements is leading to 'binge and purge' hiring cycles that create high attrition and low returns."[10] Other studies have indicated that shipyards' employment of unskilled workers has contributed to a greater number of mistakes during construction. Rand notes that building warships, in contrast with other sorts of military hardware, demands a wide spectrum of worker education and experience. Unlike aircraft or tanks, for instance, navy ships need to be able to support large crews often numbering in the hundreds—or thousands as in the case of an aircraft carrier—for months at a time. This demands the expertise of professionals whose skills are not needed for other defense-related products and who as a result can often be employed outside the defense industry. This raises the cost of retaining such workers when there is no work.[11]

Similarly, warship building demands more from shipyards than commercial shipbuilding; weapons system engineering for ships is one of the most technologically sophisticated tasks in the manufacturing world. Naval vessels in Admiral Nelson's time required a complex and balanced system of sails, rigging, masts, and hull design to maneuver and remain at sea for months or sometimes years. Today's naval warships can demand intricately shaped hull parts often made of composite parts; nuclear engineering at an advanced level; sophisticated targeting, navigating, and communications equipment; and combat systems that transform information received from a variety of close and distant sources into data that is instantly useful to a ship's officers and crew. Contemporary shipbuilding's complexity helps explain one of the causes of cost growth that the GAO identifies: a growing frequency of inexperienced shipbuilders' mistakes while ships are under construction. The GAO notes that cost growth in the case of the Arleigh Burke-class destroyer and the San Antonio class amphibious transport dock ship (LPD-17) are in part due to the fact that the shipyards that constructed these vessels had lost skilled laborers, were confronted with a high rate of turnover among new workers who required training, and suffered from the mistakes and inefficiencies that new workers are likely to cause.[12] The defense industry publication *Defense Industry Daily* confirmed the GAO's report. Besides the navy's changes to the ships' design in the middle of the project, cost increases were directly linked to the high attrition rate of workers on the shipyard that led to "scathing Navy inspector reviews that detailed shoddy construction and basic workmanship problems at (the) Avondale" shipyard in Louisiana.[13] The managers at Avondale who supervised construction of the Arleigh Burke–class destroyer reported

The U.S.S. Churchill, *an Arleigh Burke–class destroyer*

that many of the experienced workers succeeded in finding higher-paying jobs in the area as a solution to the instability and uncertainty of work on navy ships.[14] As a result, labor hours increased as inexperienced workers "took longer to finish tasks" and "made mistakes that required rework."[15] The GAO argued that the navy's fluctuating demand for ships and thus instability in the industry is the likely cause of the shipyard's loss of its experienced workforce.[16]

The unstable supplier base also causes the cost of materials to rise. In a joint statement delivered to the House Armed Services Committee in February 2007, officials from Lockheed Martin, the naval architecture firm Gibbs and Cox, the Marinette marine shipyard, and Bollinger Shipyards agreed on many of the causes of increased costs in the navy's littoral combat ship (LCS) program. The first members of this class had initially been projected to cost $220 million each: in the end, the price came out closer to three times this amount.[17] The companies pointed to "substantial supplier production issues" as an important cause of difficulties in managing expenses.[18] In one instance, the project required the purchase of HSLA- 80 steel, a high-strength, low-weight steel that is specifically designed for military use and is available from a single domestic supplier. The steel was needed for the ship's hull. The project ceased work when the supplier informed the shipyard that a "higher priority Army program would delay the delivery of the material for several months." Faced with the prospect of waiting so long, the design team improvised and redesigned the hulls to use alternate steel alloys and stay as close as possible to the production schedule.[19] Shipbuilders' dependence on a single supplier for critical parts and materials is not uncommon in the diminishing industry.

The Rand report concurred with the testimony that Congress heard. It noted that the number of firms that supply shipbuilding materials is shrinking: many of them have either merged or disappeared, thus reducing competition and causing the prices and scarcity of their products to rise.[20] Indeed, many shipbuilders rely on single sources for construction materials. As with the LCS project, shipyards' dependence on single suppliers often translates into delays and inefficiencies. The suppliers suffer from the flaws of a monopoly.[21] The Rand study also notes that shipyards rely on single-source vendors now more than ever. The Virginia class attack nuclear submarine is a good example: over 75 percent of supply vendors for this class of boats are sole sources.[22] The GAO confirms that delays in deliveries for materials often result in increases in labor and overhead costs. In its evaluation of problems with construction of Arleigh Burke class destroyers, the GAO attributed excessive overhead costs to the shipyards' demand for workers who would go for stretches of time without anything to do—as a result of delays in receiving parts and equipment—but who were needed to continue the job once the equipment arrived.[23] If you hire a craftsman to build a dining-room set, he can work on the chairs while he waits for the right materials for the table. Navy vessels are bigger and are normally built one at a time. Rarely is there an option to employ workers on another job if key parts for the one they are occupied with are lacking. The navy absorbed the expense of keeping qualified workers on the shipyard even though there was temporarily no work for them. Expensive as this is, it is cheaper than laying off workers and then trying to rehire them when the needed material arrived.

Stabilizing the shipbuilding industrial base would help reduce the construction costs of navy ships. The Rand study recommends that the navy establish longer-term contracts with shipyards and consider concentrating production in particular shipyards so that shipbuilders gain more experience quickly and shipbuilding projects can be executed more efficiently.[24] During the Cold War the navy could easily attract new recruits for jobs in shipbuilding because they could see that their naval training would eventually lead to a secure position in that part of the civilian commercial industrial base that built ships. The industrial base today would again become attractive to civilian workers if the navy can make shipbuilding steady employment. A secure industrial base for ship construction would also stimulate competition among material suppliers who could better predict future demand and make informed business decisions accordingly. This would tend to drive down the costs of their products and make their services more efficient. Obviously the one source of these incentives is the U.S. Navy itself. The direction of this argument is clear. As the nation is well served by a navy that is large and capable enough to secure the nation's global interests, the industrial base on which a healthy navy rests benefits equally when its size and skill are commensurate with the nation's changeless requirement for a powerful, modern, transoceanic fleet.

But if the navy has limited control over the annual sum Congress appropriates, it possesses greater flexibility in husbanding the money it receives. This gives the navy the ability to influence how its contractors do business. Steady, predictable, and well-disciplined management of shipbuilding will not substitute for reliable, sufficient funds to build needed vessels. But the same efficient administration can smooth the commercial environment in which shipbuilders must operate and flatten the bumps of an otherwise distracted national government's investment in a stable fleet. The navy has not practiced this efficient administration.

Over the past decade, the navy has been ambitious in its efforts to build more capable and technologically sophisticated ships. It has sought to accomplish this quickly. One important result is a marked rise in construction costs. Haste has made waste. Ship designs that were not sufficiently considered were submitted for construction along with contractual provisions that allowed shipyards to bill the navy over and above the original anticipated cost of a vessel when unexpected problems arose. Such contracts are described as cost-plus. The practice is something like asking an architect to draw up plans for a new house with the very latest technology, agreeing on a price for building it, and then further agreeing to pay additional out-of-pocket expenses if those solar heaters, wind-powered electrical generators, and waste converters don't perform as advertised. Under such circumstances a fixed-price contract is essentially a license to print money. The alternate approach in the world of ship construction is known as fixed-price contracts. Under this system, shipbuilders make bids based on their expectation of cost and the certain knowledge that they will receive no more money to build a vessel than what they were allotted when they won the bid.

Cost-plus contracts encourage neither frugality nor self-discipline on the part of either the purchaser or the contractor. The nineteenth-century English novelist Anthony Trollope named a First Lord of the Admiralty who appears in one his novels "Viscount Thrift." The joke is never lost on readers. One example of construction costs gone wild is the navy's littoral combat ship program in the middle of the last decade. As noted previously, the LCS was intended to be a small warship produced in large numbers that allowed the navy to operate close to shore in a variety of combat missions. The navy submitted an immature design to the shipbuilders and began to make adjustments after construction began. At the same time the navy wanted the LCS to join the fleet quickly and to start carrying out its several missions. It established a timeline for the LCS's construction. To encourage the contractors to keep to the schedule, the navy offered cost-plus contracts. These assured shipbuilders that they would be reimbursed for expenses that exceeded their initial cost estimate. The shipbuilders tried to keep to their schedules. However, the navy made change after change to their final plans. The contractors were required to undo work that had already been completed and sometimes build the ships out of sequence to meet the navy's deadlines. This resulted in a lot of rework: effectively doing, undoing, and then doing again the same task. Trying to construct ships that were incomplete in their design on time proved unsuccessful. It delayed construction: the first two LCS ships were delivered a year later and at costs that exceeded the initial contract by at least 60 percent.[25] The issues became so egregious that Congress cut $1 billion from the program in 2007.[26] The result was a temporary termination of the program.[27]

The navy's LCS program is just one example of the challenges that the navy's industrial base has faced with cost overruns during the past decade. Others include—as detailed previously—effective cancellation of a new class of destroyers, indefinite postponement of a new class of cruisers, and suspension of a program to construct a replacement for the U.S. Navy SEALs' ancient midget submarine. Designing and building into ships a lot of new technology is difficult. Doing it quickly is difficult and costly.

The construction of the navy's latest carrier, U.S.S. *Gerald Ford*, is another instructive example. An entirely new system for catapulting aircraft off the deck was envisioned for the carrier, a replacement for the Nimitz-class carriers that the navy has built since the late 1960s. Instead of steam-driven pistons, the new catapult uses electrical charges to generate magnetic fields that impel a carriage attached to an aircraft off the deck. Known as EMALS (electromagnetic aircraft launch system), the new catapult also generated unanticipated costs and a fifteen-month delay in the system's delivery.[28] A similar problem occurred with the ships' advanced arresting gear, which will also use electromagnetic force to "trap" planes as they return to the ship. According to the GAO, difficulties in submitting drawings of the proposed system to the navy resulted in a six-month delay in production and delivery of the system to the shipyard.[29] The ship's dual-band radar system— which combines in a single piece of equipment a ship's scanning and targeting radars—was scheduled to be built into the ship before its producers had completed the technology. The idea was sound but turned out to need more time to develop than anticipated. This caused project delays. Advanced technology is usually a benefit. The navy's recent experience has been a reminder that pacing the introduction of new technology to costs, incorporation into ships under construction, and degree of technological maturity are also critical to successful modernization. Chevrolet's electric car, the Volt, is an imperfect but instructive parallel. Among a host of other problems, its battery didn't deliver the expected mileage and performed sluggishly in cold weather. At over $40,000, it was priced at a level where only those with pocketbooks to match their enthusiasm could afford it. The lower-risk approach of other auto companies based on their legitimate concern about the maturity of existing technology is likely, over time, to prove more prudent and ultimately more profitable. The old advice about walking before running is sound, and the navy can bear eloquent witness to the cost of disregarding it.

The Washington-based think tank Center for Strategic and International Studies (CSIS) reviewed defense contract trends since 1990 and concluded that the navy has spent an increasing amount of money on research and development (R & D). The navy invested a maximum of $8 billion annually between 1990 and 2001 in R & D.[30] Beginning in 2002, this figure rose to $10 billion and in some years reached as high as $16 billion. These figures show the navy's emphasis on introducing more technologically sophisticated hardware. This investment stands to reason: under normal circumstances, times of relative peace are best suited for the research that must precede the greater technological sophistication needed to assure future naval superiority. But somewhere balance was lost. Throughout the 1990s, the navy spent no more than $8 billion on R & D. The trend changed beginning in 2002, when expenditures increased to $10 billion. After 2002 expenditures on R & D either increased or remained constant, until reaching a maximum of $16 billion in 2006. The navy's increasingly greater investment in R & D reflects what former assistant secretary of the navy George Sawyer called the acquisition team's emphasis on "capability, not production."[31] By contrast, throughout the 1980s the navy focused on production as it sought to build a six-hundred-ship fleet.[32] Sawyer observes that by 1985, all of the navy's programs were below budget and ahead of schedule. He argues that "ultimately the Navy was giving money back." While the ships that the navy purchased in the 1980s were not as sophisticated as those that the navy is currently building, Sawyer contended that the navy was able to maintain a reasonable acquisition budget because it chose to "stick with designs that worked." Sawyer argued that in recent years the navy's acquisition team has ratcheted up shipbuilding costs as it has focused on "the latest and greatest" that contractors have to offer. This has resulted ultimately in a dysfunctional relationship between the navy's acquisition team and the contractors. Part of this dysfunctionality is the navy's unrealistic time and budgetary assumptions. Sawyer attributed the delays and cost overruns that have plagued naval construction projects for the past ten to fifteen years to an unhealthy cocktail of technological overreach mixed with unachievable expectations.

The navy's LCS program is an instructive example of cost growth in recent naval shipbuilding projects that can be traced to the navy's mismanagement. In their statement before the House Armed Services Committee in 2007, officials from all the major contractors for the LCS program reported that the navy began changing its design of the ship almost as soon as the project began. In May 2004, Lockheed Martin received a list of new requirements after it had begun the construction of its final design in February of that year. The document directed fourteen thousand new technical requirements and twenty-three previously unreleased changes to such parts of the vessel as its propulsion and maneuvering, hull, control and navigation, and welding.[33] Lockheed Martin responded by adapting the design it had already begun to build. This resulted in over six hundred engineering changes to the lead ship.[34] Whatever technical benefits may have resulted from the navy's changes, the reworking required to implement them offset the schedule and began to pile delays upon delays.[35]

The LCS project also experienced significant amounts of rework as the shipyard's schedule for construction foundered between trying to maintain it and the unexpected. Because navy shipbuilding often relies on single suppliers, there are no alternatives when critical parts are delayed. The LCS's main reduction gear—the mechanical means by which power from the high-speed turbine is directed to the water jets that propel the ship—was damaged while it was being manufactured. This caused a six-month delay. The navy and the shipbuilders, however, were committed to meeting a deadline[36] and continued construction.[37] When the component finally arrived, the shipbuilders had to undo and redo all the work, which should have been completed only after the component was installed.[38] The contractors billed the navy for the added expense.

General Dynamics and Lockheed Martin were safe in signing on to the LCS program because the navy offered them cost-plus contracts: the navy would absorb expenses that exceeded the budget in order to meet the deadline. Congress identified the combination of cost-plus contracts and deadlines for completing the first vessels as a leading cause of the navy's unduly optimistic estimates in its budget. Flexibility in price mixed with rigidity in delivery schedules is no recipe for thrift. When evaluating the project in late 2007, the Senate Armed Services Committee asserted: "Long ago, we knew that we should not rush to sign a construction contract before we have solidified requirements. We also knew that the contractors will respond to incentives, and that if the incentives are focused on maintaining schedules and not on controlling cost, cost growth on a cost-plus contract should surprise no one. After the fact, everyone appears ready to agree that the original ship construction schedule for the lead ship was overly aggressive."[39]

After Congress cut $1 billion from the LCS program, the navy canceled its contract with Lockheed Martin because the contractor refused to change the terms of the contract from a cost-plus to a fixed-price agreement.[40] General Dynamics agreed to a fixed-price contract but still could not come to an agreement with the navy over the price.[41] Navy Admiral Charles Goddard stated in a Pentagon briefing that General Dynamics was simply "above the numbers we were willing to accept."[42] While one could conceivably blame the contractors for refusing to agree to a fixed-price contract, such an agreement—as one member of the defense media observed—is only fair provided that "the price target is seen as achievable based on the specifications," and "the Navy has a finished design that it will not interfere with once the contract is signed."[43] In this case, the navy could not measure up to either standard. Fixed-price contracts are meant to be planning guides that limit the purchaser's costs as they proscribe additional burdens on the contractor. They are not designed to give either party a competitive advantage over the other.

The LCS project also experienced significant cost growth because its contractors faced unanticipated scrutiny from government regulators while actual construction was under way. When Lockheed would submit a drawing for review to the appropriate authorities, it would expect a response in four to six weeks. When the answer arrived in twelve to sixteen weeks, deadlines were pushed further and further back.[44] Furthermore, oftentimes regulatory agencies were not in agreement, causing confusion concerning the design among the shipbuilders.[45] Many times regulatory agencies made significant design changes after the shipbuilders had already begun construction, leading to further rework.[46] The Rand study confirms that growing government contractual, statutory, and regulatory requirements contribute to the growth of expenses in building navy ships.[47] As the government's regulatory structure grows in volume and extent, the military feels the effects throughout. From protecting endangered species in the seas, the air, and on land to environmental impact statements on the large areas needed for realistic training to the socioeconomic and cultural effects of preparing for combat, proliferating government regulations have created a cottage industry within the military for monitoring, reporting, negotiating, and addressing federal and state regulatory requirements. This applies no less to shipbuilding. The Clean Air Act requires new paints that emit fewer toxins into the air after application. These demand research and expense in manufacturing. The Clean Water Act—reported one contractor—mandates the collection of rainwater before it enters the water supply. New regulations on asbestos, lead, methylene chloride (used, among other purposes, in paint stripping), and the use of forklifts have affected shipbuilders. The Rand study noted that compliance caused costs to rise 2 percent annually. This apparently small accretion is deceiving, especially if multiplied by even the reduced number of ships the navy builds today. For example, advance work on the navy's newest aircraft, U.S.S. *Gerald Ford*, began in 2005. The keel was laid four years later. If completed according to schedule, the ship will be delivered in 2015. The current cost is estimated at approximately $13.5 billion. At a minimum, the 2 percent annual rise that can be placed at the doorstep of regulatory compliance would increase the cost of the ship by over $16 million. Increasing regulations are a small but significant element of the spiking cost of ship construction—especially when the military budget is under greater and greater pressure. And, as though changes as a result of regulation are not already sufficiently expensive, the problem sharpens as the number of changes made throughout the construction of a ship increases when the design of a vessel is not clear, logical, and thoroughly proven before the first metal is turned. Such designs may be poor, innovative, untested, or ill-considered. For whatever reason, they are lumped together as "immature."

A GAO report released in 2007 on the rising cost of navy ships determined that shipbuilders' reliance on an immature design contributed greatly to the cost growth in the San Antonio–class amphibious assault ship.[48] A *Defense Industry Daily* article on cost increases in the project reported that "the need to tear down and rebuild completed sections of the LPD 17 was a major cause of its overruns."[49] Proceeding with a design that was not mature led to production that was out of sequence; Northrop Grumman delayed a lot of work that would otherwise have been completed before the integration of the hull until after the fact.[50] When the contractor finally accomplished these particular tasks, the defense media reported that the cost was driven up by nearly "five times the original" amount allotted for this part of the vessel. When the project was finally completed, the shipbuilders had still not succeeded in resolving the original design's ambiguities: the navy uncovered problems with the ship's steering system, reverse osmosis units, ship wide-area computing network, and electrical system two years after they had accepted delivery.

Institutional studies on the industrial base that supports America's defenses—and in particular, the navy's industrial base—are numerous and voluminous. They generally agree that there are ways to reduce cost growth and they find flaws in the navy's management of shipbuilding. The GAO argues for greater discipline in managing new technologies; designs that rely on new technologies must be mature before they are built. The Defense Department should establish a higher "confidence threshold" before committing to projects and making budget requests.[51] The navy should better manage its time for construction by authorizing construction of a new ship only after it approves its design.[52] The same report also suggests that the navy could find more effective ways of surveying and managing cost growth at the shipyards.

The Rand report makes a similar proposal. It contends that the navy should "stabilize the requirements for capability and technology" and notes that ships with more stable designs have lower cost increases, ones that correspond more or less with inflation.[53] Rand also suggests that the navy should consider building "smaller more mission-focused ships" to reduce rework expenses.[54]

Experienced professionals largely agree with the institutional findings. For example, Rear Admiral Carnevale holds that the navy's "mission has always been there." He acknowledges that the threat from foreign navies has changed, but observes that the U.S. Navy's missions of providing the stability on the high seas that American commerce and trade need, maintaining presence to protect American and allied strategic interests, responding to international crises as well as humanitarian emergencies, deterring conflict, and, if necessary, defeating an enemy continue. In fact, naval missions are multiplying as ambitious powers rise, lesser states fall, weapons of catastrophic potential proliferate, new areas of maritime interest—such as the Arctic—emerge, and our traditional European allies slowly disarm. The problem is that the navy has fewer ships than it has put to sea for nearly a century—and the possibility exists that U.S. naval force will continue to shrink. This increases the importance of building more ships based on stable designs, which U.S. shipyards could produce more cheaply and efficiently.

Other experts see the problem from complementary angles. Former assistant secretary of the navy George Sawyer, as noted above, agrees that constructing ships whose design is known and stable would increase the number of hulls the navy can use as it creates the jobs needed to sustain the shipbuilding industry. He identifies an excess of new technology as an important cause of rising prices. But he also offers explanations of why the navy favors high-technology solutions at the cost of producing a larger fleet. Sawyer argues that congressional legislation passed in the mid-1980s[55] tilted responsibility for acquisition from a balance between civilian and military leadership toward civilian control. This decreased the ability of naval officers to apply their experience to building ships. Thus the chief of naval operations' control over shipbuilding was reduced but not eliminated. Still, the changes the legislation wrought drained important operational knowledge from the process of deciding between the sometime conflicting but often concordant claims of shipbuilders and senior naval officers, both of which for different reasons were interested in the most recent, sophisticated, and expensive technology. Increasingly removed from the middle were naval officers with sufficient acquisition and operational experience to offer counterarguments, either to question their superiors' preference for overly complicated technology or to insist that industry discipline itself in its quest to manufacture and install the same complex and expensive combat solutions. The net result, as Dr. Larrie Ferreiro, director of research at the Defense Acquisition University, notes, is that the navy has found increasing difficulty in articulating to contractors precisely what it wants. The process of acquiring the ships that make up a fleet, which under normal circumstances is weighed down by bureaucracy, encumbered by honest differences of opinion about strategy, and subject to endless organizational flux, was rendered even more chaotic by the inability to communicate its needs to industry. So mistakes multiplied, the costs incurred by correcting them ascended, the number of ships launched fell, and those who constructed them saw their livelihood imperiled.

By contrast, Sawyer notes the navy's success in managing construction of the Virginia-class attack nuclear submarines. A four-star admiral retains command and control of the nuclear submarine program. This officer—as did his predecessors going back to Admiral Hyman Rickover—rules with a sleepless eye, one iron fist, and the other hand clenched just as tightly on the program's purse strings. Those who know—officers who have served aboard and commanded submarines—assist in supervising as decisions about a boat are made throughout its construction. Such cost overruns as have occurred can be laid up to dependence for critical equipment on sole sources, a fact of commercial life over which a single admiral has little control.

Others who have held senior responsibility for navy shipbuilding take similar views. Everett Pyatt, who served as principal deputy assistant secretary of the navy and then assistant secretary of the navy in the Carter and Reagan administrations, contends that with the Cold War won and in the wake of the mid-1980s congressional legislation, senior acquisition officials' interest in the most recent and untested technology supplanted the preservation of an appropriate-size fleet. Pyatt adds that as secretary of defense, Dick Cheney listened with sympathy to defense industry views and returned to the practice of cost-plus contracts, a policy that Clinton administration secretary of defense Bill Perry left untouched—and that Pyatt among others faults as needlessly expensive.

There is in sum a forest of pointing fingers to account for today's problems with the defense industrial base and in particular the navy's. But the view of the whole should not be missed in the details of the parts. The future of that portion of American industry with the experience and capability to build the warships for the U.S. combat fleet is at risk. The major culprit is decreasing orders for ships, which discourages the young from joining the workforce while the older and more experienced retire or look elsewhere for employment. Accomplices include legislation that upset the balance in naval acquisition between officers experienced in the ways of the sea and civilians who understood the demands of the Defense Department's labyrinthine acquisition process. An important, if partial, consequence has been the navy's troubled management of the acquisition process. This emphasized new technologies at the expense of constructing the larger fleet that current and likely future events require while the untested technologies were often as costly to make as they proved expensive to correct when their immaturity became apparent. The chaos fed upon itself. Where stable designs and crisply stated requirements would have allowed ships to be built at fixed costs, immature technologies accompanied by an insistence on speedy delivery opened the gates for contracts whose costs could be— and were—constantly revised upward.

The navy's problem with the industrial base that builds its ships is the nation's problem. There are many bandages that can be applied and then there are more invasive procedures. An example of the former is to purchase spare parts for ships. This would provide work that could help shipyards at the margins where businesses sink or swim. An example of the latter would be senior naval leadership's decision to emphasize building more combatants over developing and sending to sea revolutionary technologies. This does not prevent modernization. Evolutionary designs will be a slower path to more sophisticated technology, but a slower path to the most advanced technology is much to be preferred to a shrinking fleet that is already the smallest since 1916 and likely to contract further if the current course is maintained. A return of experienced naval officers to the business of acquiring ships would help assure that the impulse for the best— in this case, technology—does not sacrifice the good, in this case a U.S. maritime presence that is sufficiently large to accomplish the missions that the nation's leaders assign it. Moderation in the application of the expanding body of regulatory structure would also provide relief. These measures would all help lower costs and make more money available to build more ships. But the only effective solution that offers necessary sustenance to the industrial base at the same time that it begins to return the fleet to a size commensurate with its responsibilities and the nation's needs is to build more ships. There is no substitute for this. All other measures are half measures.

9

To Be a Great Power, or Not

ECHNOLOGY IS USEFUL, but it is not a cure for all that ails. Intelligent and imaginative U.S. Army commanders understood the importance of protecting the local population to achieve American objectives as the insurgency in Iraq intensified. In the insurgents' Iraqi stronghold of Anbar province, American commanders understood and exploited al-Qaeda's heavy-handed tactics. They succeeded in persuading local armed militias to switch sides, assist in safeguarding neighborhoods, and join the fight against armed holdouts. But superior technology is better than inferior instruments, and superior technology applied strategically can be decisive. Unmanned planes, land and surface craft, as well as submarines are likely—if their development continues—to reduce future American casualties, increase our military's ability to patrol in dangerous areas, add to the surgical ability to apply force, and greatly expand real-time intelligence of an enemy. These unmanned vehicles, as well as heightened attention to cyber warfare, are changing the character of warfare. It's not the first time.

The U.S. battleships that the Imperial Japanese Navy attacked at Pearl Harbor in 1941 existed to sink other battlewagons in a contest over command of the ocean's surface. While they were being built, however, naval aviation came into its own.

Instead of battleships' ability to throw heavy projectiles twenty or more miles, aircraft carriers could launch planes with ranges of a thousand or more miles armed with bombs, torpedoes, and cannon. This multiplied by orders of magnitude the range at which fleets could engage one another and represented an extraordinary increase in naval power's ability to influence events on shore. With planes from the aircraft carrier U.S.S. *Hornet*, Lieutenant Colonel James Doolittle led an air attack on Tokyo launched from a distance of six hundred miles less than half a year after Pearl Harbor. This innovation in naval tactics spawned another. Japan sent a carrier striking force to Midway Island in the central Pacific to seize the island's airbase and draw out U.S. carriers to punish and destroy them. The reverse came to pass. Planes from the U.S. carrier fleet destroyed the four carriers of the Japanese strike force at a distance of several hundred miles. Neither fleet ever glimpsed the other. The engagement ended the naval contest between the United States and Japan in the Pacific and prepared the way for another innovation in combat, the approach to the Japanese mainland by bitterly opposed amphibious assault. Americans' imagination in technology often has exceeded new and superior tactics. Where today's Chinese as well as the Soviets throughout the Cold War distinguished themselves mimicking Western design—called "reverse engineering"—the United States has often looked to technological innovation for an element of competitive advantage. Stealth technology, nuclear weapons, and submarines are among the better-known military results of American ingenuity.

Technology and tactics have transformed war at sea for centuries, but politics and economics have proved at least as disruptive to the established maritime order. The western Pacific had reckoned in American strategic calculations from the early nineteenth century. Commodore Matthew Perry had persuaded Japan to open trade with the United States in the mid-nineteenth century. East Asia did not command American attention until the attack on Pearl Harbor, which bore a logical connection to the militarism that infected Japanese society beginning with the return of imperial rule in 1868 known as the Meiji Restoration. The order that the United States subsequently imposed on the western Pacific was made possible by defeating Japan and forcing it to retreat from the areas it had occupied in Asia and the Pacific. Beginning with the American occupation of Japan, East Asia's economic fortunes have looked ever upward. Japan today is the world's third-largest economy. After the United States, China is the world's second-largest. The American military remains a foundation of the stability that is key to Asian prosperity. U.S. guarantees have helped keep the peace on the Korean Peninsula and in the complex relations between Taiwan and China. Sustained peace in the vast area from the Indian Ocean's western reaches to the western Pacific over the next century depends on respect for such international norms as sovereignty and the free use of air-, sea-, and cyberspace. A failure to respect these standards leads in the opposite direction, toward insecurity, a revival of age-old ethnic and national tensions, and deepening instability.

Combined with its assertion that the international waters of the South China Sea are a "core interest," claims over disputed islands in the region, and repeated incidents at sea with other states' commercial and naval shipping, China's military buildup threatens to produce the uncertainty and instability that risk the Indo-Pacific's secure future. None of this changes a fundamental premise of U.S. naval power, that the forward presence of superior forces is a condition of keeping the peace. But the oceanic nature of the Indo-Pacific region and general agreement that the United States should avoid a land war in Asia raise the difficult question of whether the naval forces that exist in the U.S. fleet today are the right size and shape for the task of countering China's current and likely future strengths and exploiting its vulnerabilities. For example, do large-deck aircraft carriers that may be vulnerable to China's antiship ballistic missiles offer the surest and least expensive answer to control the access to China's oceanic portal, the South China Sea? No. Until the safety of America's carriers from Chinese ballistic-missile attack can be assured, submarines offer a more secure and more believable means to control the seas closest to China. Would a U.S. fleet that possessed a larger number of ships that can protect the United States and its allies against medium-range ballistic missiles keep regional friends in the fold before and during a crisis? Yes. If the most powerful member of an alliance can neither limit its partners' risk nor assure a reasonable amount of their security, allies will look elsewhere for safety. And if substantial changes are required, can America afford them? Absolutely. Shipbuilding is a small fraction of the navy's budget, a minuscule percent of the total defense budget, a drop in the bucket compared to the total federal budget, and a rounding error when set alongside the U.S. GDP. Americans still have the resources. The question is whether we retain the understanding of seapower that previous generations going back to the Founders possessed, and whether we still have the will to maintain such power.

Atop the strategic heights the United States occupied during the Cold War was its lasting and versatile economic strength relative to that of the Soviet Union. Since the end of the Cold War the United States has become the world's largest debtor nation. The United States owes more money than anyone else. A former governor of the Federal Reserve estimated at the end of 2010 that if inflation does not become a serious problem, interest on the debt will rise from $847 billion in 2015 to $1.15 trillion by 2019.[1] The interest payments projected for 2019 amount to 73 percent more than the total U.S. defense budget, combat operations included, for fiscal year 2010. Current administration fiscal and economic policy has created mounting political pressure to reestablish order over the government's finances. It is inconceivable that the Obama administration failed to anticipate that one by-product of a massive increase in indebtedness would be vigorous political pressure to truncate defense spending. International developments may change political will about such cuts, but unforeseen conflicts are answered with the equipment that already exists in the national arsenal, not by increasing expenditures on forces designed for the future. The Obama administration's cuts in defense raise the question of whether the United States will have the military power to deter such known potential challenges as those that come from North Korea, China, a nuclear-armed Iran, and growing strategic uncertainty in the Middle East. In 2009, Secretary of Defense Gates canceled twenty major weapons systems. More reductions followed. He later said that he had "cancelled, capped, or ended" more than thirty programs that, if completed, would have cost more than $300 billion. In 2010, Gates announced a plan to cut $78 billion from the defense budget over the next five years. In August 2011, the Obama administration agreed to a deal with Congress in which the debt ceiling was raised. As part of that deal, the Obama administration plans to cut an additional $489 billion from defense over the next decade. This amounts to well over $800 billion in completed and projected defense cuts. To that sum must now be added the nearly $600 billion in defense cuts over the next ten years that were required if a special committee of Congress failed to agree on cutting the long-term federal deficit by the end of November 2011. They failed. So the total of cuts made plus those that are envisioned comes to more than $1.2 trillion. This may allow the Obama administration to claim that the U.S. military preserves its technological edge. But it will cut shipbuilding further and continue the disappearance of American seapower from the world's oceans. Sequestration when added to the administration's other cuts is likely to decrease naval spending from its current level of $156.4 billion per year to slightly more than $130 billion per year.[2] This will likely drop naval shipbuilding's budget from the $17.7 billion that the Congressional Budget Office (CBO) calculates is needed annually to carry out the navy's 2012 shipbuilding plan to $13.8 billion.[3] Scaling back the navy's shipbuilding budget by almost one-fourth stands a good chance of cutting the U.S. combat fleet by another 7 percent by 2025, leaving it 17 percent short of the minimum size required to perform its assigned missions. The consequence is foreseeable and inevitable: American global leadership will continue to diminish, along with the nation's ability to protect its interest in keeping conflicts at a distance from our shores.

Why does an organization that operates a global fleet spend a mere one-tenth of its annual revenues to construct ships themselves? Because the cost of basic pay, such benefits as housing and health coverage, and retirement pay consumes almost exactly what the navy spends on procurement, in 2010, approximately $44 billion.[4] Procurement also includes aircraft and such other items as the Marine Corps, weapons, and ammunition. Other budget necessaries include the considerable cost of operating ships and aircraft. For fiscal year 2010, operating ships and aircraft as well as the Marine Corps, paying for bases across the country and around the world, and maintaining in good order the arsenal of missiles, bombs, bullets, and guns carried aboard Navy Department ships and aircraft cost $43 billion.

Despite accumulating federal indebtedness, the printing of money to pay the difference between what investors are willing to lend to the United States and what the administration wishes to spend, and the growing burden of servicing what has already been borrowed, the navy hopes that it will be able to maintain the current approximate level of $15 billion per year on shipbuilding into the indefinite future. This hope is not foolish, although it represents a substantive increase over the average of $13 billion the navy has spent on shipbuilding each year over the past decade. But hope is better as a religious precept than a foundation for growing a fleet. Adding nondiscretionary federal spending to debt service produces sums that defy imaginable solution through any combination of tax increases and spending cuts: valiant efforts to preserve defense spending as well grounded as they are in necessity, the American Founders' intent,[5] and an evermore chaotic world may not succeed when put to the test of politics.

However, the United States must have a navy to defend its maritime interests, and the one that is currently envisioned by naval leadership deserves first consideration as a picture of the nation's maritime future. In 2009 the navy anticipated increasing the size of its combat fleet from about 285 ships to 322 ships by 2038. This growth would have required more money each year for shipbuilding than the average amounts the navy had received over the past thirty years and much more money than anyone thought possible. The plan was shelved. In 2011 the navy reduced to 237 the size of the fleet it anticipated at the end of the thirty-year cycle, which it normally projects.[6] But three decades is a long time. Defense budgets are more meaningful as pictures of the shorter periods for which they actually plan.

Changing the Shape of the Fleet

The Navy Plan . . . Less of the Same and a Bow to Change

In fiscal year 2011 the navy anticipated that between 2008 and 2015 it would build one aircraft carrier—in addition to the U.S.S. *George H. W. Bush*, commissioned in early 2009, thirteen nuclear-propelled attack submariners, nine destroyers, and twenty-one shallow draft vessels (called littoral combat ships [LCS], which displace slightly less than 3,000 tons and are designed for quick movement between offshore theaters where they would hunt submarines, look for and destroy mines, and attack and destroy enemy warships). Additional ships to be constructed by 2015 include two large amphibious ships (called "landing transport docks" or LPDs and displacing nearly 25,000 tons) that carry two seaborne and one airborne U.S. Marine Corps systems for conducting an opposed landing, and another large amphibious ship (called an "amphibious assault ship" or LHA and displacing 45,000 tons) whose closest relative is a full aircraft carrier. The ship is designed to carry aircraft that transport marines ashore and support them when they have landed. Four new combat logistics ships on which the fleet depends critically for resupply of such items as ammunition are scheduled to be

One of the new Joint High Speed Vessels (JHSV) currently under construction

constructed by 2015, in addition to three members of a new class of vessel, the mobile landing ship (MLP) to assist in moving equipment from logistics ships to combat vessels where no ports are available to allow such a transfer. Ten new shallow-draft, high-speed ships with flight decks that allow helicopter operations are also in the plan for 2015. Called Joint High Speed Vessels (JHSV), they will carry Special Operations Forces, army, or Marine Corps troops and/or supporting equipment and disembark them in the minimal port facilities characteristic of Third World states. A single large, seagoing tug completes the 2015 procurement program. In all, the 2009 plan would have built seventy-six ships; the 2011 plan expects to add ten fewer.

Political priorities as well as the frugality born of straitened circumstances are not the only causes of the navy's decision to build a smaller fleet in the future. The cost of building ships has been creeping up steadily since the 1980s when the average cost of ship amounted to $1.2 billion. Measured in constant (2009) dollars, this figure had climbed to $2 billion twenty years later and the Congressional Budget Office naval analyst estimated at $2.7 billion the average cost of a ship in the navy's 2009 ship-building plan. More expensive technological capability, a decrease in competition as large defense companies swallowed smaller ones, and the navy's inability to discipline shipbuilding costs contributed to the doubling of costs over the period. The navy's 2011 plan removes inflation hedges from future estimates and, by increasing the number of lower-cost support ships—like the JHSV and the mobile landing ship—allows the navy to predict a decrease of over 25 percent in the average cost of a ship. A lightly armed ferry is cheaper than a destroyer meant to go in, and emerge vic-toriously from, harm's way. None of this denies that the average number of ships the navy builds in a year has dropped precipi-tously since the 1980s when that number stood at 17.2. In the 2011 plan, the average number of ships the navy plans to build is 9.2. The fleet's continued shrinkage is the product of many causes. Steadily contracting numbers of ships purchased annu-ally is one of the surest distress signals.

However, the measures of a fleet's strength have been debated since classical times when, for example, the Athenian navy sought advantage by increasing the number of banks of rowers and armoring their warships. Numbers remain extremely impor-tant, but speed, armor, firepower, maneuverability, survivability, and most of all the suitability to national strategy of the missions that fleets are designed to carry out weigh heavily in measuring naval strength. The new littoral combat ships that the navy plans to have built by 2015 emphasize high-speed movement between coastal waters that may be separated by large distances and a growing ability to fight in littoral areas close to coasts. The less expensive shallow-draft JHSVs aim at a related objective, the swift arrival of equipment and/or ground troops for the kinds of irreg-ular wars that the United States has fought in Iraq and Afghanistan as well as the ability to operate close to shore and help train small states' maritime forces to defend their own coasts. Devoting scarce resources to these and such other vessels as the mobile landing ship—which permits transit of cargo from large logistics vessels to land where port facilities are minimal, unavailable, or nonexistent—show naval leadership's understanding that a portion of American interests has changed significantly since the end of the Cold War. Instead of creating a fleet designed chiefly to neutralize the Soviets' blue-water threat and project aircraft carrier–borne airpower in support of large-scale ground operations to defend Western Europe, the navy is emphasizing greater participation in humanitarian operations; training friendly and partner states' coastal navies; taking part in antipiracy operations; destroying swarms of small enemy craft operating close to coasts, such as the force that Iran possesses in the Persian Gulf; conducting mine warfare, especially at key choke points in major sea routes; and preventing the shipment by sea of weapons of mass destruction to American or allied ports. All these missions draw U.S. naval force away from the safety of the open seas and toward more dangerous coastal waters where threats from low-cost, very quiet diesel-electric submarines must be added to the possibility of shore-launched missile attacks, land-based aircraft, mines, and land-bracketed spaces that constrain the freedom of maneuver and easily visible horizons enjoyed on the high seas. At the same time, American naval leadership senses the danger in China's rise as a naval power and the possibility of a modest return of Russia's naval force. These facts are an open secret. Every naval officer knows them, but political correctness and administration policy have muzzled open discussion, especially where it is needed most: in public justification of the naval budget, which aims to preserve traditional large combat ships while adding the partnerships and humanitarian missions associated with littoral operations.

In sum, U.S. naval leadership recognizes threats from the shore that could reduce or deny the navy's ability to approach land closely enough to influence events on it. Naval leaders also see the political advantages of operating in benign coastal areas where partnerships with other navies and humanitarian assistance or disaster relief could demonstrate value to U.S. national leadership's focus on the unconventional conflicts that now occupy the U.S. military's land forces. The other prong of naval strategy, the less publicly visible one, is the navy leadership's growing appreciation of the traditional naval threat that China poses today and could pose far more seriously in the foreseeable future.

The looming problem is cost. Even the smaller ships the navy proposes to build—the littoral combat ships—come at a substantial price, approximately $550 million per ship, which does not include the cost of the separate antisubmarine warfare, anti–surface ship warfare, and minesweeping systems— perhaps as little as $100 million each—that can be moved from one vessel to another in its class as operational circumstances require. The navy plans to buy fifty-five vessels and a smaller number of the individual fighting systems that can be moved from one LCS to another. The next three aircraft carriers—of the new Gerald Ford class—that the navy must build if it is to maintain a fleet of eleven such ships will cost between $11.4 billion and $13.8 billion each[7] and the airplanes aboard each ship another $10 billion. The DDG-1000 class destroyer of which the navy originally intended to build thirty-two sank when costs exploded.[8] The current plan is to purchase three vessels, which are expected to cost $3 billion per ship.[9] The less expensive destroyers, the Arleigh Burke–class, which will be substituted for the more expensive DDG-1000 class, are projected to cost approximately $1.75 billion each. Building new nuclear-propelled submarines to replace those that are nearing the end of their useful service lives will also be expensive. For example, the replacement to the Los Angeles–class attack submarine, of which forty-five were built, the Virginia class, is expected to cost approximately $2 billion each and the navy anticipates

The 1,000 ton deckhouse of the future U.S.S. Zumwalt, a DDG-1000 model, being lowered into its future position

building two each year beginning in 2011. The two LPDs mentioned above that the navy plans to build by 2015 come with a price tag of $2 billion each. The LHA is expected to cost $3.4 billion without its aircraft.

Other large potential costs must also be reckoned. Convinced that a redundant force offers the greatest power to persuade a potential enemy state that a nuclear attack against the United States or its allies would be suicidal, the United States cleaves to the general idea of nuclear deterrence forces that was developed in the Cold War. Its chief virtue was considered to be its division into three parts: missiles launched from land-based silos, large aircraft capable of delivering weapons at transcontinental distances, and Ohio-class submarines that patrol the world's oceans armed with solid-fuel missiles whose multiple and independently targetable warheads can reach well over four thousand miles. Each submarine has space for twenty-four such missiles and there are fourteen of these nuclear-powered Ohio-class vessels. These submarines will begin reaching the end of their useful service life in the late 2020s. The replacement cost of an individual submarine is estimated at approximately $7 billion. The navy's 2011 plan calls for a reduction—from fourteen to twelve—in the number of the ballistic missile–carrying fleet, so the bill would total about $85 billion (current dollars) when the Ohio class had been replaced. The new subs—like their predecessors—answer national strategic goals rather than the more strictly speaking maritime strategic missions of the rest of the fleet. Thus, the question of whether the navy would be required to fund these submarines from the sum it allots to shipbuilding—or whether Congress would add money to the navy's shipbuilding accounts—remains open and deeply important to the navy's ability to carry out the remainder of its shipbuilding program. Additional costs can be anticipated if national leadership decides that more ships capable of shooting down enemy missiles are required.

Among these unknowns, the Congressional Budget Office finds one point clear. The 2011 plan to build 276 ships from 2011 to 2040 will *not* result in the 322-ship fleet that the navy says is needed to accomplish its missions. Navy estimates count on an annual shipbuilding budget of $16 billion for the next three decades, or about 6.6 percent higher than their average over the past thirty years. The CBO estimates that $21 billion would be needed annually for each of the next thirty years to achieve the navy's goals, and that the disparity between the money the navy hopes for and what it needs to build the envisioned fleet will not produce a 322-ship force but one that is composed of 237 ships. The CBO's figures show that instead of growing by 12 percent, the size of the navy will shrink by 16 percent. Their projections envision a fleet that is over one-fourth smaller than what the navy needs in 2040.

The point should not be lost in a flurry of numbers and long-range estimates. The navy sees a requirement for a larger fleet in the future than the one it sails today. But between the increasing cost of ships the navy wants to purchase and the possibility of decreasing resources to pay for them, the likelihood is that the U.S. fleet will diminish substantially over the next thirty years.

The least likely solution to the problem of dwindling resources and rising cost is that the threat will vanish or wither. China's economic growth could weaken and sweep away Beijing's steady progress toward expanding naval power. The price of oil might dive and stay low, depriving Russia of the resources to increase its military forces and renew its ability to project global power. And diplomacy or the threat or use of force could drive the wind from the sails of Iran and North Korea's nuclear ambitions. But these are a frayed thread from which to hang the future of U.S. maritime dominance. Another improbable is a swift national recovery from the United States' indebtedness and its accompanying ills. Continued long-range national debt lessens the chance that more resources will be available to pay for the navy's shipbuilding plans.

The evil twin of spiraling expense is dwindling fleet size. No matter how much military capability is squeezed into a single platform, one vessel cannot be in two places at the same time. Impressive advances in naval technology may moderate this fact by extending the range of their weapons. But distance is likely to continue to tyrannize. A ship patrolling off San Diego is not likely soon to be able to locate and sink a submarine maneuvering in the approaches to Zhanjiang. Introducing the littoral combat ship is a change that acknowledges the shift—at least for now—of naval warfare away from blue toward green (i.e., coastal) waters. But the rest of the fleet is molded in the expectation that large, expensive vessels with a host of combat systems are as well suited to face down smaller unconventional coastal threats from piracy to dangerous illicit cargoes as they are to address the burgeoning challenge of a maritime-oriented China. The corollary assumption is that a fleet of this shape is as applicable to the future as it once was to the solitary challenge of a continental-looking Soviet Union.

A New Navy Fighting Machine: Larger Fleet, Lower Cost

A different approach is to start by questioning the assumptions on which the navy has designed its future fleet. The most fundamental argument here is that the navy faces two challenges in the future. Unlike the navy's declared policy, *The New Navy Fighting Machine* (NNFM), a study written for the Defense Department's Office of Net Assessment[10] by Captain Wayne Hughes, U.S.N. (ret.), along with several other faculty members from the Naval Postgraduate School and offered in a report that was made public early in 2010, sees threats from both small, irregular, unconventional warfare fought largely in coastal areas *and* from the growing naval and military power of China. The remainder of the NNFM asks and answers questions of how to fit design, cost, and size to these twin threats. Does a shrinking naval force of expensive ships equipped to perform a variety of tasks provide the United States the global presence and capability that a larger but less costly fleet might? Do large-deck aircraft carriers that displace 100,000 tons and carry one hundred planes with a crew of five thousand still make sense when they may be increasingly threatened, for example, by China's antiship ballistic missiles? Could a larger number of smaller carriers provide better value and more security? As coastal navies strengthen and the Chinese navy expands its reach, is the U.S. Navy's concentration over the past several decades on projecting force ashore—using missiles and aircraft—as important as its earlier emphasis on being able to sweep the sea of enemy ships? Where today's large aircraft carriers are vulnerable to missile attack, submarines could prove very useful in such areas as the South China Sea, which is China's oceanic door to the world. Submarines can patrol unseen, armed with cruise missiles that threaten an enemy's ability to command and control his forces. They can threaten surface combatants and commercial shipping. They can help enforce blockades. Nuclear-powered submarines are very expensive. Could diesel-electric submarines offer a way to increase the size of the U.S. fleet while reducing its cost? Would a larger U.S. naval force composed of "capable-enough" vessels that can perform a single mission well rather than the current design of ships equipped for all warfare challenges at sea give the U.S. greater global presence, visibility, and influence—and at lower cost?

These are some of the ideas contained in the Hughes study, which takes its intellectual inspiration from Rear Admiral Bradley A. Fiske's 1916 book, *The Navy as a Fighting Machine*, specifically Fiske's aim to unify the design of ships with tactics and national security policy including military strategy. Rather than change the mix of ships in the fleet—as the navy has proposed—the Hughes study examined the fundamentals of the United States' need for naval power in the twenty-first century and attempted to conceive a force that matched ship design and purpose to foreseeable events. This evolutionary alternative to the navy's current shape seeks cost savings in combining smaller but more numerous ships designed for a single purpose together with the ships in the navy's fleet today whose large size makes them inviting targets and whose multiple missions increase costs significantly.

Equally important, the Hughes study parts company with the navy's official and largely indifferent attitude toward China as expressed most sharply in naval leadership's strategically unaccountable refusal to mention the word "China" in the new maritime strategy the navy published in the autumn of 2007. Sensibly designed forces depend vitally on answering the question, "What are they intended to accomplish?" Hughes's strategic maritime alternative offers an intelligent, coherent answer: increase America's ability to influence China in Asia by being able to:

1. Use submarines to sink Chinese naval and merchant ships and mine the approaches to China's ports;

2. Threaten Chinese shipping at sea with airborne reconnaissance and surface patrol vessels operating under the protection of the main U.S. battle fleet;

3. Field small, inexpensive coastal warships that can defend such Asian allies, friends, or partners as Indonesia, Malaysia, the Philippines, South Korea, Taiwan, and Vietnam;

4. Protect energy and mineral resources in the contested islands of the South China Sea and surrounding disputed ocean areas;

5. Use satellites and long-range unmanned aerial vehicles for reconnaissance and U.S. Air Force long-range bombers that can threaten effective escalation if such threats are needed to keep a conflict from widening;

6. Maintain land-based fighter aircraft in such regional bases as those in Japan, Okinawa, and South Korea as a hedge against Chinese expansion of a possible naval conflict to include American allies' territory;

7. Rather than risk an aircraft carrier, place new and powerful coastal combatants in Taiwanese waters where they can survive attack and materially assist in blocking a mainland attack.

The sum of these objectives would be a profound change for the U.S. Navy. Missing from the above list of seven is a major role for what has been at the heart of U.S. naval force since World War II, the aircraft carrier. The objective in a naval conflict with China would be to deny its ability to use the seas for commerce, warfare, and the intimidation of its enemies or America's friends. The vulnerability of large American aircraft carriers to China's antiship ballistic missiles and the limited range of the aircraft aboard U.S. carriers shift the burden of projecting effective power from large-deck carriers and toward submarines and aircraft that depart from and return to bases that are beyond China's shore-based missiles and long-range aircraft. Large-deck supercarriers, which displace about 100,000 tons, and their hundred aircraft—such as the United States has operated for decades—are significant targets. The loss of a single one with its crew of five thousand would be a major blow to U.S. naval power and to national prestige. The Hughes study argues that smaller carriers that displace a weight equal to one-third or less than the current ones, and of which more than one hundred were deployed in World War II, would—as a result of their bigger number—allow greater U.S. aircraft carrier presence around the world and usefulness in the small and irregular wars whose end no one today sees. This would not require mothballing the supercarrier fleet, but rather replacing some of its vessels as they reach the end of their useful service life so that the U.S. aircraft carrier fleet increases from its current level of ten to sixteen carriers, of which there would be six supercarriers and ten "light" carriers. This would reduce the size of the navy's carrier-borne aircraft to 620, or 12 percent fewer than current levels.[11] The cost of the lighter carriers is expected to be one-fourth to one-third the cost of the navy's new U.S.S. *Gerald R. Ford*–class supercarrier. The study warns that with current shipbuilding budgets and increasing costs, the navy's fleet of supercarriers will diminish to a total of eight in the next twenty years unless smaller carriers are introduced.[12]

But if the navy and some of its critics divide over China's importance as a justification for future U.S. seapower, there is agreement about the future of naval operations near the world's shores. Indeed, a basic tenet of the Hughes study coincided with a conclusion the navy had already reached. Littorals matter more as new powers emerge and nations scramble to protect their immediate surroundings against such threats as those that weak states, proliferation, piracy, and resource competition offer. These threats have long since supplanted the Cold War jockeying of small states amid the crosswinds of competing and hostile ideologies. U.S. maritime strategy, the Hughes reports agrees, should take advantage of opportunities in these coastal areas at the same time that it defends itself against threats.

The East African coast, northern coast of South America, and western Persian Gulf coast are good examples where partnerships and assistance serve American interests in stability and security. Friendly relations as the result of military-to-military training, the provision of medical services, and humanitarian and disaster relief as needed would help offset China's interest in establishing the East African coast as a base of operations in the event of a naval contest for control of the Indian Ocean through which much of China's oil supplies flow by tanker. Partnerships and training along with similar humanitarian aid would also help contain Venezuela if it becomes a serious threat in the region. Firm working relationships with friendly Persian Gulf coast states is good policy where the prospect of a nuclear-armed Iran would profoundly alter the strategic status quo in one of the world's most important bodies of water.

But if partnerships and cooperation offer opportunity close to shore, the same geographic areas also come with risk. More dangerous forms of naval operations in littoral areas include turning back threats from land-based missiles,[13] swarms of small missile-armed boats—such as are characteristic of Iran's Revolutionary Guards—mine clearing, and defending against hostile and very quiet diesel-electric submarines if, for example, the United States needs to land amphibious forces in the face of determined opposition in the future.

The danger to ships from forces ashore has waxed and waned over the centuries. Oar-driven galleys whose masters preferred to hug coasts because the size of the crew, cargo, and armament restricted space for water and food risked raids from darting smaller vessels that stayed in port except to plunder. As Byzantine power slacked in the tenth century, Venice had to provide its own protection against pirates who hid in the coves and inlets of islands along the Dalmatian shore and sallied out to prey on passing Venetian ships, even merchantmen armed for naval combat.[14] Almost six centuries later, Christian refugees from Ottoman rule in the Balkans—known as Uskoks—used small twenty-oared boats that swarmed out of land bases in the northern Adriatic to attack both Turkish and Venetian shipping.[15] Great wind-driven sailing ships loosened large navies' ties to land and sharpened naval warfare's focus on enemies' threat to life- or empire-sustaining seagoing trade. But technology in the form of mines and torpedoes heightened the threat to warships operating in coastal areas at the beginning of the twentieth century. Today's missiles represent a return to greater danger in the world's littorals.

Current U.S. maritime strategy depends on a mixture of high-performance and expensive ships for noncombat and combat missions in the littorals. The navy's idea of a global fleet station, for example, puts a mother ship off the coast of an area of immediate interest to the United States, like the Caribbean, along with smaller shallow-draft vessels. The mother ship is the command and supply center. The smaller ships ferry medical supplies as well as uniformed personnel who provide a range of services from humanitarian to military training. The navy envisions four such global fleet stations. Keeping a single large naval vessel at sea demands at least three similar ships in waiting: one that is training so that it can relieve the on-station ship when its six-month deployment is over, another that is undergoing intermediate maintenance, and a third that needs to be dry-docked for major overhaul. Four global fleet stations require twelve ships. Will these ships be selected from among those that are now in the fleet, for example, large amphibious platforms that cost a minimum of $2 billion each? The Hughes study recommends ships with less combat capability, since they are not intended to go in harm's way, and that cost one-eighth the price of one of today's large amphibious ships. The idea is straightforward enough: designing and building ships to perform a single mission—in this case a peaceful one—is cheaper than calling on the resources of large, battle-hardened, multipurpose vessels intended to defend against modern firepower. The Hughes study alternative aims at creating a naval force in which costs are moderated by increasing the number of vessels and decreasing the number of tasks each is designed and built to accomplish.

The navy's littoral combat ship, as its name indicates, is designed to operate in the coastal waters that abut those of the world's land ribbons experiencing rapid population increases. It is a mixture of the old idea of building ships that can perform many functions and the Hughes notion of constructing vessels at lower cost intended for a single purpose. The LCS was designed so that different weapons systems, contained in boxes called modules, could be moved quickly from one member of the class to another. So an LCS that can track down and destroy submarines one day can be speedily transformed into a vessel that hunts for surface targets on another. The LCS's high speed— between 44 and 47 knots—allows it to move quickly from one region to another. The vessel has been the subject of prolonged debate within naval circles, not because there is doubt about the need for a ship smaller and cheaper than a destroyer that can transit swiftly among distant trouble spots and protect against missile boats, mines, and submarines. Rather, skeptics have argued that the LCS is too large to function successfully in coastal areas, too small to operate on the high seas, and too expensive in any event. Still, LCSs are being built. The navy will have the opportunity to see how usefully they can do what they are designed to do. Most important, the idea of a single class of ship that can be transformed to conduct several different missions will be tested, as will the usefulness of a ship specifically intended to play a major role in coastal waters. Critics of the LCS, however, ask whether costs could not be reduced by experimenting with modular ships that other navies have built and that incorporate the same design.

There are in fact several alternatives to the 3,000-ton LCS. One is ships that have already been built with characteristics designed for the same littoral purposes, for example, the Danish navy's Flyvefisken 450-ton multirole patrol craft, which uses modules to change its mission from hunting for mines to searching for and destroying submarines to attacking surface ships. It costs less than one-fourth as much as what is projected for the

LCS with its weapons module. A larger vessel that already exists in the littoral-focused Danish navy with the same modular technology is the 3,500-ton Thetis-class patrol frigate. Like its smaller sister, the Thetis class can be easily and quickly equipped with modules that allow it to conduct antisubmarine warfare, anti–surface ship warfare, and other related littoral missions. The Thetis class costs about half what is expected for the LCS. Purchasing such a ship or two of its class would give the navy a chance to learn the strengths and weaknesses of the modular approach and decide whether, or if, changes are needed in its ideas of using such vessels for operations in coastal waters.

Another alternative is nonmodular design. Instead of building one vessel into which different warfare systems can be inserted, a nonmodular means of addressing the challenges of littoral warfare would produce smaller, more numerous ships that serve a single purpose. Rather than constructing a host of relatively large and expensive LCS-class combatants that can switch missions using different exchangeable equipment, the navy could purchase ships whose sole purpose would be to clear mines, or hunt subs, or search for and destroy surface ships. This would also offer a less expensive solution to the challenges of littoral warfare because it would give more contracts to American shipyards, which need work to preserve skills and retain skilled employees. It would also produce a larger fleet and, thus, one that is better equipped to demonstrate sustained American naval presence in those areas of the world where it is most needed.

The littoral ship is not the only class in which simplicity could result in lesser cost, a larger fleet, and the strategic good of a more widely distributed global navy. A fundamental assumption of American naval design as technology adds threats from the air and beneath the surface to those that already exist from surface vessels and shore batteries has been to proof each individual member of the surface fleet against the gamut of multiplying dangers. The NNFM asks whether defending all ships equally well is worth value when threats vary widely between the low and high end of warfare at sea; cost matters increasingly, and more combatants are needed to fulfill the navy's global missions as technology and political changes weigh importantly. Hughes, for example, contends that improving missile technologies are shifting the advantage in warfare at sea in favor of the attacker at the expense of the defender. China's antiship ballistic missile, which is intended to put out of action or sink a ship as large as an aircraft carrier, is a good example. Another is the proliferation of high-speed, low-observable antiship cruise missiles. The NNFM argues in favor of smaller antimissile frigate-size ships that can defend against submarines and destroy enemy ships as a means of increasing the navy's sea control ability. This, too, represents an important deflection from the approach of recent decades when navy strategy emphasized the use of missiles and aircraft to protect a battle group's ability to destroy land targets. The rise of China's navy and littoral warfare shifts emphasis from projecting power ashore toward traditional sea control. Because the Pacific is so vast and maintaining supply lines across it so difficult, and because the Chinese population outnumbers America's by about 4.3:1, threatening to sink China's navy or interrupt its commerce at sea is a better option than a land war in Asia. It is clearly better to isolate a conflict to the seas than to exchange missile attacks on each other's homeland.

As with its other proposals, the forcefulness of the NNFM's ideas is complemented by the moderation of its recommendations. Gutting the navy's current surface fleet is not in the picture. What *is* in the picture is reducing from the current number of eighty-six to thirty the number of traditional large, multipurpose surface ships—8,000 tons or more—equipped with expensive and highly capable computer tracking and targeting systems for the prudent reasons of maintaining advanced technology and sustaining shipyards that produce them. These reductions would be balanced by adding ninety frigate-size combatants (2,500 to 3,000 tons) whose ability to defend themselves from submarine threats and sink enemy ships could be purchased at about $400 million each. Again, this change in force would bend U.S. naval power toward winning and thus deterring a naval conflict in the western Pacific, instead of its far more destructive alternatives. However, single ships that can deliver naval gunfire, neutralize submarines, protect against missile threats, sweep the seas of hostile vessels, and threaten land targets remain a valuable deterrent, especially to persuade a potential enemy that the United States still possesses the ability to strike land targets where necessary. This ability would be preserved—but at a lower cost than that incurred by the large, multipurpose surface vessels that are the backbone of the navy's current surface fleet. The NNFM would create a fleet of simple, low-cost corvettes, each armed with land attack missiles to retain the navy's striking power ashore. Again, the details should not be allowed to obscure the strategic insight. The NNFM proposes the same capability that exists in the fleet today, or even more capability, by fielding smaller, less expensive, and more numerous vessels that increase effectiveness, safety, presence, and global reach.

Nowhere is the contrast greater between the U.S. Navy's current traditions and the NNFM's ideas than in submarine warfare and design. Admiral Hyman Rickover, whose career spanned sixty-four years—he enrolled as a midshipman at the U.S. Naval Academy in 1918 and retired as a full admiral in 1982—built the nuclear submarine fleet, starting with the launch of U.S.S. *Nautilus* in 1954. Under his iron-willed and imaginative leadership, the navy's submarine community marched together with the discipline of a Roman legion in defense of the range, staying power, and stealth of boats whose nuclear propulsion systems allow them to remain submerged for months and do not need to be refueled for decades—if at all. One signal benefit, especially during the Cold War, was the ability of ballistic missile–carrying subs, known as "boomers," to patrol the world's oceans undetected without risking detection by surfacing. This helped assure the Soviets that a nuclear first strike—even an unimaginably successful one against U.S. land-based intercontinental ballistic missiles and long-range aircraft—would not leave the United States bereft of the ability to retaliate in kind. Today, all U.S. submarines are nuclear-powered.

However, there is a price for the speed, range, and stealth of nuclear-powered submarines, whether they are built as part of the nation's nuclear deterrent or equipped to launch missile strikes at land targets or to hunt other submarines and surface ships. The current class of attack submarines—the Virginia class—range up to $2.5 billion each. The improvements that the navy would like to make will increase the cost to $3.3 billion per boat. Current plans call for the navy to build forty-six attack submarines from 2013 to 2042, twenty-seven of the $2.9 billion type and nineteen of the $3.3 billion improved class. Highly capable submarines as these are, their missions are global and the need to relieve their crews and service the submarines substantially reduces the number of boats that can be concentrated in a single oceanic region.

As early as 2008, the *New York Times* was reporting that although American submarines' technological prowess will continue, analysts had warned that China will possess a larger submarine fleet within a decade.[16] If China concentrates its submarine fleet in and around the South China Sea and if the United States, with an inferior-size submarine fleet, maintains its global commitments, the United States would be seriously outnumbered in a contest where subsurface warfare figures heavily. The vulnerability of large American surface combatants to China's antiship ballistic missiles is fair warning that submarine warfare—to establish control of the South China Sea and the Malay archipelago's choke point that straddles the sea lines of communication between China and Middle Eastern oil—would be decisive in deterring or, if need be, winning a naval contest between the United States and China. The NNFM regards the prospect of the large quantitative difference between Chinese and American submarine forces as a menace to American power in the region. It recommends building cheaper, air-independent propulsion (AIP) submarines that can recharge their batteries without surfacing and then patrol extremely quietly on the electricity stored in their batteries. If the NNFM's estimate that four AIP subs can be purchased for the price of one nuclear-powered boat is correct, and if the U.S. Navy is able to overcome its nuclear submarine community's opposition to nonnuclear propelled submarines—or even their construction in a U.S. shipyard for the Egyptian navy—the United States would be able to outnumber Chinese submarines in the area of most likely contest. As with aircraft carriers, the NNFM pictures a submarine fleet that mixes the expensive boats that the United States has used successfully since the Cold War with less expensive but more numerous submarines that have the advantage of running more silently than nuclear-propelled boats—thus acknowledging the political, economic, and military reality of an increasingly powerful China. The United States would retain the extraordinary endurance of nuclear-propelled submarines while adding to the fleet the stealth and numerical advantage of less expensive but still highly capable AIP submarines. Technology at costs significantly lower than what the United States now pays would turn China's access denial strategy against it. The broad military objective is to make the international waters that surround China sufficiently treacherous for Chinese warships and merchant ships to prevent or defeat any challenge to the continued stabilizing presence of American seapower.

Finally, the New Navy Fighting Machine option seeks cost savings in changing the kind of ships that the navy currently plans to purchase for the Marine Corps. Some of these ships, as noted earlier, can displace up to nearly half the tonnage of a supercarrier and cost more than $4 billion. They are expensive because they are big and they are big because they are designed to carry the aircraft and equipment required to land marines in the face of sustained deadly enemy fire. Such a landing has not taken place since Operation Chromite, the opposed landing at Inchon during the Korean War in September 1950. Since then marines have fought all over the world from the Caribbean to

Southeast Asia to Iraq and Afghanistan. But the United States has not conducted an opposed amphibious landing in sixty years. The NNFM would retain naval gunfire and air support of marines ashore along with ships that carry necessary supporting combat matériel. The United States would keep its unique and elite combat force along with the American military's powerful advantage of being able to land forces from the sea almost anywhere in the world.

The shape and size of the New Navy Fighting Machine are its distinguishing characteristics. The plan acknowledges the likelihood of increased tension in the future as a result of nontraditional, low-intensity conflict—for example, piracy, terror, drug trafficking, illegal immigration, and seaborne transit of highly dangerous weapons of mass destruction—in the world's coastal areas. It also recognizes China's rise as a potential threat stretching from the western Pacific to the western Indian Ocean. Major naval competition may revert to a primarily two-way rivalry, as during the Cold War. But the Soviet navy looked wistfully to cutting off the United States from Europe in the event of a major land war on the Continent and put ballistic-missile submarines to sea as part of Moscow's nuclear force. Their listless economy did not depend on seaborne imports and exports. China's vibrant economy does, and such dependence is a vulnerability because Beijing's disputes with its neighbors and claims to archipelagos and wide swaths of international waters point toward the quest for regional hegemony and its attendant dangers. The robustness of China's economy—at least for now—is also a strength that permits the construction of a modern, technologically sophisticated military including navy. The NNFM incorporates two fundamentals of good strategy: blunting a potential adversary's strength and threatening him at his point of greatest weakness. Building smaller U.S. carriers that are more difficult and numerous targets for China's antiballistic missiles and whose loss would damage the overall U.S. fleet less than the sinking of a supercarrier complicates China's plan to deny access to American seapower in the region. A larger force of American submarines and greater numbers of smaller surface ships equipped with cruise missiles that could hold at risk China's communications and intelligence-sharing network also assure the continued ability of American seapower to operate effectively in the region. Building a force large enough to maintain effective American presence in the seagoing areas that China identifies as core interests would help prevent a war from escalating, defend allies, encourage continued regional stability, and discourage a protracted naval engagement of disastrous consequences to China's economy, and the world's.

Smaller, more numerous ships would also increase American seapower's overall survivability, increase its capacity to respond globally, demonstrate continued U.S. interest in preserving the safety of the world's oceans, and extend the stabilizing presence of power that seeks no higher goal than the preservation of an international order that has been a major objective of both U.S. foreign and naval policy for over a century.

The proposed New Navy Fighting Machine aims at a second fundamental strategic objective, matching ends to means. It projects shipbuilding costs that will not exceed the naval budget's current level, or about $15 billion per year over several decades. Cost calculations are always disputable and deserve close scrutiny. But the New Navy Fighting Machine's idea of a maritime force that adapts to foreseeable international political circumstances deserves the most serious consideration. The idea is based on the assumption that America's position as a great power and its exceptional beneficence in exercising this power are an international good the absence of which would encourage chaos and guarantee a substantial loss of U.S. and allied security. The NNFM aims to fill the need for greater U.S. seapower in the world's coastal regions as well as to deter China from the regional hegemony that its modernizing and enlarging navy would permit. A shrinking fleet is a certainty if current ship design and expense are maintained. Replacing it with a considerably larger fleet[17] whose ships, while individually less muscular than today's, would preserve the United States' aggregate seapower. Such a fleet would also retain political leverage the misuse or lack of which doomed the Athenians in their contest with Sparta, neutered Napoleon's attempt to control all of Europe, and most recently stopped Germany and then Russia from sundering an essentially maritime grand alliance.

The Third Way: Technology Reshapes American Seapower

By force of character and intellect, Fleet Admiral Sir Jacky Fisher, a sometime professional partner of Winston Churchill when the latter was First Lord of the Admiralty,[18] championed the technology that transformed the Royal Navy from the metal-coated chrysalis of the late nineteenth century into a turbine-powered, large-gunned capital ship fleet prepared for submarine warfare and balanced on the cusp of naval aviation. Fisher saw where new technology could radically expand the Royal Navy's lethality and adaptability, and he largely succeeded in compelling change in a famously hidebound organization.

Fisher's example and the pace of technological change since his time remain an inspiration, especially today when it is a commonplace that advances in information technology have far surpassed those in the mechanical and industrial arts. A third alternative future for American seapower is based largely on exploiting today's—and tomorrow's—technology to transform the U.S. combat fleet into a highly flexible instrument whose adaptive powers will assure continued naval dominance long into the future.

The late vice admiral Arthur K. Cebrowski, along with Stuart E. Johnson, senior research analyst at the Rand Corporation, offered an alternative vision of a future fleet that is the intellectual descendant of the ideas that Fisher turned into facts. Published in 2005, the paper—*Alternative Fleet Architecture Design (AFAD)*—offers an assessment of the strategic and financial challenges to American seapower and finds answers in using technology to increase commanders' knowledge, share this knowledge among entire fleets, and confound a potential enemy with greater numbers of faster, cheaper, smaller, more maneuverable ships, all the while retaining the ability to shunt American naval power back and forth between smaller and larger threats as they emerge and transmogrify.

AFAD's commentary on the changes that separate today and the future from the Cold War era is an unintended primer in the extraordinary elasticity of human-devised perils that issue from the seas and their rims, as well as testimony to the potential malleability of seapower in turning back these changeable threats. AFAD correctly notes that large combatants bristling with a host of blue-water defensive and offensive systems such as the ability to hunt submarines, engage other surface ships, and destroy air targets served their Cold War purposes well. The Soviets had constructed a battle fleet to contest American seapower's ability to resupply its NATO allies across the Atlantic, to repulse the Western alliance's possible use of seapower in support of land forces if the Cold War turned hot on the European continent, and to protect the nuclear weapon–tipped ballistic missiles carried aboard submarines upon which Moscow partially depended as a deterrent to nuclear attack. Thus Soviet naval power manifested itself on the high seas where it could threaten U.S. forces from beneath, above, and upon the ocean's surface. Sensible was the design of ships that could defend themselves from these multitudinous dangers.

AFAD, again sensibly, argues that this threat has vanished, along with the political landscape from which it materialized. In its place is a range of possibilities that are as geographically as they are kinetically diverse. A destroyer built to locate and kill submarines and destroy missiles is not the most suitable ship or cost-effective method for hunting down young Somali pirates in wooden boats with outboard motors. As AFAD notes, "we have designed and built one Navy and are operating another."[19] More troubling, recent history, that is since the end of the Cold War, keeps turning out to be a poor guide to the future. While the Balkan wars smoldered and burned in southern Europe, peace-keeping became the U.S. military's overwrought buzzword. The future would be a long procession of negotiating skills, multinational cooperative ventures that kept warring factions apart, the supervision of elections, and the reeducation of U.S. troops about the use of force. The terrorist attacks against U.S. targets in 2001 put paid to all that. The "shock and awe" of the U.S.-led coalition against Saddam enjoyed its fifteen minutes of fame followed by a growing concentration on counterinsurgency expertise that continues as U.S. forces oppose the Taliban in Afghanistan. Johnson and Cebrowski argue that the future may prove to be equally unpredictable. Reaction against involvement in Iraq and Afghanistan could end significant U.S. military action overseas. More virulent and deadly terrorist attacks could produce the opposite response. China's military capabilities are increasing while its intentions remain a subject of debate.

AFAD divides the application of future U.S. seapower into two camps: "intervention" and "strategic advantage." The former connects U.S. post–Cold War military action in the Balkans, Haiti, Somalia, and the Middle East and counts on more of the same. Rogue states and such nonstate actors as terrorism and insurgency continue to threaten the United States sufficiently to produce U.S. or U.S.-led coalition military force. This is the world of what has heretofore been called nontraditional warfare. Mines, swarming small craft, short-range but lethal missiles and aircraft, and midget submarines infest key littoral areas and navigational choke points around the world. These complicate safe passage through coastal regions, as well as the use of military force where vital U.S. interests are at stake and other efforts to protect these interests have proven useless. "Strategic advantage" assumes that military force on land is not an option but that the United States retains its interest in acting and being perceived as a major power, including specifically safeguarding the world's key shipping lanes. "Strategic advantage" means contesting China's possible claim to regional hegemony or more expansive potential ambitions without invading it on land.

The AFAD alternative holds that intervention and strategic advantage share a dependence on good, timely intelligence; smooth command, control, and communications; effective protection against ballistic and cruise missiles; and continued refining of the U.S. military's ability to strike targets with close to absolute precision. But intervention and strategic advantage diverge importantly in other respects.

For the former, the Johnson-Cebrowski collaboration emphasizes greater attention to the communications and command networks that weave together more closely the different military forces—army, navy, air force, marines, Special Operations, and possible Coast Guard—whose cooperation is ordinarily essential for successful land operations. Other skills needed for an interventionist future include a greater naval ability to move heavy ground forces around quickly; an improved ability to defeat the threats in littoral waters mentioned above; more developed logistics in supplying from the sea a force that had been placed ashore; and greater combat support from the sea for troops on land including Special Operations Forces.

Improving and further developing these interventionist abilities points in a markedly different direction from guaranteeing the strategic advantage needed to preserve U.S. power in the face of a potential naval peer competitor, that is, China. To achieve the second objective, AFAD would stress improvements in the surface navy, the ability to prevent an enemy from projecting his own power at a distance, antisubmarine warfare, sea-based nuclear deterrence, and sea-based national missile defense. The interventionist future is a series of flash fires and brushfires whose extinguishing contains and thwarts larger, more damaging conflagrations. Defending strategic advantage means being prepared to prevent or put out a searing inferno in which the nation's future as a great power is on the line.

In principle the Alternate Fleet Architecture Design's image of an interventionist versus strategic advantage future resembles the bimodal idea—littoral *and* blue-water capabilities—of the New Navy Fighting Machine alternative, with one profound exception. The NNFM would build a large fleet of smaller craft for brushfires and also a sizable fleet of less expensive, larger vessels to fight the inferno. AFAD is similarly focused on a smaller, cheaper, and more numerous fleet. But it would construct a single force whose ability to convey information, adapt, and swiftly shuttle different sets of combat skills from one ship to another could smother a kitchen fire as handily as it could stifle a continent-spanning wildfire. AFAD does not offer compelling evidence that technology can achieve such advances in information sharing and adaptability but implies that they are possible.

However, the differences between the two options for the future of U.S. seapower should not be allowed to obscure their similarities. Like NNFM, AFAD sees grave problems ahead for the navy's shipbuilding budget. In 2005 AFAD questioned the assumptions on which the navy based its plans to increase the size of the fleet. These included continued growth in the Defense Department budget and additional funds for the wars in Iraq and Afghanistan. Both of these assumptions have turned out to be groundless. Funding for the Middle Eastern wars was folded into the Defense Department's annual budget following the 2008 presidential elections, and in the spring of 2011 President Obama proposed a $400 billion cut in defense spending over a twelve-year period. The AFAD was prescient. When it was written, the navy's official and approved goal was to build a 375-ship fleet. Two years after the Johnson-Cebrowski report was published, the navy lowered its guns a bit and aimed at a 313-ship fleet. In 2009 admirals began publicly to question whether the 313-ship goal would survive. Anticipated additions to the fleet of the littoral combat ship will increase the navy's target, but the long-term prospects for fleet growth as outlined above remain dim.

AFAD's answer to both the budget squeeze and constructing

an ambidextrous fleet that can conduct interventions and protect strategic advantage is technology. It sees a quantum leap in our detailed knowledge of distant seagoing threats. This valuable data would be distributed at once among American naval commanders in a form to be used for striking enemies before they have a chance to attack U.S. ships. Sensors would blanket large ocean areas. They would signal the position of targets. Secure communications would relay the information to U.S. and allied commanders on the scene, their superiors, and unmanned vehicles that orbit above and patrol on and below the sea's surface. Subsequent sensor-provided data would help in destroying targets once they had been identified. This, in simplified form, is what the Johnson-Cebrowski document means by *network-centric warfare*. Although executing it in the form AFAD describes is complicated, the objective has been known to naval commanders for centuries: to use ships that can communicate with one another—formerly by lights or flags—and separated by the distance of nearly a horizon to extend the commander's knowledge of an enemy's whereabouts.

At the receiving end of this modernized and much expanded field of useful vision are ships whose hull design, speed, shape, maneuverability, construction out of composite materials, sea keeping, stealth characteristics, and advanced propulsion—for example, electricity—will give birth to a larger fleet of smaller, less-detectable vessels. Greater automation will reduce manning requirements and save money. Unmanned vehicles will provide information that extends commanders' field of vision while surveillance that does not rely solely on acoustic information exposes the deep. As a result, torpedoes launched from the air and encased in vapor bubbles—allowing them to reach hypersonic speed—would convert the seas into boundless graveyards for enemy shipping. The word "fire" would be disassociated from the word "gun" when electromagnetic propulsion replaces chemical-based powders as the motive source for rounds launched from ships. The enormous power of these weapons will eliminate the need for explosive warheads, relying instead on the kinetic energy of a round moving at several times the speed of sound to destroy a target hundreds of miles away.

Combining network-centric warfare with the technological advances mentioned above would change ship design. AFAD argues that the navy can design and field smaller, cheaper ships without reducing the entire fleet's combat effectiveness. An added support to combat effectiveness is the ability to exchange specific missions swiftly from ship to ship, called modularity. As noted earlier—and as the navy is currently building into its littoral combat ship—modularity allows the same hull to be quickly reconfigured to perform a different mission. A ship that had been used to search for and destroy mines can, with the exchange of modules equipped for different missions, be changed into one that hunts for and sinks submarines. In other words, more information would be usefully shared among stealthier ships. The ships would possess greater speed and sea-keeping ability. These advantages would be combined with powerful new weapons technologies, both manned and unmanned, as well as the widespread interchangeability of weapons systems. Together these advances would permit the building of a new navy composed of smaller, cheaper, and more numerous ships.

AFAD holds that precise weapons "decouple" punch from size. That is, once a target can be sunk or put out of action with a single particularly lethal shot, the need for large magazines that store bulky rounds vanishes (a battleship's single 16-inch shell tipped the scales at slightly less to considerably more than 1 ton and required between four and six bags of powder that weighed one hundred pounds each). Similarly with survivability: smaller ships that can dart about like minnows are harder for an enemy to see and target. They are proportionately more survivable, and require less cladding with heavy armor. AFAD argues that these advances in technology will allow the navy to substitute massive hulls for speedy ones. Parallel technological advances will vastly improve the sharing of essential combat information and, thus, the unified action of a large number of smaller vessels operating toward the same combat ends but dispersed—to the enemy's confusion—over a wide swath of ocean.

The decoupling, AFAD holds, of power from size is matched by a similar separation of distance from the precision required to strike a target. In other words, the distance from a target at which a weapon is released has been separated from its chance of striking the target. Global positions systems (GPS) and inertial guidance systems carried aboard speeding weapons—for example, those provided by gyroscopes—represent large advances over World War II when it took one to two thousand sorties to destroy a single target. AFAD notes that between then and the next significant series of air strikes in Europe, the Kosovo campaign, technology had progressed so that a single sortie could be reasonably certain of destroying more one target. At the same time, lightweight building materials are reducing the weight of unmanned aerial vehicles as their ability to fly undetected—stealth—improves. The result is a trove of information about an enemy relayed from secure platforms that are highly capable of providing a timely and unbroken stream of intelligence to track and destroy an elusive target, for example, a terrorist leader.

AFAD logically connects advancing technology with the ability to exploit it. The navy's LCS is a prototypical example. So are computers that allow customers to modify or include such features as hard-drive capacity and CD writers. The Johnson-Cebrowski paper peers into the future and sees widely differing threats that possess increasingly adaptable and threatening technology. U.S. seapower, they predict, must choose between slow, expensive decay and swift, technological adaptability: between the drawn-out processes that have characterized design and production in the Cold War period and, for example, the modularity of the LCS that allows a single hull to be converted for different missions as circumstances require. They argue that large expensive, multipurpose ships are too valuable to lose, especially in low-intensity conflicts, whereas smaller, networked vessels, which in the aggregate can accomplish the same objectives as larger vessels, can survive losses without substantially endangering the success of a particular mission. Moreover, smaller, faster, more numerous, and more maneuverable vessels substantially complicate an enemy's problem in defending itself and attacking an opposing force.

Specific ideas of the shape of the Johnson-Cebrowski fleet include reducing the size of aircraft carriers from their current level of about 100,000 tons to no more than 57,000 tons, substituting Very Short Take-Off and Landing (VSTOL) versions of the Joint Strike Fighter aircraft that the Defense Department is now building in common for each of the services that use fixed-wing, multirole fighters; using longer-range conventional strike aircraft once technological advances in catapult machinery make launches from the smaller carriers' decks possible; and substituting, in part, diesel-electric submarines for the larger and far more expensive nuclear-propelled boats in the U.S. submarine fleet today. The argument in favor of a fleet that would include smaller carriers is the same in practical terms as it is in theoretical ones: larger, more costly ships are individually more survivable, but smaller, cheaper carriers are harder for an enemy to target because of their greater speed and maneuverability.

Johnson and Cebrowski's idea of future warfare is debatable at every turn, tactical, strategic, and financial. But it is consistent with the direction of technology since classical times. Greek city-states lightened the offensive and defensive equipage of their soldiers to allow them greater maneuverability and striking power. Knights shed armor as gunpowder replaced crossbows and killing distances increased. Postmedieval princes sacrificed massive and fixed stone fortifications for cannon. Cannons were transformed from huge bulky siege engines into lighter weapons that could be maneuvered on a battlefield to mow down an enemy's line.

Swiftness, agility, and superior range have been seen as better defenses than mass or armor from the Greek peltasts—quicker, more lightly armed and armored troops than their heavier hoplite brethren—to today's advanced strike aircraft whose ability to launch rockets at a safe distance from enemy fire is among their best defenses. A major theme of warfare is that striking the enemy before he can hit you is better than trying to absorb his blows. The heavily armored French nobles enmeshed in the mud of the Agincourt battlefield who were assaulted by less encumbered English archers with their long-range bows might have survived if they could move faster and shoot farther. In exactly this ability did aircraft carriers surpass the battleship navy. Swarms of carrier-based planes could reach the enemy fleet at far greater distance and with at least as much lethality as a battlewagon's tremendous shells.

Hughes and Cebrowski work from the same idea: their host of sensors thrown over a massive geographic area linked together by an electronic blanket. Its fibers transmit and receive decisive information among a numerous, coordinated, and dispersed fleet that is larger and less expensive in its individual parts than the current fleet. The imagined fleet's size and diffusion confound the enemy and minimize the damage of possible losses. Its coordination assures swiftness, a wider range of possibilities for striking an enemy, and the adaptability that commanders require to outmaneuver an unpredictable opponent. These advantages, both Hughes and Cebrowski agree, characterize the fleet design they recommend and apply as much to defeating the asymmetric enemy they see in an interventionist future as they do to the peer competitor the United States faces if preserving strategic advantage becomes the nation's major challenge of the future.

The third and final significant alternative to the current U.S. shape and size of U.S. seapower comes from Robert Work, a Marine Corps veteran, strategic analyst, and undersecretary of the navy in the Obama administration. Work's ideas, which appeared in a 2008 paper, "Charting a Course for Tomorrow's Fleet," are less radical than either the Hughes or the Johnson-Cebrowski option. Work sees the defeat of violent Islamist radicalism, the rise of China or perhaps resurrection of Russian military power, and proliferation of weapons of mass destruction as the important security challenges that face the United States in the foreseeable future. Similar to the two alternatives noted above, he identifies a need for both greater naval capability and affordability. "Charting a Course for Tomorrow's Fleet" is alarmed that U.S. naval power today must approach a potential opponent too closely to launch effective strikes safely. The Soviet Union's demise effectively ended the threat to U.S. seapower of land-based reconnaissance and strike aircraft. Correctly, Work notes that this threat has reappeared today in the form of Chinese land-based naval aviation, which, for example, can strike targets more than nine hundred miles distant. Work finds a more general and parallel vulnerability as the number of states with nuclear weapons grows and China's navy enlarges. He explicitly rejects "a major expansion of ships" and agrees with the U.S. Navy's attempt to seek greater maritime security in partnerships with friendly states' naval forces.

Also included in his paper's prescriptions is acknowledgment that subsurface threats are on the rise both in the world's coastal regions and as a result of China's expanding submarine fleet. The solution? Increase the rate at which the United States builds and deploys existing nuclear-powered attack submarines and look to technology to design and manufacture the unmanned submersible vehicles and weapons to counter growing threats beneath the surface of the world's littorals. "Charting" looks to modular design that would fit both the United States' and the UK's ballistic submarine boats, thus cutting costs for each naval service. Consistent with its modest adherence to overall current U.S. naval programs, the Work report embraces the idea of global fleet stations. The stations are a way to preserve a stabilizing U.S. presence in a region—at sea instead of ashore—using a host of different naval vessels and skills from different parts of the U.S. government to establish and/or firm up relations with partner navies as well as supply medical and humanitarian services in such places as off the African coasts, in the Caribbean, and along

South America's east coast. "Charting" also emphasizes seabasing, an idea that is arguably as old as continuous blockades,[20] as a means of supplying American force independently of the politics that restrict use of land bases. "Charting" places great store in increasing the sea services' ability to move logistics quickly around the world and improve the efficiency of the navy's supply vessels, both of which are worthy objectives. Seapower's ability to replenish itself is to command of the oceans *and* the ability to conduct global military operations as sunlight is to agriculture. No sun, no wheat. No logistics support, no global U.S. military.

The Work plan also aims to reduce shipbuilding costs. But again its proposals are modest compared to the other alternatives described in this chapter. While increasing—from two to four—the number of littoral combat ships purchased annually, it would cut back construction of aircraft carriers from one supercarrier every four years to one every five—which means that over the standard thirty-year picture that the navy has traditionally drawn of its shipbuilding plans, the number of aircraft carriers would be reduced by one. Other cost savings would be found in simplifying ship design to cut back on the number of different vessels the navy designs, builds, and maintains; and improving networks among ships at sea, thus increasing their massed power.

"Charting" looks to the conclusion of the thirty-year period its changes are meant to shape and envisions greater flexibility for American seapower that operates with smaller navies to protect against terrorism and illegal seaborne trafficking, including the possible transit of nuclear material. A combat fleet that is able to fight at greater distance from danger would counter larger traditional threats, such as those that China and growing numbers of nuclear power are likely to present. A merging of ship types and increased modularity would generate savings in the costs of logistics, training, and maintenance. The fleet would grow modestly, by about 17 percent over its current level of approximately 286 ships.

10

Changing American Maritime Strategy

THE ALTERNATIVE TO a large transformation in the shape and character of the fleet that would preserve American seapower's presence, reach, and combat power is a profound change in the United States' role as a maritime power. Unless the public and the political class's understanding of the nation's economic and political stake in retaining our position as a transoceanic seapower increases by large steps, such a change appears to be increasingly likely. The most visible evidence is the possibility that in 2013 the cuts to the Defense budget requested by the Obama administration, added to monies scheduled to be "sequestered" as a result of the failure of a bipartisan congressional committee in the fall of 2011, will result in a reduction of approximately $1 trillion over the succeeding decade. In November 2011 Secretary of Defense Leon Panetta answered a congressional request for information about programs that must be eliminated if funds are sequestered from the defense budget. He wrote that among other major weapons systems, the F-35 bomber, the littoral combat ship, and the next generation of ballistic-missile submarines would all go. The House Armed Services Committee estimates that sequestration will result in a navy that is about 16 percent smaller than the current one, and nearly one-fourth smaller than the 313-ship fleet that navy leadership has maintained is needed for the tasks that U.S. military strategy asks of it.[1] Left to the military service chiefs was the task of explaining the consequences. Marine Commandant General James Amos reminded Congress the same month that deep cuts in training, personnel, and equipment would result in an unready force, one that cannot respond quickly to crises, cannot quickly replace units returning from deployment around the world with those that are ready to take their place, and cannot easily supply troops in the field. He warned Congress that the depleted force left by major reductions in the defense budget would curtail the marines' ability to support its troops on the ground if—as planned—the USMC version of the F-35 is canceled. And he called attention to the United States' strategic interest in the protection of the six choke points through which most of the world's commerce pass, as well as the navy and marine's quiet success in keeping these channels safe for international commerce.[2] Amos invited Congress to consider what the world system of commerce would look like if, undeterred by receding U.S. seapower, the choke points that separate Asia from the Middle East are overtaken by the piracy that now afflicts the Gulf of Aden. Admiral Jonathan Greenert, chief of naval operations, reflecting on the large cuts in the number of ships that would result from sequestration, told congressmen that instead of maintaining a presence around the world, U.S. seapower would be required to return to American waters and cross oceans as crises occur. In naval terms this is called "surging." Greenert added that "if we're not there, it's hard to influence and you can't surge trust and confidence. You have to build it."[3] Greenert and Amos also expressed deep concern about American companies' ability to build ships. Greenert repeated that the industrial base that supports seapower will also suffer as orders for ships fall precipitously. "In 1998," he said, "we had six shipbuilder companies, today we have two." He added that the number of shipyards will decrease "to five in 2013."[4] Amos talked about irreversible damage to the naval industrial base for naval shipping and said that such harm "could be terminal." However, a congressional hearing is not a good setting for detailed explanations. Admiral Greenert's and General Amos's sketches of the consequences of eviscerating the defense department budget have practical consequences that would end the era of predominant American seapower that took shape in the early twentieth century and solidified during World War II.

Seapower today—as it has been throughout history—is as complex as the intersection of oceans with land and is as essential to international commerce as the lines that connect busy ports with one another across the world's great oceanic distances are invisible. A nuclear device slipped into a small freighter that calls at several ports in southern Asia before sailing on to Europe and the United States could prove more devastating than all the great-power jockeying over mineral rights in the South China Sea. The detonation of such a device could generate irresistible political pressure to refocus the missions of already overstretched U.S. naval forces away from maintaining the order that American commerce needs on the high seas and protecting American and allied interests in global crises toward guaranteeing the safety of America's coasts against another such catastrophe. Preventing that freighter from moving its deadly cargo requires monitoring the shore and sometimes the open seas. Stopping or at least impeding piracy, illicit drug trade, human trafficking, and arms smuggling also demands similar attention to areas close to shore. The same smaller forces are the right ones for working with coastal navies in African, Asian, and South American states whose chief naval interests are to defend their home waters and protect their sovereignty. Good working relations with these states advance the interests of American diplomacy and security. The partnerships developed over years of cooperation and training help assure the safety of the world's coastal regions against the threats noted immediately above and relieve the demands on U.S. seapower.

On the other hand, reassuring allies in Asia that the United States will remain a Pacific power and discouraging Chinese ambitions insofar as they aim at hegemony through regional naval dominance require larger ships that can project effective combat power ashore, deny China the use of surrounding international waters, and, if need be, sink China's combat fleet. Large combatants have also proved necessary and useful in the Iraq and Afghanistan wars and in keeping open the sea-lanes that connect Middle Eastern oil with the world. Taking the safety of these sea-lanes for granted is unwise, as was suggested in late December 2011 when the deputy chief of the Iranian parliament, Hossein Ebrahimi, threatened to close the vital choke point of the Strait of Hormuz if the West imposed oil sanctions on Iran.[5] U.S. seapower today aims at both the missions that require less firepower and those that require superior firepower. The choice that faces U.S. seapower in the form of radical cuts to the U.S. defense budget is either to cut all forces so that the pain is shared equally or selectively to abandon or attenuate some missions in favor of others.

At a strength of approximately fifty ships, American seapower today is concentrated in the western Pacific and in the Indian Ocean. The former assures our allies that the United States remains a Pacific power and will continue its stabilizing presence in the region. At the same time, China's leaders are encouraged to believe that their possible initiation of combat operations in the area would be ill advised. At the same time a smaller concentration—about thirty combatants—patrols the Indian Ocean. Fewer than a dozen sail the Mediterranean, notwithstanding its increasing political volatility, and about half this number is dedicated to partnership, presence, and cooperative efforts in South American waters. Another forty-five ships are unequally divided between the East and West Coasts of the United States, preparing to relieve vessels that have completed their foreign tours. The remainder of the U.S. fleet is in intermediate or long-term maintenance and overhaul, awaiting the scheduled work needed to sustain ships over a life span of thirty or more years. For all intents and purposes, U.S. seapower is effectively concentrated in and divided between the adjacent foci of the West Pacific and Indian Ocean. During the Cold War the geographic foci of U.S. seapower were the Mediterranean and the western Pacific. This put large combat naval forces on the flanks of the Soviet Empire. U.S. seapower's larger size also meant that the foci were composed of more ships, including capital ships. Crises, humanitarian missions, and disaster relief were more easily answered because the forces concentrated in the Mediterranean and west Pacific were larger than those that the United States can bring to bear today. If shipbuilding continues to decrease, along with the monies available for operating the fleet, U.S. naval forces in the western Pacific and Indian Ocean will shrink and U.S. political leaders then must choose between diminishing, however temporarily, the strength of U.S. forces in the world's most strategic regions and dispatching individual vessels or squadrons to respond to crises. The question future presidents ask in a crisis will not be—as it was in the past—"Where are the carriers?" but rather "Dare I spare either of those that are deployed in the world's most strategic and volatile regions?" And if the answer is that neither a carrier nor its accompanying vessels can be spared, it is a certainty that painstakingly developed cooperative efforts with coastal navies around the world will come a cropper as ships formerly dedicated to these missions are redirected to the minimal needs of American fleets in the Indian Ocean and western Pacific. The task of preserving order in troubled parts of the world's coastal regions would fall to small, weak states with small, weak navies or coast guards.

However, depending on how much U.S. seapower contracts, worse strategic outcomes are imaginable . . . and possible. Better to concentrate one's forces where they can be effective than to divide them and risk being able to accomplish anything. Declining defense budgets based on political agreement to "share the burden" equally between defense and nondefense costs and a new perception that defending the nation is no longer the central government's first responsibility could force U.S. leadership to choose between focusing on the western Pacific or the Indian Ocean. The most obvious consequence is that the region deserted by U.S. seapower would immediately become either less stable, a likely event in the Persian Gulf where competing powers would contest for dominance, or more stable as in the western Pacific where a single power, China, is most likely to emerge on top. Neither possibility is attractive to the United States' interest in balanced regional power, freedom of navigation, and dependable allies. Both would encourage a widespread appearance that the United States—like Great Britain at the dawn of the twentieth century—was in slow but inexorable retreat. If U.S. seapower is confined by a shrinking fleet to covering only one of the world's two most strategic regions, its ability to respond persuasively elsewhere to terrorism, the certainty of currently unforeseeable crises, irregular warfare, and a host of other emergencies that could determine a distant region's future stability is not in jeopardy. It is finished.

Other alternatives present themselves as U.S. seapower shrivels. But as with much else in life, the less one puts in, the less one takes out. Spending what's needed on a new building's ventilation or electrical system will produce a more efficient and safer structure than skimping on vital systems. A truncated ability to build and equip major combatants would still leave American seapower with choices, albeit much reduced ones. Amphibious and much smaller vessels could remain deployed overseas and able to train other nations' naval, marine, and coastal forces. Such naval competencies as construction battalions, explosive ordnance experts, riverine operations, and certain kinds of intelligence and of course Special Operations Forces (SEALs) could help suppress piracy, illicit traffic, and probably discourage forms of terror that are benign by comparison to the Taliban's seizure of Afghanistan or its related attacks on the United States in 2001. If terrorism and drug running or gunrunning were to become the major seaborne threats to American or allied interests, such a navy would fit the bill handsomely. However, if large threats to oil tankers departing the Persian Gulf or a Chinese navy, emboldened by the evanescence of U.S. seapower, persisted or enlarged, the waning force would have lost its power to influence events. What strength survived would be a small core, not a bristling and lethal mantle. It could be overmastered by any opposing fleet with greater combat power and the ability to add and sustain superior firepower.

There are still more alternatives to the transoceanic force whose shape U.S. commerce and foreign policy has determined over the past century. Most prominent among them is largely to reduce the practice of stationing naval forces abroad and to preserve a smaller force of aircraft carriers, large surface combatants, and submarines in or very near American waters. This would save the large costs of keeping fleets at sea. It would also end the global presence of American seapower. As crises emerged, American combatants could be dispatched to the affected area. It's a troubling solution. Even if maintained on the ready, weeks are required to move a large battle force from either U.S. coast to the Indian Ocean, the eastern Mediterranean, or the western Pacific. The U.S.S. *Independence* battle group's homeporting in Japan allowed it to reach the area of the Taiwan Strait in short order when China fired missiles in the area as Taiwan's presidential elections approached in March 1996. Of diplomatic interest, the United States could also claim at the time that U.S. carriers routinely patrolled in the region, a slender and manifestly self-interested justification but also an unimpeachable one. No such argument would be possible if an American president were required to send an aircraft carrier battle group or two across the Pacific in a similar future crisis. A fire truck's departure to the scene of a reported conflagration has no effect on what firemen find when they arrive at the scene. The same cannot be said of a decision to flush an aircraft battle group from U.S. waters and send it halfway around the world. This deployment would affect the calculations of hostile states or terror groups. It would vastly complicate the political decision to take action as U.S. government officials squabbled over whether sending naval force would reduce or sharpen tensions in a crisis. Effective seapower within sight or just over the horizon presents no such problems. Quite the opposite. It assures friends and dissuades those who might consider becoming enemies. The end of global American presence cannot possibly be offset by regularly scheduled or even sporadic global patrols. Who would purchase a burglar alarm that functions intermittently at known and infrequent intervals or one that is activated occasionally and spasmodically? What sort of deterrence does an annual visit from the U.S. fleet provide where a real potential threat exists? What kind of ally or friend would look to seapower of this kind for assurance and leadership? The answers to these questions provide no comfort for American security. A navy that must shrink substantially or virtually end its presence in the areas of greatest national interest has historical antecedents in the Dutch and English experience noted earlier. Their experiences point toward a decline in national greatness and power that cannot be managed by modulating crew sizes or tinkering with the disposition of forces, alliance management, or diplomacy.

The same must be said of continuing on the current course of American seapower. Trying to perform the same tasks with forces that are being slowly dissolved by budget reductions merely postpones the inevitable. A large triangle that is shrunk while preserving the same angles retains the same shape but not the same size. It is similar, not congruent. A navy ravaged by budget cuts but one that still preserves the same kinds of vessels could provide everything that current American seapower offers but in smaller and smaller portions. Forces would still be sent to the Indian Ocean and western Pacific, but they would grow weaker as they shrank. Ships that provide ballistic-missile defense would continue to sail, as would other combatants that protect allies and project power. But their number, reach, and staying power would all dwindle. Who would want a bridge precisely similar to the existing one but too short to reach from one bank of the river to the other?

There is no end of cost-saving ideas: increased automation, decreased crew sizes, and changing crews aboard ships on station rather than changing the ships themselves have all been proposed and sometimes put into effect—with very mixed results. Mine countermeasure ships in the Persian Gulf, for instance, have been routinely found in poor condition by the replacement crew: maintenance and repair problems are left for the incoming crew to resolve. Still, a few of these notions are good and have or will provide savings either in financial or strategic form. Other ideas are trendy and will be discarded as their lack of value becomes clear. Still others are imposed because the fleet's size is decreasing while its missions remain the same or increase. A normal ship deployment lasts about six months. On January 20, 2012, the all-purpose amphibious ship U.S.S. *Bataan* (Landing Helicopter Dock, LHD 5) had been on duty overseas for 303 days, thus surpassing the navy's all-time longest deployment of an amphibious ship. Asking sailors to leave their families for six months is asking a lot. Increasing this separation to nearly a year is asking for moral problems, maintenance issues, and a shortening of ships' useful service lives. Efficiency this is not. But no combination of worthwhile efficiencies or tinkering at the margins will produce the sums needed for naval rearmament. Americans will have to decide whether they want to remain the world's great naval power or accept the consequences of allowing another to assume this role.

One idea offers significant financial relief, not only for American seapower but for U.S. defenses as a whole. Most Western liberal democracies have decided that military service is no longer the duty of its citizens and that financial benefit, as in the private sector, is the best way to fill their ranks—from when personnel join the military until death. In the United States the cost of substituting pay for what had once been seen as duty comes out to more than half the defense budget. The All-Volunteer

Force—as ours is called—would have surprised the Founders who believed that militias would be the backbone of the nation's defense led by a small, active-duty professional corps. Were the United States to return the larger part of responsibility for defense to the part-time National Guard and Reserves, the growing separation between civilian and military society would be healed at the same time that a system was restored whose civic benefits the nation enjoyed for most of its history. Since most of its individual members would earn their living as civilians, moving the bulk of U.S. forces into the National Guard and Reserves would also promote a shift away from financial gain and toward civic duty as the primary reason for enlistment. Not least, a return to larger militia forces and a smaller active-duty military would save the nation trillions of dollars in less than a decade, money that could be spent on modernizing the military and assuring its proper size.

Still, other strategies would mitigate the cost of naval rearmament. One example of a strategic approach that would produce a whole greater than the sum of its parts is the military's evolving idea of naval and air cooperation called the Air-Sea Battle. It knits together air force and navy aircraft, allied bases, a hardening of support functions throughout the western Pacific, and increased attention to defending against ballistic missiles in the service of blunting China's ability to deny U.S. seapower access to the region in the event of hostilities. It's a sensible response to the strategic problem of China's antiship ballistic missiles, which are part of their broader effort to deny U.S. forces access to the western Pacific. There is nothing to gain from a rise in tensions between the United States and China and much to be lost by a violent outcome of protracted enmity. American seapower's ability to sustain its traditional role as regional peacekeeper and cornerstone of an association of democratic states that also includes those who fear Chinese hegemony is the best assurance of the entire area's continued stability and prosperity. U.S. battle fleets' uninterrupted ability to patrol in international waters off the coast of East Asia will go a long way toward offering this assurance.

Strategic gain could—and should—also be sought in fabricating, at least for a small group of dedicated and highly intelligent officers, the relative calm that characterized the period between World Wars I and II. This requires assigning some of the best officers—who would otherwise receive major commands at sea or senior positions on joint staffs—to think about everything from China to terror to technology and test their ideas in war games and fleet maneuvers. There is precedent for this, but it resulted from happenstance, not design. With little else to do from the demobilization that followed the end of World War I until shortly before 1941, the navy and Marine Corps were able to think about the future and design and experiment with new technologies and tactics. In this more-than-two-decade breather, American seapower prepared the basis for what would become successful aircraft carrier tactics during the war and designed the planes to execute them. It conceived the notions of advanced bases and the coordination of infantry, airpower, and naval gunfire that are integral to amphibious warfare as we know it today. It thought through the strategy of securing a string of islands to secure American lines of communication as they approached the Japanese mainland. War games that tested these innovations demonstrated their value and focused commanders' attention as it stimulated their imaginations. Indeed, after the war Fleet Admiral Nimitz wrote, "The war with Japan had been reenacted in the game rooms here [at the Naval War College] in so many different ways that nothing that happened during the war was a surprise—absolutely nothing except the kamikaze tactics toward the end of the war; we had not visualized those." With increased global demand for U.S. seapower today and decreased numbers of ships to meet demand, the navy and Marine Corps lack the breathing space and time to think through and test ideas about future warfare that their predecessors enjoyed in the 1920s and '30s. The likelihood of slashed defense budgets adds urgency to finding this breathing space. Defeating enemies by overwhelming them with a wealthy nation's industrial output has been a hallmark of American strategic culture since the Civil War. But Americans have not forgotten how to imagine or innovate, as the U.S. space program, extraordinary advances in information technology, and the sophistication of weapons demonstrate. The same qualities of mind and the remove to test them are needed to understand how American seapower can retain its dominance.

Conclusion

THE STRATEGIC RECASTINGS of American seapower away from the form in which it currently exists would signal an important retreat from the powerful transoceanic presence, deterrence, and war-fighting missions that U.S. seapower has performed since World War II. Removing the fleet from either the western Pacific or the Indian Ocean/Persian Gulf region accepts either the likelihood of Chinese hegemony in Asia or economically crippling instability at the world's largest oil spigot. Dividing a reduced force incapable of adequately performing its mission in either theater demonstrates strategic frailty, tactical imprudence, and financial impotence.

Salvaging a global presence for its own sake is no better an alternative. Allowing U.S. seapower's carrier forces to wither along with the abilities of unmanned carrier-launched aircraft whose impressive capabilities can safely be predicted in the near future will surely save money. But the substitution of amphibious and smaller craft that are useful for developing working relationships in the world's littorals for the punch of large vessels that project fearsome power over long distances admits that we have all but conceded our interest in preventing major international crises and resolving them in our favor if need be. The presence of American seapower around the world would be minimally preserved, but it would command a lower level of respect than is merited by battle groups able to defeat an enemy's navy and deliver persuasive force from hundreds of miles away from a target.

Holing up in American waters awaiting a crisis to respond to is a worse option. Since the chief objective of such a strategy is to save money, the available fleet would necessarily be smaller. Its dispatch would be a predictable fountain of domestic political friction in a crisis and an endless source of uncertainty as allies wondered what succor they might expect in the event. More certain is it that erstwhile allies would look elsewhere for security. Thus would American military power recede as its alliances disintegrated. The twin misfortunes would go on reinforcing each other simultaneously, weakening the United States.

Cutting back American seapower also promises nothing except advancing powerlessness, the suspicion of allies, and global challenges to American security. Fewer carriers and their accompanying vessels reduce the ability to patrol the major areas of American interest in the Indo-Pacific region, soon forcing the same dilemma as having to choose between focusing U.S. seapower on the western Pacific or the Indian Ocean/Persian Gulf. Further cutbacks would end the possibility of maintaining an effective presence in either region. Fewer amphibious ships and combatants designed to operate in the world's littorals would restrict the United States' ability to work with coastal powers whose vigilance helps protect against local instability and such specific threats as the shipment of dangerous and illicit cargoes. Cutbacks in the navy's logistics would chip away at the fleet's ability to supply itself at a distance from homeports. Eventually the United States' ability to respond to crises would also be imperiled. The fleet that has been constructed over the decades would be proportional to its former self, but the shape left would resemble silhouette more than substance.

No rejiggering of American seapower, strategic or otherwise, will preserve the security that the world still enjoys as a result of

American maritime dominance. Every alternative based on immediate or drawn-out decreases in fleet size ends in choices that diminish the navy, either in its large task of securing American and allied interests against threats from growing powers like China that could become peer competitors or medium-size powers like Iran whose geographic position could also cause serious harm. The same cuts—whether directed at types of vessels or how frequently they are deployed, or whether they are to be largely returned to U.S. home waters—limit or effectively end U.S. seapower's global presence and its partnerships with coastal navies that assume burdens, which if abandoned will add broad swaths of ocean to failed and failing states as threats to global security. Other misfortunes that can be safely predicted include a reduction in the number of vessels equipped with ballistic-missile defenses, an unwelcome development as nuclear weapons and ballistic missiles proliferate in tandem with the United States' reduced access to foreign land bases nearest the most likely threats and on which defenses against such weapons could be placed.

The best answer to these undesirable consequences was understood most clearly by the American Founders, who in the preamble to the Constitution included providing "for the common defense" among the government's first responsibilities. This does not mean that the defense budget should be allowed to expand without question or limit, and the arguments in chapter 5 offer suggestions for the less bureaucratized and more accountable defense organization that would save billions. But the Founders also possessed a commonsense understanding of strategy. It is reflected in the Constitution's writing. The Constitution grants Congress the power to raise armies and qualifies it by restricting the appropriation of money for raising an army to no more than two years. The same article gives Congress the power to "provide and maintain a Navy"[1] with no restriction on the time for which public funds can be appropriated in advance to support the navy. Based on experience, the Constitution's writers were aware that a standing army could do far more harm to citizens' liberty than a navy. They also understood that navies take longer to build, equip, man, and train than armies. This was as true in 1787 as it is today. Thus, whatever financial pain will be required of the defense budget, the burden—if shared equally by the military services—will fall most heavily on the navy. Its ships take longer to build than any other service's fighting platforms. Its personnel take longer to train to combat readiness. And the effect of its exit from the world's oceans will be more profound for each dollar subtracted from its accounts than if the land or air services were to experience the same decreases. The logical strategic conclusion is that budget cuts should be weighted not so much to preserve, but to increase, American seapower. Unfortunately this counters the prevailing Defense Department culture over which the catchall jargon "jointness" descended in the mid-1980s. Jointness is like the elephant described by the blind mice in the children's story. One mouse feels the tusk and describes the pachyderm as a spear. Another touches the trunk and describes the elephant as a snake. And so on. To some, jointness means that the military should save money by building different variants of the same equipment, for example, the Joint Strike Fighter. For others, jointness means increased cooperation in operating—from crisis response to nation-building to combat. To others still, jointness means more commonality in education and more equal participation from each military service among the huge staff that serves the chairman of the Joint Chiefs as well as the staffs that work for the U.S. military's geographic combatant commanders. For still others, it means an equal division of the budget. And for some it means all of the above . . . and more. Some of these ideas are sensible. Others are strategically dubious. Foremost among the latter is the notion of an equal distribution of appropriated money. Strategy requires forgoing some options in favors of others to advance a larger objective. If the supply of money or equipment is limitless, strategy is unnecessary. If—as is the United States' current predicament—money is increasingly limited, the government must decide what comes first. This is critical in the domestic political argument over spending and taxation. It is also critical in judging how important a strong defense is and how best to use the monies allocated to defense. Cutting the budgets of each of the military services equally fulfills the politically correct requirement of jointness. But it makes no more sense than for a family facing a smaller income to reduce what they spend on health care and education by the same amount they spend on buying new appliances or repairs to the home. The latter can be delayed or minimized. The former are imperative. American seapower can be preserved and increased by the unequal distribution of defense reductions. Now is the right time to distribute defense resources strategically. With the end of American engagement in the Middle Eastern wars, the likelihood of a large- or similar-scale use of U.S. ground forces in the foreseeable future is much diminished. If an unforeseen need arises, suddenly land forces can be reconstituted more quickly than seapower. Simultaneously, the future of American influence in Asia, our alliances, economic power, and the region's stability are all at risk in large measure due to China's growing military assertiveness. American seapower is critical to preserving our position as a Pacific power and a large investment in it and the industrial base on which its future health depends would assure both China and our allies in the region that the U.S. commitment to strength in the region is beyond question. There is no better solution to the immediate problem of sustaining and augmenting American seapower in the face of radical defense budget decreases than a strategic division of financial resources among the United States' military services.

The navy itself is in a weak position to make this argument because it counters the regnant go-along-get-along culture of jointness. The current U.S. administration's hopeful attitude toward China, Iran, and other potentially troublesome states and non-state actors also muffles naval—or any military—leadership arguments that robust seapower is an incentive to peace from the Straits of Hormuz to the South China Sea.

Thus, attention to American seapower's future inevitably returns to technology with the occasional dollop of strategy. The navy's current plan for the next thirty years is the most conservative. It seeks modest changes in the character of the fleet complemented by modest alterations in strategy. Its maritime strategy's attention to partnerships with foreign navies and humanitarian/disaster relief missions explicitly recognizes the importance of low-level hostilities such as terrorism, illegal trafficking, and piracy. The idea of global fleet stations is a new variation on an ancient theme that bolsters sustained U.S. presence around the world, sidestepping the diplomatic problems of basing and providing the pleasing although strategically uncertain rationale that offshore presence is somehow sufficient to achieve major goals of U.S. foreign policy. On the positive side, it gradually knits strong partnerships in both this hemisphere and Africa, where additional U.S. presence serves humanitarian ends, and it might hedge against China's intensifying interest in the region's resources. The littoral combat ship fleet now under construction helps turn this recognition into reality. The idea of using different modules as a quick means of changing the littoral combat ship's fighting mission is an innovation that could influence naval shipbuilding generally and perhaps result in significant savings. The navy acknowledges the importance of cyber warfare, unmanned vehicles, advanced weaponry, and the need to operate in the western Pacific, unimpeded by China's avowed intent to deny access to the U.S. fleet. But while the access denial issue in the western Pacific is seen as a threat, there remains a supreme and quiet confidence among today's U.S. naval officers that China is not to be taken seriously as a threat, now or in the future. Signs of cracks in this self-assurance exist, such as the one noted above in then chairman of the Joint Chiefs Admiral Mullen's 2010 admission of "being genuinely concerned" about China's military programs. But these are the exception. For the most part, the American sense of absolute seagoing dominance is complemented by official U.S. policy of failing largely to see or admit that a strategic competition exists between Washington and Beijing. The consequence is the navy's reluctance and inability publicly to justify its mission to Congress and the American people as maintaining stability in the western Pacific by deterring China's oceanic ambitions. At the same time large-deck supercarriers; big, expensive, nuclear-powered submarines; and multipurpose surface ships remain very much the meat-and-potato regimen of fleet composition. The question of their abilities in the face of future threats recedes before the looming issue of affordability. If affordability and the possibility of additional substantial cuts in the defense budget overlap or converge, fleet size will be profoundly and negatively affected, with the most dire consequences for U.S. seapower and, thus, status as a great power.

The most radical naval future is the vision that Cebrowski and Johnson offer: networks and sensors that transform the fog of war into an infinitely visible crystalline sphere; fleets of unmanned air, surface, and submersible unmanned vehicles to peer into the distant corners of an operational area; the modularity that gives an entire fleet the transformative ability of the Homeric sea god Proteus who could turn himself into a lion, a serpent, a leopard, or a tree; and stealth capabilities to compare with Hades' cap of invisibility. These changes would create a bigger fleet of ships better equipped to take on both large and small future threats, and whose individual parts—that is, ships'— smaller size, the authors argue, would save real money.

Closest to the navy's current program is the alternative that the Work paper proposes. Its simplification of certain ship designs and support for modularity, small cutbacks in the purchase of capital ships, and increases in networking are intended to result in the savings that are needed for modest fleet growth.

In the middle between Work and Cebrowski-Johnson is the Hughes alternative. It eschews both Work's evolutionary approach and Cebrowski-Johnson's revolutionary prescriptions. The Hughes alternative aims at a large fleet of small and very small vessels for many littoral missions and warfare at the lower end of the spectrum generally—and finds costs savings in designing smaller craft for lesser threats. At the same time, it would reduce the size while increasing the number of larger combatants demanded by such traditional Mahanian sea control missions as deterring or, if necessary, defeating China's navy.

The similarities among the several alternatives are more interesting than the differences. All four alternatives see the emergence of a more chaotic world. They agree—as do virtually all strategic forecasts—that weapons of mass destruction will proliferate. They accept that simultaneous threats at the low and high end of conflict magnify the complexity of making a cohesive maritime strategy that defends the United States' and its allies' particular interests. They are united in connecting America's overarching national interest with retaining its supremacy at sea. All four alternatives, including that of the navy, agree that naval warfare must address both littoral and blue-water threats, the former because access to a hostile coast should be assured at the same time that other threats—like piracy, trafficking, and terrorism—are countered. Blue-water means China for all the alternatives, even if the navy refuses to say so publicly. All four alternative naval visions of the future see common hulls with large interchangeable parts (modularity) as a route to greater flexibility in adjusting the shape of fleets and a possible means of saving money. Each of the four alternatives sees an extension of seapower's reach and power in the continuing development of unmanned vehicles.

All agree that unmanned combat systems—in this case aircraft—could help patch the hole that China's antiship ballistic missile has likely punctured in naval aircraft carriers' ability to approach the mainland safely and conduct strike missions, whether in defense of allies or to retaliate against possible Chinese aggression in the region. Absent the requirements for humans in the cockpit and the limitations of human endurance in piloting a high-performance combat aircraft, unmanned vehicles can stay aloft much longer and fly much farther than the current

Conclusion

or next generation of strike naval aircraft. Their reduced weight and size, combined with stealth, would allow them to loiter over a target area, giving commanders thousands of miles away options that do not currently exist with manned aircraft whose range demands that they fly to a target, deliver their payloads, and return. One of the navy's large contractors successfully completed the first flight of an unmanned naval strike aircraft in February 2011. Northrop Grumman's X-47B has an anticipated operational range of four thousand miles, more than three times the range of the current generation of carrier strike aircraft, the Super Hornet, and well over twice the range of the next generation of carrier strike aircraft, the F-35C. The first efforts to land the unmanned plane on a carrier deck are scheduled for 2013.[2] As the range of these pilotless vehicles lengthens, so does the distance at which carriers can safely launch strikes. Similar developments in unmanned surface vessels and submersibles unite the navy and alternative visions of U.S. seapower in the shared goal of decreased cost and increased surveillance and effective combat power as a partial solution to the access China seeks to deny the U.S. fleet in the western Pacific.

All four alternatives agree on the importance and necessity of reducing the cost of building ships. Excluding the navy, three of the alternative visions agree that smaller aircraft carriers offer possible cost savings and a reduction in the risk that sails with the current and future generations of large-deck carriers paralleled by a larger and more diffuse presence of carrier-borne aircraft. Excluding the navy again, each of the three alternatives identifies the need for nonnuclear-powered submarines albeit for different purposes. Work, the closest to the navy's current program, argues in favor of a "midget" submarine for carrying Special Operations Forces (SEALs) clandestinely to their targets. Such a vessel must be too small for nuclear propulsion. Its introduction into the fleet, tiny though it is, might help smooth the way for a reexamination of the navy's decades-old attachment to building only nuclear-propelled submarines.

This attachment made sense during the Cold War when the U.S. global cat-and-mouse contest with Soviet submarines gave advantage to boats that could remain submerged for months. But China does not present the same strategic competition that the Soviet Union did. Rather than submarines that shadow each other, peer into potentially hostile ports, and prepare to pounce in the event of war, undersea competition with China means developing the ability to cut off its imported energy, hold its seaborne commerce at risk, and threaten its fleet. This more traditional seagoing contest of wills and China's growing investments in large numbers of extremely quiet diesel-electric submarines strain U.S. seapower's ability to deter China with the U.S. fleet of very expensive nuclear-powered submarines that limited resources can support and can only be concentrated in the western Pacific approaches if they are withdrawn from other missions around the world. The Hughes and the Cebrowski-Johnson reports' explicit recommendations for adding cheaper, more numerous diesel-electric submarines to the U.S. fleet are sensible and deserve the most serious consideration.

The same thought should be given to ideas contained in all three non-navy-written alternatives that question the future usefulness of large-deck aircraft carriers. Strike aircraft remain an effective instrument for projecting power, placing an enemy's valuable assets at risk, and providing a stabilizing, calming presence in a crisis. But China's antiship ballistic missile, the close proximity of the Chinese mainland to the western Pacific compared to the thousands of nautical miles over which U.S. forces are stretched, and the array of China's land-based naval aviation suggest that the littoral surface waters surrounding the Chinese mainland will become increasingly dangerous for huge targets, like U.S. supercarriers. The loss of a single supercarrier, to a Chinese antiship ballistic missile, for example, would be an immense blow to American national prestige, a powerful incentive to U.S. escalation, and a major loss of naval power with highly uncertain prospects of quick wartime replacement. The argument that the threat of Chinese antiship ballistic missiles is substantially less-ened because they are land-based is weak. The missiles can be deployed on mobile launchers, which make them difficult to find and destroy. Substituting smaller, lower-cost carriers that sail with fewer aircraft for some of the large-deck carriers as the large-deck carriers are retired from the fleet would keep the U.S. arse-nal stocked with supercarriers for missions where access was not a serious problem while adding to the fleet more numerous, less easily targeted carriers whose possible loss would not be crip-pling where access is a serious problem.

Without positive change, the future of U.S. seapower is called into question by the increasing costs of the ships that com-prise the fleet today and the navy's persistent attachment to many of the same vessels notwithstanding large global strategic changes that continue to change the character of the United States' most likely international competitors. Increasing personnel costs raise the same question about the future of U.S. seapower. So does the lack of strategic focus on the single greatest threat to America's dominant global maritime position, China. And before long, the heavy financial burden of paying back money that the national government has borrowed will press the same question about the nation's ability to hold on to its position as a great military power. Intelligent, more adaptable, lower-cost proposals exist that would preserve that part of the nation's industrial base devoted to build-ing combat vessels. Constructing more ships will preserve critical skills and grow a workforce with the know-how to preserve America's maritime strength. The same ideas incorporate the understanding that American seapower must temper its focus on projecting power ashore with the older, Mahanian mission of commanding the seas by being able to sink an opponent's com-mercial and naval shipping. The alternatives that now exist to the existing fleet are sensible and deserve serious consideration. They acknowledge—as does the navy—the need to balance the turning back of threats close to the shore against those that could materi-alize on the high seas, and that chief among the latter threats is the unfolding enlargement of China's ambitions joined with its rapidly advancing technology and application to a powerful navy. Smaller, cheaper, and more numerous combatants, ships designed so that outdated systems can be swiftly replaced by the most recent technology, and substantive transformations to design and deploy smaller aircraft carriers and diesel-electric-powered submarines are all likely to save money. They are certain to complicate a competitor's problem in denying the United States seaborne access to strategic parts of the world's oceans. All of this requires adapting, retaining, and improving the American sea services' flexibility. Nations that adapted their navies, like Britain and the United States in the years before World War II, retained and infused their international power. States like Venice that failed to adapt to new technology—for example, oceangoing sailing vessels rather than rowed galleys—found that technological rigidity contributed to the loss of naval superiority. The same loss befell Spain when it could no longer afford a powerful fleet. The United States faces both the challenge of adapting its fleet to changed circumstances and footing the bills. Costs may be reduced, but only to a certain point. Effective navies are not cheap. The retort to this, of course, is that ineffective navies are far more expensive to the nation as a whole.

What Needs to Be Done

With the large budget cuts that the Obama administration has already made to the military and those that are likely in the president's second term, the immediate future for American seapower is bleak. The Navy acknowledges this in its estimate that the size of the fleet will stay below 310 ships over the next thirty years. Three hundred and five ships is a reasonable expectation but only—according to the non-partisan Congressional Budget Office's estimate[3]—if the Navy's shipbuilding budget is increased by 19 percent over its current level, a large amount in absolute terms and a very large sum in a time of major budget cuts. The 305-ship fleet represents another notch down for the Navy whose target for the past seven years has been 313 ships. Before the 313-ship objective the Navy had planned on a fleet as large as 325 ships. Over the years the decrements are too few to qualify as the thousand natural shocks that end in demise, but over time they must have a similar result.

What should be done? First, decisions about how to divide a shrinking military budget should be based on strategy, not the politically correct equal apportionment of pain across the three military departments. Such division is a deep bow to political correctness. It is a major slab of the altar at which the Pentagon has prayed for over twenty-five years. In operating and training forces together jointness makes sense. In dividing defense resources equally jointness is strategic poison. It silences the individual military services from explaining, both to policy-makers and to the public, their particular role in defending the nation.

Take, for example, the Pacific. The U.S. has a large and growing interest in the stability of East Asia and its progress toward greater self-governance. The Pacific—and the west Pacific in particular—are naval theaters of operations. China's productive region lies along its Pacific coast, which is bordered near and far by strings of island nations like Japan, Taiwan, and the Philippines or peninsular states such as South Korea and most of Southeast Asia, whose southern borders are the Indo-Pacific oceans and whose northern borders abut China. The current disputes between China and its neighbors over territorial rights in the South China Sea have their origin around the time of the 1991 exit of U.S. naval and air forces from the Philippines. Subtract or diminish American seapower in a strategically critical oceanic region and power relationships readjust, stability diminishes, and established alliances shake. If the Obama administration expects that its pivot to Asia can succeed in sustaining America's influence in the region based purely on diplomatic maneuver, it will fool no one, especially China. Alberto del Rosario, the foreign affairs secretary of the Philippines, a nation that Imperial Japan ravaged in World War II, said publicly in December 2012 that he "would welcome very much" the rearmament of Japan as a counterpoise to China.[4] This startling about-face in a region where memories are long shows how seriously regional powers regard China's unchecked rising military. American seapower needs the resources to assure allies, control the seas if necessary, and restrict a potential conflict to the seas rather than risk its expansion to the Asian land mass.

After the last decade of Middle Eastern wars, there will be no appetite in the U.S. for land conflicts in the foreseeable future. Such conflicts may come, but it is far easier to swiftly increase ground forces than more technologically complex naval and air forces. A strategic division of defense monies is needed to cut the Army and increase the Navy and Air Force's combat strength particularly as it applies to conducting successful and joint operations in the west Pacific. An additional reason for bolstering naval forces is that although the pivot to Asia was supposed to shift American focus away from Iraq and Afghanistan, the Middle East is growing more unstable as is demonstrated most notably but not exclusively by the prospect of an Iranian nuclear weapon. Hamas' increasing rocket and mortar attacks on Israel in November 2012 caused then-Secretary of State Hillary Clinton to interrupt her visit to Asia and return to the Middle East. A clearer proof does not exist that while we may have lost interest in the Middle East the Middle East remains very much interested in us. This will continue, Asia pivot or not. The U.S. Sixth Fleet today is largely a fleet in name alone. The Mediterranean has seen war for most of its history. The Arab Spring's cold outcome requires a return of U.S. naval power to the region—in the form of a reinvigorated and powerful U.S. Sixth Fleet. A strategic, rather than equal, division of defense budgetary pain is necessary to build the naval forces required in both the Mediterranean and the west Pacific.

Additional and substantial defense resources can and should be sought from substantively changing the way the Defense

Department is managed. Despite decreases in manpower and equipment from their Cold War levels, the Pentagon's bureaucracy has flourished and increased its striking similarity to Soviet central planning. The multiplying layers of bureaucracy and enlarging staffs in the Secretary of Defense's office, the vast civilian agencies that do everything from auditing contracts to purchasing non-military equipment, such as pencils and toilet paper, and the burgeoning Joint Staff all but guarantee an absence of accountability in the design, execution, and evaluation of major weapons programs. The metastasizing bureaucracy darkens the important identification of requirements for major weapons systems with an equally stultifying and dilatory cloud. Decreasing the size of these mega-staffs, flattening management structures, and returning responsibility and accountability for procurement to the military services while maintaining financial and policy control with the Secretary of Defense would save billions. Relieving officers for cause would help improve efficiency, morale, and combat effectiveness. General George Marshall fired 600 officers before a single U.S. soldier was deployed to fight in World War II. By late 2006 no general officer had been relieved in the U.S.' Middle Eastern wars. The worthwhile effort to increase accountability cannot be advanced by a less-than-stellar fitness report but would have real meaning if the consequence of serious failure in acquisition no less than operations were to be relieved. Today the only cause for being fired is crossing the Pentagon's social red lines. This keeps tongues from clucking but has no effect on military efficiency. Personnel policy should complement management policy in saving monies that could be better spent on bolstering our defenses rather than on expanding the bureaucracy and its refined ability to obfuscate.

The Obama administration has largely muffled the question of sequestering defense monies: the administration will want deep cuts in defense, sequester or no. Future military budgets will reflect this regardless of the political maneuvering over the so-called fiscal cliff that followed the 2012 elections. The coming cuts, unless countered by a surprising injection of strategic resolve and good sense, will place growing pressure on the nation's ability to defend its interests and those of its allies, for today and long into the future. This in turn will encourage schemes that have the ring of credibility but are in fact nice names for more of the weakness exhibited in a fulcrum-less pivot to Asia. Indeed, the pivot is a tongue-in-groove companion to the new American vacuum in leadership as demonstrated most plainly by the hands-off policy toward the Syrian civil war—and a general retreat from positive engagement in the Middle East. How will U.S. policy handle these problems? In speeches. "Off-shore balancing" has become a cottage industry for analysts and academics. They advocate prodding others into standing in for the leadership that we are unable or unwilling to supply ourselves. Offshore balancing includes maintaining reduced naval forces offshore. Expecting to maintain influence through offshore balancing is like a child who expects that he can control the motion of the toy horse he mounts outside the supermarket. Offshore balancing is a prescription for growing international irrelevance. Thus, the kind of naval forces we build is as grave an issue as the cost in dollars and inefficiency of the multiplying defense bureaucracy.

Other navies are growing. China is increasingly assertive as demonstrated by its ambitious naval plans and provocations in the South China Sea. Iranian hostility toward Israel should not be seen as an end point in the ruling mullahs' plans. With or without Israel, the temporal jewel of Saudi oil beckons as does the shining grail of subduing the Sunni world. Russia continues its own effort to reclaim naval presence and influence. Naval competition over the next three decades will grow, not diminish.

Instead of a slowly disappearing fleet, the U.S. should set and meet the goal of increasing its navy, at a minimum, to 350 ships in ten years. Reversing the current administration's plan to decommission twenty-two frigates and seven cruisers years before their usefulness to the fleet has expired will help advance the goal of a 350-ship fleet, about the number recommended by the 2010 Quadrennial Defense Review Independent Review Panel.[5]

Still, more ships will have to be built than are currently planned. Quality should not be allowed to suffer, but the most advanced technology should bow to numbers. The best is ever the enemy of the good. In this case, the best would be large numbers of ships with matchless technology for combating threats from the air, surface, and subsurface simultaneously. A small fleet of the same vessels is unacceptable because they cannot cover the large areas of the world where dominant American seapower will either retain our ability to command the seas or inferior seapower will surrender this command. The moderate course is a larger fleet of combat vessels whose numbers permit sufficient geographic reach and whose ships' fighting abilities reflect the savings to be had through rigorous supervision of cost, scrupulous examination of changes to ship design as vessels are built, multiyear procurement, competition, and other management changes that would re-assert the cost discipline that characterized naval shipbuilding when the fleet was twice the size of the current one.

Design should also be subject to serious reconsideration aimed at increasing the fleet's size. Introducing aircraft carriers that are smaller than the giants we build today expands the entire fleet's global presence and diminishes the vulnerability of the navy's current class of aircraft carrier that, while immensely powerful, is increasingly and troublingly vulnerable to missile attack. The consequences of the loss of so great a ship along with its crew of 5,000—and more—could lead inexorably to war. Smaller carriers, perhaps a third the size of current ones, are less expensive, more difficult to target and while the loss of one would be a major blow, it might be sustained without going to war. A carrier fleet based on a mixture of today's class of immense ships and smaller ones would be larger than the one that exists, more adaptable in responding to crises, less vulnerable to the growing missile threat, and cheaper to operate.

Similarly with submarines. Diesel-electric submarines cannot stay submerged for as long as nuclear-powered ones, but when using their electric motors underwater they are significantly quieter than their much bigger and far more expensive nuclear brethren. Equal consideration should be given to air-independent propulsion (AIP) for submarines with a very small crew or none at all. An attack submarine force that mixed diesel-electric and AIP submarines with nuclear ones would reduce costs, increase the overall stealth of American seapower's submarine arm, and add options for fleet commanders as the size of their forces grew.

In other places, ship design needs to be more robust. Time will tell whether operating in the world's littoral areas justifies the impressive cost of the littoral combat ship's high speed and whether U.S. combatant commanders value the ship's interchangeable modules of different warfighting abilities. The LCS possesses a thin ability to protect itself from airborne threats and time is needed to return to port to change the modules that determine its mission. These limitations argue in favor of the larger and more traditional frigate, which can simultaneously perform the range of likely naval combat missions—from antisubmarine warfare, to air defense, to anti-surface ship operations. Contested areas of the sea may for the foreseeable future move closer to land as in the South China Sea, the Persian Gulf, and the Eastern Mediterranean. But airplanes, missiles, swarming small-boat tactics, mini-submarines, and suicide missions do not make proximity to the shore safer than the high seas. Naval shipbuilding should anticipate the increase of littoral threats by building larger more powerful combatants whose salient virtue lies in defeating the anticipated range of threats at once rather than in moving quickly from one theater to another.

None of these changes are easily made. Tradition, resistance to change of those invested in existing equipment, and senior naval and civilian officials who have spent their careers designing, operating, repairing, and learning today's combat systems are nothing new. The same interests fought ironclads, steam-propulsion, oil rather than coal-fired ships' engines and carrier aviation, to name a few. To have tried to argue the father of American nuclear propulsion, the late Admiral Hyman Rickover, out of his attachment to nuclear-powered ships would have been like trying to persuade Captain Ahab to abandon his search for Moby Dick and fish for anchovies. But the Navy *has* changed over the years. And it will be necessary to change again as reduced budgets intersect with increasing threat.

Changes in the way seapower is designed and built are critical to efficiency and savings. The design and cost of ships that are the core of the fleet will determine if the U.S. is prepared for emerging threats. No less important is how we think about seapower. Irregular warfare is important as the SEALs' increasing role in strategically decisive engagements show. But the more traditional form of warfare among states will be with us for a long time. Nothing is more important than the ideas that shape both irregular and traditional warfare. The navy's most recent—2007— maritime strategy concentrated on deterring wars not fighting and winning them. *A Cooperative Strategy for 21st Century Seapower* emphasized humanitarian assistance and disaster relief along with partnerships with other navies as key instruments in a mission that America has rarely embraced, preventing wars from occurring. The word "China" did not appear once in the document.[6] Military modernization and a rise in territorial incidents with Beijing's South China Sea neighbors since the publication of that strategy six years ago are powerful arguments for taking China seriously. War with China is undesirable. About this there is no disagreement. But is the chance of conflict diminished more by not speaking of it—as the 2007 maritime strategy failed to do? Or are we better off accepting the fact of strategic competition with China and preparing sensible plans that have been practiced again and again? The Latin adage, *si vis pacem para bellum* (if you want peace, prepare for war) applies with particular urgency. Yet the current administration does not want to consider war with China. In language and deed it has reversed the old Latin: its policy is better expressed by switched the nouns: *si vis bellum para pacem* (if you want war, prepare for peace). In 2010 the Obama administration changed the name of the annual report to Congress on China's military, which had been known as *The Military Power of the People's Republic of China*. The new version was given the anodyne title, *Military and Security Developments Involving the People's Republic of China*. Actions followed words. The pivot to Asia is chiefly a diplomatic initiative as demonstrated by the president's sensible outreach to Burma. The military element of the pivot consists of a detachment of Marines in faraway Darwin, Australia, and a small shift of U.S. ships from the Atlantic to the Pacific. This will impress neither our allies nor China. Our thinking, and in particular American seapower's thinking about China, has to change. The surest way to prevent disputes between China and such of our friends and allies as Taiwan, Japan, and South Korea or the Philippines from turning into actual conflict is through increased U.S. naval presence in the region accompanied by more exercises with friendly navies, and serious thought followed by exercises designed to test different ideas about how best to defeat China if disputes lead to conflict. Our interest in peace and stability in the region is best served if China's leaders never think that they could engage and defeat U.S. forces in and beyond the Western Pacific.

The U.S. has four large tasks ahead if it is to guarantee the nation's command of the seas and with it, both the international order that a century of American diplomatic and military effort has established as well as our status as the world's leading power. The tasks are: dividing the defense budget strategically rather than according to the requirements of political correctness; saving substantial sums by returning accountability and good management practices to the construction of naval equipment; increasing the size of the fleet through important changes in design and types of combatants; and thinking through and testing the ideas that are essential to assuring American victory in any confrontation with China's emerging military power. If we succeed in these difficult tasks American seapower will emerge stronger and more robust than ever.

However, the most important change that precedes any of these recommendations is to restore the national agreement that the future of the United States as a great power cannot be separated from a transoceanic presence as the world's dominant combat fleet. If the understanding that the United States' ability to shape great events, preserve a balance of power in Asia, maintain an international system favorable to liberty, assure the safety of the world's oceans, communicate with and expand our global alliances, and win naval contests decisively as well as influence the outcome of continental ones disappears, those who predict decline for the United States will see their predictions borne out. So long as the United States remembers that seapower is the effective keel of the nation's success as a great state, America's security and that of a stable, increasingly democratic world will be assured.

Notes

Chapter 1: American Seapower in Distress

1. "An Analysis of the Navy's Fiscal Year 2012 Shipbuilding Budget," Congressional Budget Office, June 2011, http://www.cbo .gov/sites/default/files/cbofiles/ftpdocs/122xx/doc12237/06-23 -navyshipbuilding.pdf, and "An Analysis of the Navy's Fiscal Year 2013 Shipbuilding Budget," Congressional Budget Office, July 2012, http://www.cbo.gov/sites/default/files/cbofiles/attachments/07-25-12 -NavyShipbuilding_0.pdf.

2. "Defense Spending and the Super Committee," Foreign Policy Initiative Analysis, September 12, 2011, http://www.foreignpolicyi.org /content/fpi-analysis-defense-spending-and-super-committee-0.

3. Bill Gertz, "Gates Warns of 'Hollowing Effect,'" *Washington Times*, May 24, 2011, http://www.washingtontimes.com/news/2011 /may/24/gates-warns-of-hollowing-effect/.

4. Testimony of Eric J. Labs before Subcommittee on Seapower and Expeditionary Forces, January 20, 2010, http://www.cbo.gov/ftpdocs /108xx/doc10877/01-20-NavyShipbuilding.shtml#80.

5. As related to author by U.S. ambassador to Turkey Robert Strausz-Hupé in November 1986.

6. Petty Officer 2nd Class Elizabeth Merriam, "U.S. Ship Arrives in Cameroon Early with Emergency Supplies for Chad Refugees," Africa Partnership Station, February 10, 2008, http://www.africom.mil /getArticle.asp?art=1639.

7. "The Escalating Ties Between Middle Eastern Terror Groups and Criminal Activity," remarks of David T. Johnson, Assistant Secretary of

State, Bureau of International Narcotics and Law Enforcement Affairs, January 19, 2010, http://www.state.gov/p/inl/rls/rm/135404.htm.

8. U.S.N.S. stands for United States Naval Ship, a term of reference for such noncommissioned navy ships as research and hospital ships that perform noncombatant support roles.

9. http://www.hafen-hamburg.de/en/content/container-port-throughput -global-comparison.

10. Edward Gibbon, *The History of the Decline and Fall of the Roman Empire* London, 1837, T. Cadell, Vol. IV, Ch. XXVI, p.411 http://books .google.com/books?id=Hy8OAAAAQAAJ&pg=PA411&lpg=PA411&dq=were +constantly+exposed+to+the+invasion+and+passage+of+the+barbarians .&source=bl&ots=PHhJQnSq5l&sig=sGRNT53___OASFBSLRLaSv FsOKo&hl=en&sa=X&ei=YKbFULrYEqPayAHc3YDACA&ved=0CDMQ6 AEwAQ#v=onepage&q=were%20constantly%20exposed%20to%20the %20invasion%20and%20passage%20of%20the%20barbarians.&f=false

11. Deuteronomy 30:19.

CHAPTER 2: ALFRED THAYER MAHAN: SEAPOWER AS AN INSTRUMENT OF DEMOCRATIC EXPANSION

1. Charles Lipson, *Reliable Partners: How Democracies Have Made a Separate Peace* (Princeton, NJ: Princeton University Press, 2003).

2. A. T. Mahan, *The Influence of Sea Power upon History, 1660–1783* (New York: Dover Publications, 1987), p. 63.

3. Ibid., p. 5.

4. Ibid., p. 50.

5. Ibid., p. 29.

6. Ibid., p. 22.

7. Ibid., p. 32.

8. Ibid., p. 1.

9. Ibid., p. 50.

10. Mahan would be unmoved by contemporary arguments that attempt to manage and negotiate the end of competition between powerful states. Scarcity of necessity produces competition. But the recognition of scarcity as the first economic principle assumes that the good of one's state is superior to the good of other states. This forces each state to look upon itself as exceptional in its own desires.

11. Mahan, *The Influence of Sea Power upon History, 1660–1783*, p. 50.

12. Ibid., p. 52.

13. For example, the current commander of the People's Liberation Army Navy, Admiral Wu Shengli, has called China an "oceanic nation." The notion of oceanic states, that is, ones that are particularly suited to exercise seapower, comes straight out of Mahan, who pointed to geography as one of several conditions that determine a nation's link to the sea. See Toshi Yoshihara and James R. Holmes, *Red Star over the Pacific: China's Rise and the Challenge to U.S. Maritime Strategy* (Annapolis, MD: Naval Institute Press, Annapolis, 2010), p. 18.

14. Ibid., p. 23.

15. Ibid., p. 55.

16. Ibid.

17. Alexis de Tocqueville, Harvey Claflin Mansfield, and Delba Winthrop, translators, *Democracy in America* (Chicago: University of Chicago Press, 2000), p. 526.

18. Ibid., p. 527.

19. Ibid., p. 528.

20. Ibid., p. 529.

21. So much of the Dutch character and expansion is a reaction against their geography.

22. Mahan, *The Influence of Sea Power upon History, 1660–1783*, p. 49.

23. Ibid., p. 66.

24. Ibid.

25. Mahan questioned the depths of the American manpower reserves and foresaw that drafting reserves from the mechanical classes would likely be most successful. Did he fear that the increase of the middle class will sap imperial military strength? Did he foresee the ridged divide between military and civil society?

26. Ibid., p. 48.

CHAPTER 3: THE ROOTS OF AMERICAN SEAPOWER

1. *The Works of John Adams* (Boston: Charles C. Little and James Brown, 1851), vol. 4, chap. 7.

2. Ibid.

3. Polybius, *The Rise of the Roman Empire*, translated by Ian Scott-Kilvert (Harmondsworth, UK: Penguin Books, 1979), book 1, chap. 10.

4. John Adams, Special Session Message to Congress, May 16, 1797.

5. Ibid.

6. Ibid.

7. Ibid.

8. Alfred Thayer Mahan, *The Influence of Sea Power upon History, 1660–1783* (Boston: Little, Brown and Company, 1890), 12th edition, chap. 7, p. 280.

9. Thomas Jefferson, Special Message to Congress on Gunboats, February 10, 1807.

10. Thomas Jefferson, *Notes on the State of Virginia*.

11. "Paris," in *The Autobiography of Thomas Jefferson* (New York: Literary Classics of the United States, 1984, Chap. 7, p. 76.

12. Ibid. p. 65.

13. Thomas Jefferson, Special Message to Congress on the Wreck of the U.S.S. *Philadelphia* in Tripoli, March 20, 1804.

14. Theodore Roosevelt, *The Naval War of 1812* (New York: G. P. Putnam's Sons, 1882), p. 397.

15. Ian W. Toll, *Six Frigates* (New York: W. W. Norton & Co., 2006).

16. Ibid.

17. Ibid.

18. Roosevelt, *The Naval War of 1812*, p. 134.

19. James Madison, Message on the Special Congressional Session, State of War and Diplomacy, May 25, 1813.

20. Quoted in Toll, *Six Frigates*, p. 385.

21. Ibid., p. 381.

22. Ibid.

23. Ibid., p. 439.

24. Ibid.

25. Ibid., p. 454.

26. Ibid.

27. James Madison, Special Message to Congress on the Treaty of Ghent, February 18, 1815.

28. Thomas Jefferson to James Monroe, January 1, 1815.

29. John Locke, *Second Treatise of Civil Government*, chap. 2, sec. 6.

30. John H. Schroeder, *Shaping a Maritime Empire: The Commercial and Diplomatic Role of the American Navy, 1829–1861* (Westport, CT: Greenwood Press, 1985), p. 91.

31. *Historical Statistics of the United States*, Millennial Edition On Line, edited by Susan B. Carter et al. (Cambridge: Cambridge University Press, 2006), tables Ee362/2, Ee363, Ee364.

32. David G. Surdam, *Northern Naval Superiority and the Economics of the American Civil War* (Columbia: University of South Carolina Press, 2001), table 11.3, p. 158.

33. Ibid.

34. Quoted in George W. Baer, *One Hundred Years of Sea Power: The U.S. Navy, 1890–1990* (Stanford, CA: Stanford University Press, 1994), p. 59.

35. Samuel Eliot Morison, *The Two-Ocean War* (Boston: Little, Brown and Company, 1963), p. 9.

36. Quote from Sir Peter Gretton, *Maritime Strategy: A Study of Defense Problems* New York: Praeger, 1965, p. 43.

37. Chester W. Nimitz quoted in Baer, George W. *The U.S. Navy, 1890–1990, One Hundred Years of Sea Power*, Stanford University Press, Stanford, CA, p. 286.

38. Ibid. p.399.

Chapter 4: The Future of American Seapower

1. National Bureau of Economic Research, "Determination of the December 2007 Peak in Economic Activity," http://www.nber.org/cycles/dec2008.pdf.

2. "The Budget and Economic Outlook: An Update," Congressional Budget Office, p. 22, http://www.cbo.gov/ftpdocs/117xx/doc11705/08-18-Update.pdf. http://www.cbo.gov/publication/43907

3. Editorial, "Mr. Obama's Defense Cuts," *Washington Post*, April 20, 2011, http://www.washingtonpost.com/opinions/mr-obamas-defense-cuts/2011/04/20/AFlMqNEE_story.html.

4. http://www.whitehouse.gov/omb/budget/hisoricals

5. Ibid., p. 5 (of 13).

6. "Corrected-U.S. Fiscal 2007 Budget Deficit Falls to $163 Bln,"

Reuters, October 11, 2007, http://www.reuters.com/article/2007/10/11 /usa-budget-idUSWBT00770120071011.

7. "U.S. Sets $223B Deficit Record," *Washington Times*, March 7, 2011, http://www.washingtontimes.com/news/2011/mar/7/government -posts-biggest-monthly-deficit-ever/.

8. Michael Mullen, "Mullen: Debt Is Top National Security Threat," CNN U.S., August 27, 2010, http://articles.cnn.com/2010-08-27 /us/debt .security.mullen_1_pentagon-budget-national-debt-michael-mullen ?_s=PM:US.

9. Remarks of General Michael Hayden, USAF (ret.), "Rethinking the Future International Security Environment," Seminar Series, January 20, 2011.

10. Callum Borchers, "Defense Secretary Leon Panetta Warns Against 'Disastrous' Spending Cuts," *Political Intelligence,* May 27, 2012, http://www.boston.com/politicalintelligence/2012/05/27/defense -secretary-leon-panetta-warns-against-disastrous-spending-cuts /IYJWZ7foT1bdEZxgddZV9K/story.html.

11. Admittedly here the comparison of large federal deficits to black holes stretches since astronomers agree that black holes exist as the nuclei of most galaxies, serving, if no other useful purpose, as a valuable source of scientific information.

12. Base Realignment and Closure, the means by which Congress and the Defense Department decreased military bases at the end of the Cold War.

13. *Report of the National Commission on Fiscal Responsibility and Reform*, The White House, December 2010, p. 25.

14. *Report of the Sustainable Defense Task Force*, June 11, 2010.

15. Ibid., p. 19.

16. Dr. Eric J. Labs, senior analyst for naval forces and weapons, "The Long-Term Outlook for the U.S. Fleet," Congressional Budget Office, Slide #16, http://www.hudson.org/index.cfm?fuseaction=hudson _upcoming_events&id=683.

17. Andrew S. Erickson and Adam P. Liff, "PacNet #16—Understanding China's Defense Budget: What It Means, and Why It Matters," Center for Strategic and International Studies, March 10, 2011, http://csis .org/publication/pacnet-16-understanding-chinas-defense-budget-what -it-means-and-why-it-matters.

Notes

18. Statement of Eric J. Labs before the U.S. House Committee on Armed Services, March 9, 2011, p. 2.

19. http://www.defense.gov/speeches/speech.aspx?speechid=1747.

20. http://www.npr.org/blogs/thetwo-way/2013/02/06/17130043/citing-uncertainty-pentagon-will-not-deploy-aircraft-carrier-to-persian-gulf.

CHAPTER 5: AMERICA ADRIFT

1. For example, in March 2010 the China National Offshore Oil Company announced its purchase of half of the Argentine oil and gas firm Bridas. In October of the same year another large Chinese energy company, Sinopec, agreed to invest over $7 billion in the Brazilian operations of the Spanish company Respol. Jaime Daremblum, "The Chinese Dragon Sweeps Through Latin America," PJ Media, May 13, 2011, http://pjmedia.com/blog/the-chinese-dragon-sweeps-through-latin-america/.

2. Lee Kuan Yew speech before U.S.-ASEAN Business Council 25th Anniversary Dinner, October 27, 2009.

3. China Military News (cited by Reuters), October 22, 2009, http://www.reuters.com/article/2009/10/21/us-usa-china-military-idUSTRE59K2N420091021.

4. Takehiko Yamamoto quoted in Eric Talmadge, "Japan, Worried About China, May Boost Its Submarine Fleet," Associated Press, October 26, 2010, http://www.cnsnews.com/news/article/japan-worried-about-china-may-boost-its-submarine-fleet.

5. "Australia: Bids to Boost Military Ties with China," Stratfor Global Intelligence, April 28, 2011, http://www.google.com/hostednews/afp/article/ALeqM5gxK_iwnDDp-DdyZ1JcmpkYv3qLyg?docId=CNG.329c6cccb28bef19304d6977b2e73a97.5e1

6. "The Long-Term Outlook for the U.S. Navy's Fleet," Statement of Eric J. Labs, senior analyst for naval forces and weapons, before the U.S. House Subcommittee on Seapower and Expeditionary Forces, January 20, 2010, http://www.cbo.gov/ftpdocs/108xx/doc10877/01-20-NavyShipbuilding.shtml.

7. George Ziezulewicz, "Taxed by Wars, Aging Air Tankers Suffer Fleet Fatigue," *Stars and Stripes*, October 18, 2010, http://www .stripes.com/taxed-by-wars-aging-air-tankers-suffer-fleet-fatigue-1.122207.

8. *Quadrennial Defense Report*, United States Department of Defense, February 2010, p. 60.

9. Roger Cliff et al., *Entering the Dragon's Lair: Chinese Antiaccess Strategies and Their Implications for the United States* (Santa Monica, CA: Rand Corporation, 2007), p. xiv.

10. David Brooks, "National Greatness Agenda," *New York Times*, November 11, 2010.

11. Megan Carpentier, "Fiscal Commission Co-Chairs Simpson and Bowles Release Eye-Popping Recommendations," TPM, November 10, 2010, http://tpmdc.talkingpointsmemo.com/2010/11/deficit-commission-co-chairs-simpson-and-bowles-release-eye-popping-recommendations.php.

12. George Baer, *One Hundred Years of Sea Power* (Stanford, CA: Stanford University Press, 1993).

13. Steven Lee Myers and Jane Perlez, "No Movement on Major Disputes as Clinton Meets with Chinese Leaders," *New York Times*, September 5, 2012, http://www.nytimes.com/2012/09/06/world/asia/no-movement-on-key-disputes-as-clinton-meets-with-chinese-leaders.html?_r=0.

14. "Vietnam Demands Release of Vessels Seized by China," *Voice of Vietnam* online, May 25, 2012, http://english.vov.vn/Politics/Vietnam-demands-release-of-vessels-seized-by-China/234874.vov.

CHAPTER 6: CHINA AND THE COMING THREATS TO DOMINANCE

1. Joseph Needham, *Science and Civilization in China* (Cambridge: Cambridge University Press, 1971), vol. 4, p. 563.

2. Ibid., p. 569.

3. Ibid., p. 642.

4. Ibid., pp. 401, 698.

5. Ibid., p. 467.

6. Ibid., p. 421.

7. Ibid., p. 452.

8. Edward L. Dreyer, *Zheng He: China and the Oceans in the Early Ming Dynasty, 1405–1433* (New York: Pearson Longman Library of World Biography, 2007), p. 106.

9. Ibid., p. 112.

Notes

10. Needham, *Science and Civilization in China*, vol. 4, p. 488.

11. Ibid., p. 489.

12. Quoted in Toshi Yoshihara and James R. Holmes, *Red Star over the Pacific: China's Rise and the Challenge to U.S. Maritime Strategy* (Annapolis, MD: Naval Institute Press, 2010), p. 171.

13. "Oceanic Odyssey Remains a Treasure," XINHUA online, July 8, 2004, http://news.xinhuanet.com/english/2004-07/08/content _1583224.htm.

14. Geoff Wade, *The Zheng He Voyages: A Reassessment*, Working Paper Series No. 31, Asia Research Institute, National University of Singapore, October 2004, pp. 7, 8.

15. Dreyer, *Zheng He*, pp. 24 and 31.

16. Ibid., p. 31.

17. Wade, *The Zheng He Voyages: A Reassessment*, p. 15.

18. Dreyer, *Zheng He*, p. 81.

19. Alfred Thayer Mahan, *The Influence of Sea Power upon World History, 1660–1783* (Boston: Little Brown and Company, 1890), 12th edition, preface, p. 20.

20. Dreyer, *Zheng He*, p. 162.

21. Ibid., quoted on p. 30.

22. Bernard D. Cole, "More Red Than Expert: Chinese Sea Power During the Cold War," in *China Goes to Sea*, edited by Andrew S. Erickson, Lyle J. Goldstein, and Carnes Lord (Annapolis, MD: Naval Institute Press, 2009), p. 327.

23. Andrew S. Erickson et al., *China's Future Nuclear Submarine Force* (Annapolis, MD: China Maritime Studies Institute and The Naval Institute Press, 2007), p. 85 (footnoted to John Wilson Lewis and Xue Litai, *China's Strategic Seapower: The Politics of Force Modernization in the Nuclear Age* [Stanford, CA: Stanford University Press, 1994]).

24. Melvyn R. Paisley, author's notes, 1986.

25. Gabriel Collins and Michael Grubb, "Strong Foundation: Contemporary Chinese Shipbuilding Prowess," in *China Goes to Sea*, edited by Andrew S. Erickson, Lyle J. Goldstein, and Carnes Lord (Annapolis, MD: Naval Institute Press, 2009), pp. 344 and 345.

26. Mahan, *The Influence of Sea Power upon History, 1660–1783*, chap. 1, introduction.

27. Ibid., chap. 1, sec. 5.

28. Ibid., chap. 1, penultimate paragraph.

29. The World Bank, http://data.worldbank.org/country/china.

30. Ibid.

31. Ibid.

32. "US-China Trade Statistics and China's World Trade Statistics," The US-China Business Council, http://www.uschina.org/statistics/tradetable.html.

33. Ibid.

34. "Top US State Exporters to China, 2010," The US-China Business Council, http://www.uschina.org/public/exports/2000_2010/2010-top-us-state-exporters.pdf.

35. Yoshihara and Holmes, *Red Star over the Pacific*, p. 2.

36. Admiral Robert F. Willard, Commander, U.S. Pacific Command, before the House Armed Service Committee, January 13, 2010, p. 2.

37. Jeremy Page, "China Flexes Naval Muscle," *Wall Street Journal*, August 11, 2011, http://online.wsj.com/article/SB10001424053111903918104576499423267407488.html.

38. *Annual Report to Congress: Military Power of the People's Republic of China, 2009*, Council on Foreign Relations, March 2009, p. 50.

39. Ibid., p. 40.

40. Zhu Shanshan, "Navy Talent Drive Fuels Carrier Buzz," *Global Times* (the website of *People's Daily*, the official Communist Party of China newspaper), May 11, 2011, as reported by B. Raman, Paper no. 4485, South Asia Analysis Group, May 13, 2011, http://www.globaltimes.cn/NEWS/tabid/99/ID/653696/Navy-talent-drive-fuels-carrier-buzz.aspx

41. Clarissa Ward, "First Chinese Aircraft Carrier Revealed," ABC News, June 9, 2011, abcnews.go.com/Blotter/Chinese-aircraft-carrier-revealed/story?id=13800990#.ULhAEdPjm_0.

42. Yoshihara and Holmes, *Red Star over the Pacific*, p. 89.

43. Mukul Devichand, "Is Chittagong One of China's 'String of Pearls'?" BBC News, May 17, 2010, http://news.bbc.co.uk/2/hi/business/8687917.stm.

44. *Annual Report to Congress: Military Power of the People's Republic of China, 2009*, p. 54.

Notes

45. Aly-Khan Satchu, "South Africa–China Trade Ties: President Zuma Bids to Shore Up 'Gateway to China' Status," *Christian Science Monitor*, August 25, 2010, http://www.csmonitor.com/World/Africa/Africa-Monitor/2010/0825/South-Africa-China-trade-ties-President-Zuma-bids-to-shore-up-Gateway-to-China-status.

46. *Report: Chinese Develop Special "Kill Weapon" to Destroy U.S. Aircraft Carriers*, U.S. Naval Institute, March 31, 2009, http://www.usni.org/news-and-features/chinese-kill-weapon.

47. *Annual Report to Congress: Military and Security Developments Involving the People's Republic of China, 2010*, [http://www.defense.gov/pubs/pdfs/2010_CMPR_Final.pdf] p. 2 (and) "Chinese Develop Special 'Kill Weapon' to Destroy U.S. Aircraft Carriers."

48. Andrew S. Erickson and David D. Yang, "On the Verge of a Game-Changer," *U.S. Naval Institute Proceedings* Vol. 135/5/1,275 (May 2009), p. 27.

49. *Report to Congress: The Military Power of the People's Republic of China, 2004*, sec. 4 (Force Modernization), subsection: Air Defense Systems.

50. Bernard D. Cole, *The Great Wall at Sea: China's Navy in the Twenty-First Century* (Annapolis, MD: Naval Institute Press, 2010).

51. Ronald O'Rourke, "China Naval Modernization: Implications for U.S. Navy Capabilities—Background and Issues for Congress," Congressional Research Service, October 17, 2012, p. 35.

52. *A Modern Navy with Chinese Characteristics*, Office of Naval Intelligence, Suitland, Maryland, 2009, pp. 21 and 49.

53. Ronald O'Rourke, *Navy Force Structure and Shipbuilding Plans*: Background and Issues for Congress, December 10, 2012, p. 9 hhttp://www.fas.org/sgp/crs/weapons/RL32665.pdf

54. "Adm. Mullen 'Genuinely Concerned' About China's Military Buildup," CBS News "WorldWatch," June 10, 2010, http://www.cbsnews.com/8301-503543_162-20007340-503543.html.

55. Dr. Carlyle A. Thayer, emeritus professor, School of Humanities and Social Sciences, the University of New South Wales at the Australian Defense Force Academy at Center for Strategic and International Studies conference on maritime security in the South China Sea, Washington, DC, June 20–21, 2011.

56. "Top Chinese General Warns US over Attack," *Financial Times Asia-Pacific*, July 15, 2005, http://www.ft.com/cms/s/2/28cfe55a-f4a7 -11d9-9dd1-00000e2511c8.html#axzz1LPSeQ2fu.

57. Elisabeth Bumiller and Michael Wines, "Test of Stealth Fighter Clouds Gates Visit to China," *New York Times*, January 11, 2011, http://www.nytimes.com/2011/01/12/world/asia/12fighter.html.

58. "CCTV Military Channel Director: Bin Laden Is the Greatest National Hero in the History of Arab World," http://chinascope.org /main/content/view/3537/150/.

59. "US, South Korean Naval Exercises Postponed," Voice of America, July 12, 2010, http://www.voanews.com/english/news/asia /US-South-Korean-Naval-Exercises-Postponed-98335404.html.

CHAPTER 7: WHAT IS LOST CAN NEVER BE REGAINED

1. Early in 2012 former First Sea Lord Alan West said that it is "bonkers" for the United Kingdom to have so small a number of the combat vessels that are the backbone of the fleet. Chris Parry, "Britain Has to Decide upon the Royal Navy's Role," March 19, 2012, *The Telegraph*, http://www.telegraph.co.uk/news/uknews/defence/9153258 /Britain -has-to-decide-upon-the-Royal-Navys-role.html.

2. "Henry VIII and His Navy," Royal Museums Greenwich, http://www.rmg.co.uk/explore/sea-and-ships/facts/navies-and-warships/henry-viii-and-his-navy.

3. Thucydides, *The Peloponnesian War*, 1.33-2, p. 22, in *The Landmark Thucydides*, edited by Robert B. Strassler (New York: Simon & Schuster, 1996).

4. Frederic C. Lane, *Venice, a Maritime Republic* (Baltimore: Johns Hopkins University Press, 1973), p. 29.

5. Ibid., p. 421.

6. Alfred Thayer Mahan, *The Influence of Sea Power upon History, 1660–1783* (Boston: Little, Brown and Company, 1890), 12th edition, chap.1, p. 37.

7. Ibid.

8. C. R. Boxer, *The Dutch Seaborne Empire, 1600–1800,* History of Human Society series, edited by J. H. Plumb (New York: Knopf, 1975), chap. 4, p. 86.

9. Germain Antonin Lefevre-Pontalis, *Jean de Witt: Grand Pensionnire de Holland*, quoted in Mahan, *The Influence of Sea Power upon History, 1660–1783*, 12th edition, chap. 2, p. 96

10. J. Ellis Barker, *The Rise and Decline of the Netherlands* (New York: E. P. Dutton & Co., 1906), chap. 14, p. 272.

11, Ibid., p. 287.

12. Jonathan I. Israel, *The Dutch Republic: Its Rise, Greatness, and Fall 1477–1806* (Oxford, UK: Clarendon Press, 1995), p. 971.

13. J. Ellis Barker, *The Rise and Decline of the Netherlands: A Political and Economic History and a Study in Practical Statesmanship* (New York: Smith, Elder & Co., 1906), chap. 20, p. 415.

14. Ibid., p. 414.

15. Ibid., p. 416.

16. Speech at the Guildhall (London), January 19, 1904, quoted in Aaron L. Friedberg, *The Weary Titan: Britain and the Experience of Relative Decline, 1895–1905* (Princeton, NJ: Princeton University Press, 1988), p. 72.

17. Paul M. Kennedy, *The Rise and Fall of the Great Powers: Economic Change and Military Conflict from 1500 to 2000* (New York: Random House, 1987), p. 201.

18. Internet Modern History Sourcebook, Fordham University, http://www.fordham.edu/halsall/mod/indrevtabs1.asp.

19. Quoted in Friedberg, *The Weary Titan*, p. 97.

20. Ibid., p. 100.

21. Niall Ferguson, *Empire: The Rise and Demise of the British World Order and the Lessons for Global Power* (New York: Basic Books, 2003), p. 227.

22. Friedberg, *The Weary Titan*, p. 146.

23. Quoted from ibid., p. 163, Lord Lansdowne, "The Defense of Esquimalt," January 8, 1897.

24. Robert K. Massie, *Dreadnought* (New York: Random House, 1991), pp. 470–76.

25. Peter Orszag, "Estimated Costs of U.S. Operations in Iraq and Afghanistan and of Other Activities Related to the War on Terrorism," Statement of Director of Congressional Budget Office before U.S. House Committee on the Budget, October 24, 2007, pp. 1 and 9,

http://www.cbo.gov/ftpdocs/86xx/doc8690/10-24-CostOfWar
_Testimony.pdf.

26. The Royal Navy, http://www.royalnavy.mod.uk/.

27. Royal Navy, from The National Archives, http://www.telegraph
.co.uk/news/uknews/defence/8049674/Navy-to-reduce-to-smallest-size
-ever-to-save-carriers.html

28. Air Chief Marshal Sir Michael Graydon, General Sir Michael
Rose, Vice Admiral Sir Jeremy Blackham, Air Commodore Andrew Lam-
bert, and Allen Sykes, *Inconvenient Truths—Threats Justify Prioritising
Defence*, United Kingdom National Defence Association, September
2011, p. 11. http://www.uknda.org/File/Inconvenient%20Truths%20Tue
%2027%20Final%20%20%28F1.3%29.pdf.

29. Ibid., p. 12.

30. *Report of the Sustainable Defense Task Force*, June 11, 2010, p. vii.

31. Sameer Lalwani and Joshua Shifrinson, "Whither Command of the Commons?" New America Foundation, Washington,
DC, September 13, 2011, http://newamerica.net/publications
/policy/whither_command_of_the_commons.

32. Ibid., p. 16.

33. Ibid., p. 17.

34. Ibid., pp. 2–3.

35. Ibid., p. 6.

36. Ibid.

37. Ibid., p. 8.

38. Ibid.

CHAPTER 8: CAN AMERICA STILL MANUFACTURE ITS OWN WEAPONS?

1. "Electromagnetic Railgun," Office of Naval Research, http:/
/www.onr.navy.mil/Media-Center/Fact-Sheets/Electromagnetic
-Railgun.aspx.

2. Spencer Ackerman, "Video: Navy Fires Off Its New Weaponized
Railgun," *Wired*, February 28, 2012, http://www.wired.com /danger-
room/2012/02/railgun-real-gun/.

3. Polybius, *The Rise of the Roman Empire*, translated by Ian Scott-Kilvert (Harmondsworth, UK: Penguin Books, 1979), book 1, chap. 20, p. 63.

4. Ibid., p. 62.

5. David Berteau, Presentation to Naval Postgraduate School's 8th Annual Acquisition Research Symposium, May 10–12, 2011.

6. Rear Admiral Joe Carnevale, U.S.N. (ret.), holds a master of science degree in naval architecture and marine engineering from MIT and, among other assignments in defense acquisition, has served as supervisor of shipbuilding at the Pascagoula (Mississippi) shipyard and as director for surface combatants in the office of the deputy assistant secretary of the navy.

7. Rear Admiral Joe Carnevale, interview, September 1, 2011.

8. Mark V. Arena, Irv Blickstein, Obaid Younossi, and Clifford A. Grammich, *Why Has the Cost of Navy Ships Risen?* National Defense Research Institute, The Rand Corporation, 2006, pp. 51–52.

9. Ibid., p. 55.

10. "Cost Overruns, Budget Uncertainties Hurting USN and Contractors," *Defense Industry Daily*, March 18, 2005, http://www.defenseindustrydaily.com/cost-overruns-budget-uncertainties-hurting-usn-and-contractors-0196/.

11. Arena et al., "Why Has the Cost of Navy Ships Risen?" p. 5.

12. *Defense Acquisitions: Improved Management Practices Could Help Minimize Cost Growth in Navy Shipbuilding Programs*, Government Accountability Office, February 28, 2005, pp. 41, 60.

13. *Cost Overruns, Budget Uncertainties Hurting USN and Contractors*.

14. "Defense Acquisitions: Improved Management Practices Could Help Minimize Cost Growth in Navy Shipbuilding Programs," p. 41.

15. Ibid.

16. Ibid.

17. "Littoral Combat Ship Costs, Rising Again," *Defense Industry Daily*, February 11, 2008, http://www.defenseindustrydaily.com/Littoral-Combat-Ship-Costs-Issues-Rising-Again-04730/.

18. Statement of Fred Moosally, Kevin Moak, Richard McCreary, and Mike Ellis, House Armed Service Subcommittee on Seapower and Expeditionary Forces, February 8, 2007.

19. Ibid.

20. Arena et al., "Why Has the Cost of Navy Ships Risen?" p. 52.

21. Ibid., p. 53.

22. Ibid., p. 54.

23. "Defense Acquisitions: Improved Management Practices Could Help Minimize Cost Growth in Navy Shipbuilding Programs," p. 40.

24. Arena et al., "Why Has the Cost of Navy Ships Risen?" pp. xix.

25. Christopher P. Cavas, "LCS: 'Considerable Cost Overruns,' " *Navy Times*, January 11, 2007, http://www.navytimes.com/news/2007/01/dfnLCScostsweb07011/.

26. "US Navy Sinks LCS-4 Construction," *Defense Industry Daily*, November 4, 2007, http://www.defenseindustrydaily.com/navy-sinks-lcs-4-construction-04134/.

27. Ibid.

28. *Defense Acquisitions: Realistic Business Cases Needed to Execute Navy Shipbuilding Programs*, Government Accountability Office, July 24, 2007, p. 14.

29. Ibid.

30. Jesse Ellman, Reed Livergood, David Morrow, and Gregory Sanders, *Defense Contract Trends: U.S. Department of Defense Contract Spending and the Supporting Industrial Base: An Annotated Brief by the CSIS Defense-Industrial Initiatives Group, Center for Strategic and International Studies*, May 2011, p. 14.

31. Interview with George Sawyer, November 4, 2011.

32. Ibid.

33. Statement of Fred Moosally et al.

34. Ibid.

35. Ibid.

36. "Defense Acquisitions: Realistic Business Cases Needed to Execute Navy Shipbuilding Programs," p. 11.

37. Ibid.

38. Statement of Fred Moosally et al.

39. Ronald O'Rourke, *Navy Littoral Combat Ship (LCS) Program: Background, Issues, and Options for Congress*, Congressional Research Service, April 29, 2011, p. 48.

40. Zachary A. Goldfarb, "Rising Costs Plague Navy's Shipbuilding Programs," *Washington Post*, October 8, 2007.

41. "US Navy Sinks LCS-4 Construction."

42. Ibid.

43. Ibid.

44. Statement of Fred Moosally et al.

45. Ibid.

46. "Defense Acquisitions: Realistic Business Cases Needed to Execute Navy Shipbuilding Programs," p. 11.

47. Arena et al., "Why Has the Cost of Navy Ships Risen?" p. 56.

48. "Defense Acquisitions: Realistic Business Cases Needed to Execute Navy Shipbuilding Programs," p. 10.

49. "Cost Overruns, Budget Uncertainties Hurting USN and Contractors."

50. Ibid.

51. "Defense Acquisitions: Realistic Business Cases Needed to Execute Navy Shipbuilding Programs," p. 17.

52. Ibid., p. 18.

53. Arena et al., "Why Has the Cost of Navy Ships Risen?" pp. xviii–xix.

54. Ibid.

55. Goldwater-Nichols Department of Defense Reorganization Act of 1986.

CHAPTER 9: TO BE A GREAT POWER, OR NOT

1. Lawrence B. Lindsey, "The Fiscal Trap: Quantitative Easing Won't Solve Our Deeper Problem," *Weekly Standard* 16, no. 12 (December 6, 2010): 10, http://www.weeklystandard.com/articles/fiscal-trap_519582.html.

2. Eric J. Labs, Congressional Budget Office naval analyst, briefing to Surface Navy Association, January 12, 2012.

3. Ibid.

4. Rear Admiral J. T. Blake, *Department of the Navy Fiscal Year 2010 President's Budget, May 7, 2009*, http://www.finance.hq.navy.mil/FMB/10pres/10Press_Brief.pdf.

5. Article I, Sec. 8 of the U.S. Constitution lists the powers of Congress. After providing for it to collect taxes and pay debts, Congress's first listed duty is "to provide for the common defense." Such other congressional powers as borrowing money, establishing rules on natural-

ization, bankruptcy, and courts lower than the Supreme Court are listed after defending the nation. Similarly with the executive branch: Article II begins by providing for the president's election. Its second section lists first the president's responsibility as commander in chief of the United States' armed forces. The same section describes the president's power to make treaties, command the militia, and appoint ambassadors. The organization of the Constitution and the writings of its authors in such documents as *The Federalist Papers* agree that defending the nation is government's first responsibility.

6. Congressional Budget Office analyst Eric J. Labs in prepared testimony, "The Long-Term Outlook for the U.S. Navy's Fleet," January 20, 2010, before the Subcommittee on Seapower and Expeditionary Forces, Committee on Armed Forces, U.S. House of Representatives, http://www .cbo.gov/ftpdocs/108xx/doc10877/01-20-NavyShipbuilding.pdf.

7. Ronald O'Rourke, *Navy Ford (CVN-78) Class Aircraft Carrier Program: Background and Issues for Congress*, Congressional Research Service, December 10, 2012.

8. *National Defense Authorization Act for Fiscal Year 2007*, Report of the Committee on Armed Services, U.S. House of Representatives, p. 69.

9. Ronald O'Rourke, *Navy DDG-51 and DDG-1000 Destroyer Programs: Background and Issues for Congress,* Congressional Research Service, June 14, 2010.

10. The Office of Net Assessment (ONA) is the Defense Department's most prominent and reflective source of strategic thinking. Its job is to look at future U.S. military capabilities and compare them to those of other likely competitors and make sense of the comparisons. Andrew Marshall, one of the United States' leading strategic thinkers, has directed ONA since it was established in 1973.

11. Wayne Hughes, *The New Navy Fighting Machine: A Study of the Connections Between Contemporary Policy, Strategy, Sea Power, Naval Operations, and the Composition of the United States Fleet*, prepared for the Director of New Assessment, Office of the Secretary of Defense, August 2009.

12. Ibid.

13. The July 2006 Hezbollah attack on a 1,200-ton Israeli corvette patrolling waters ten miles off the Lebanese coast killed four sailors and

set the Israeli warship on fire. This is an accurate indication of the risk to naval vessels from land-based missiles, a risk that the placement of longer-range, more potent missiles aboard small boats is likely to increase.

14. Frederic C. Lane, *Venice, a Maritime Republic* (Baltimore: Johns Hopkins University Press, 1973), p. 24.

15. Ibid., p. 386.

16. David Lague, "Chinese Submarine Fleet Is Growing, Analysts Say," *New York Times*, February 25, 2008, http://www.nytimes.com /2008/02/25/world/asia/25submarine.html.

17. Two hundred and forty-eight vessels for coastal work plus four hundred small inshore patrol craft; 411 blue-water ships; and nine ballistic-missile submarines and nine ships for ballistic-missile defense. In Hughes, *The New Navy Fighting Machine*.

18. 1911 to 1915.

19. Stuart E. Johnson and Arthur K. Cebrowski, *Alternative Fleet Architecture Design*, Center for Technology and National Security Policy, National Defense University, August 2005, p. 7.

20. Thucydides mentions blockades in several places in *The History of the Peloponnesian War*, for example, the Athenian blockade of Chios in book 8, chap. 24.

CHAPTER 10: CHANGING AMERICAN MARITIME STRATEGY

1. Max Boot, "Slashing America's Defense; A Suicidal Trajectory," *Commentary*, January 2012, p. 17.

2. General James F. Amos, Statement to House Armed Services Committee on the Future of the Military Services and the Consequences of Sequestration, November 2, 2011.

3. Admiral Jonathan W. Greenert, Hearing on the Future of the Military Services and the Consequences of Defense Sequestration, published in *Quantico Sentry*, November 3, 2011, p. 17, http://www2 .quanticosentryonline.com/news/2011/nov/03/full-transcript-hearing -future-military-services-a-ar-1432761/

4. Ibid., p. 6.

5. "Iran Reiterates Threat to Close Hormuz Strait if Oil Exports Sanctioned," *Xinhua English*, December 18, 2011, http://news.xinhuanet .com/english/world/2011-12/19/c_122442363.htm.

CONCLUSION

1. United States Constitution, Article I, Sec. 8.

2. As reported in *Aviation Week* and *Space Technology*, December 5, 2011.

3. O'Rourke, Ronald, *Navy Force Structure and Shipbuilding Plans: Background and Issues for Congress*, October 25, 2012, Congressional Research Service, Washington, DC.

4. Pilling, David; Landingin, Roel; Soble, Jonathan, "Philippines Back Rearming of Japan," *Financial Times,* December 9, 2012, http://www.ft.com/cms/s/0/250430bc-41ba-11e2-a8c3-00144feabdc0.html#axzz2Efu1QKev

5. Hadley, Stephen J., Perry, William J, et al. *The QDR in Perspective: Meeting America's National Security Needs In the 21st Century*; The Final Report of the Quadrennial Defense Review Independent panel, p. 58 http://www.usip.org/files/qdr/qdrreport.pdf.

6. Conway, General James T. Roughead, Admiral Gary; Allen, Admiral Thad W.; *A Cooperative Strategy for 21st Century Seapower*, October 2007 http://www.navy.mil/maritime/Maritimestrategy.pdf.

Acknowledgments

MY THANKS TO THE SMITH RICHARDSON FOUNDATION FOR ITS generous support throughout the writing of this book. For its enthusiasm and confidence, I am also obliged to Hudson Institute and in particular to Arthur Milikh, Adam Logan Taylor, and Zachary Taylor for their assistance with research and suggestions. A better editor than Dan Crissman I could neither have expected nor hoped for. Finally, I am beholden to my wife, Mihaela, and son, Gabriel, for their understanding of the demands on my time away from their loving presence that this project necessarily, but not always joyfully, entailed.

Index